The
Good Beach Guide

A guide to over 150 of Britain's best beaches

Edited by
RICHARD CAINES
MARINE CONSERVATION SOCIETY

EBURY PRESS  LONDON

The author would like to thank the following people for providing information and help in producing this book: Jenny Norman and other MCS staff, district and local councils, The National Trust, Tourist Authorities, The Townswomen's Guild, coastal wardens and members of the Marine Conservation Society.

Published by Ebury Press

First impression 1988
Reprinted twice 1988
Revised and updated 1989
Revised and updated 1990

British Library Cataloguing in Publication Data
The good beach guide. – New ed.
1. Great Britain. Beaches
I. Caines, Richard (Editor) II. Marine Conservation Society
551.4'57'0941

ISBN 0-85223-852-5

Designed by Gwyn Lewis
Illustrations by Kate Simunek
Maps by ML Design

Typeset in Souvenir by Textype Typesetters, Cambridge
Printed and bound in Great Britain at The Bath Press, Avon

Contents

Foreword
by David Bellamy

A day trip or holiday at the seaside is a traditional summertime activity for many British families and visitors to our country. Weather permitting, a paddle or swim in the sea can be an additional treat and add to the fun.

Sadly, however, a visit to the seaside nowadays is not always the pleasure it should be. Instead of golden sands and a clear blue sea, you may well be confronted with beach and waters spoilt by oil, rubbish, and even raw sewage. All too often the sea is used as an outlet for the waste products of our society which means that many of our beaches fall far below the standard established by the EC for safe bathing.

Q Why, in 1990, should we be faced with the problem of bathing in our own, and other peoples', diluted sewage?

A We shouldn't, and money *must* be found to alleviate the problem. Simply dumping further out to sea is not the answer.

Q Why should we throw away multi millions of tonnes of potential energy and potential organic fertilizer and cause massive pollution of the sea at the same time?

A We shouldn't. We should be using our rubbish and our sewage in the cogeneration of energy and the manufacture of organic soil conditions.

By buying this book you will be supporting the very important work of the Marine Conservation Society who are coming up with the right answers, thus protecting the marine world for us all to enjoy.

HAPPY HOLIDAY

The Marine Conservation Society is a rapidly expanding national conservation organisation formed to protect Britain's seashore and coastal waters by campaigning and lobbying on issues which threaten the seas. It also undertakes research and education to help develop a better understanding and awareness of the marine environment.

Already the Society can be proud of its achievements. It forced a ban on competitive spearfishing which threatened to decimate fish stocks in inshore areas. It successfully fought to have marine nature reserves included in the Wildlife and Countryside Act and has already seen the first statutory reserve declared – Lundy Island. It has actively promoted the creation of voluntary marine conservation areas, the most recent being the Seven Sisters in Sussex. The Society has achieved a major victory in the fight against pollution by getting the Government to ban the use of anti-fouling paint containing the poisonous chemical TBT. Joining forces with the Coastal Anti-Pollution League, it has forced the authorities to make massive increases in the amount of money spent on cleaning up our bathing waters.

The Society is currently tackling the pollution problems of the North Sea, quality of our beaches, the threats to sharks, the trade in corals and shells and the impact of fish farming on our coastal waters and their wildlife.

Membership is £12.00 a year (see page 207) and you will receive the quarterly magazine 'Marine Conservation' updating you on all the campaigns and issues affecting the sea, and how you can help.

Help make the proper protection of our seas, their resources and their wildlife a reality. Join the Society now.

Heinz Guardians of the Countryside is a major British conservation programme sponsored by Heinz in association with World Wide Fund for Nature. Its objective is to help protect those wildlife species and habitats in greatest danger, thus safeguarding them for future generations.

Marine conservation initiatives via the MCS under the programme have included the funding of coastal wardening at several sites during the summer season; sponsorship of a marine conservation officer to co-ordinate a variety of national campaigns such as research into the habits of dolphins and basking sharks; and publication of the Marine Conservation Society's Coastal Directory.

Through the programme, protection of a number of important marine sites has been achieved, including the Helford River and sites in Devon, Dorset and Northumberland as well as the purchase of Cape Cornwall (including Priest's Cove) for the National Trust.

Introduction

Everyone's expectations of a day at the seaside are different. Some people look for quiet and solitude, an escape from the hustle and bustle of their everyday life. Others look for just the opposite – amusements and bright lights, ice cream and rock, sun-bathing by day and dancing by night.

Britain has more than 7,000 miles (11,000km) of coastline, with literally thousands of beaches, varying from long, sweeping sandy bays gently lapped by sparkling clear water, to tiny rocky coves. There are banks of groyne-ribbed shingle, flat golden sands pounded by Atlantic rollers, and secluded coves ringed by cliffs with rocky outcrops and pools waiting to be explored. In addition, there are the resort beaches, traditional promenades with their Victorian piers, pavilions, bandstands, funfairs and amusements. And every beach is someone's favourite!

'Why is my favourite beach not included in the guide?'

We have not attempted to describe every British beach; the beauty of many is the very fact that they remain undiscovered. The guide is a selection, a mere 150 of Britain's beaches, a mixture of popular holiday resorts, quieter secluded bays and some faraway places – hopefully a beach to suit every taste. Use the guide as a starting point for exploring the delights of our beautiful coastline. Part of the fun is searching out your own personal favourite.

For beaches which are not featured, the Golden List within each regional chapter may be of help, too, but again, this is a mere starting point. However, some very good beaches *are* missing from the guide because water quality monitoring by the water authorities or River Purification Boards found that they did not meet the minimum

EC standard for clean bathing water. Details of all the monitored beaches are given in the Golden List within each regional
section.

Any beaches where there have been reports of significant
pollution of the shore, whether industrial or domestic, are also
excluded. We have not included beaches where there is major
industrial development on the shore, beaches which are shadowed
by power stations (nuclear or conventional), construction yards,
refineries, or gas and oil terminals. If a beach is used for military
purposes, there are times when it is a danger area with restricted
access and therefore cannot be considered as a good beach.

In choosing good beaches we also felt that they had to be
reasonably accessible; having to scramble down wet cliffs is
probably not the ideal way to start a relaxing day on the beach.
Beaches should also have reasonable parking facilities for beach
users. Parking on narrow roads and verges should be avoided; it is
not only very damaging, but also causes problems for the local
people, rescue services and other visitors. Although there are lots
of little secluded beaches, particularly in Scotland and Wales, most
are only accessible to the walker who is prepared to explore the
remoter areas of Britain.

The Blue Flag Award

The Blue Flag Award is part of the programme of awards for good
beaches run by the Foundation for Environmental Education in
Europe. The Blue Flag is awarded to beaches which have a high
standard of water quality, are cleaned daily during the bathing season
and have good facilities, toilets, lifesaving equipment, first aid etc. On
these beaches there is strict control of domestic animals, and driving
or racing on the beach are prohibited. Provision is also made for
environmental education, public information and safety.

Twenty-one British beaches received the Blue Flag Award in 1989.
Eighteen of these are featured in the guide: these are marked with a
flag symbol. Three are excluded because they either failed to meet
the EC standard for clean bathing water in 1989 or other information
we received was detrimental. This failure highlights the fluctuating
nature of the pollution of our shores, and the constant need for action
to clean up our beaches and seas.

The next annual Blue Flag Awards will be announced on 5th June
1990, World Environment Day. Look out for the latest winners.

The Clean Beach Award

The Clean Beach Awards mentioned in the text were won by beaches both for the general level of amenities provided for the public and for the efforts made by the local authorities towards promoting beach safety and the provision and use of litter bins. The awards are made by the Tidy Britain Group to encourage high standards of beach maintenance.

Visiting Beaches

There is intense pressure at many beauty spots where the number of people visiting the beach and surrounding area leads to damage, particularly when cars are parked close to the beach. Sand dunes are particularly vulnerable, their protective covering of marram grass is easily damaged and, once lost, the wind blows the sand away, destroying the dunes. Only by taking care of what is often a fragile environment will we be able to continue to enjoy the unspoilt beauty of our coastline. So please remember to follow the seashore code whenever you are down at the beach and:

TAKE NOTHING BUT PICTURES

WASTE NOTHING BUT TIME

LEAVE NOTHING BUT FOOTPRINTS

Help us to help you

If, on a visit to any of these beaches, you find pollution problems, or a change in facilities, please write to the Society and let us know. A form has been included at the back of the book to help you. Don't ever think that you are powerless in the fight to save our beaches and seas.

Marine Pollution

Over the past few years, the deaths of thousands of common seals, massive blooms of algae, and the deaths and breeding failure in sea-bird colonies on the Orkney and Shetland islands, have highlighted the problems of our seas as never before. The causes have been the subject of fierce debate but few would deny that pollution is a major threat to the health of our seas and wildlife, and that something must be done to clean them up.

Pollution occurs when we introduce any substances into the sea which are harmful to wildlife, which threaten human health or reduce marine activities and amenities. An enormous range of such substances enters our seas – deliberately, accidentally, or through sheer negligence – often creating pollution problems far from their source.

Golden sands littered with rubbish, raw sewage at the water's edge, oil on the rocks and lumps of tar on your flip-flops. These are the highly visible signs for the holiday-maker. But there are other pollutants which remain unseen: for example, poisonous chemicals, pesticides, and radioactivity. Such pollutants may be invisible but their effects are not, and they can be equally or more damaging. The sea has no fences and therefore the effect of a pollutant never occurs in isolation, it spreads through the environment, combining with other pollutants to create a highly poisonous cocktail.

Types of Marine Pollution

Waste can be classed under three main types: domestic, industrial and agricultural. *Domestic waste* includes sewage, silt, oil, lead, tar and de-icing chemicals which are used on the roads. *Industrial waste* includes, for example, radioactive waste, toxic chemicals, thermal discharges, refuse and oil from ships, as well as degradable organic waste from the paper, pulp and food processing industries. *Agricultural waste* – fertilizers, herbicides and organic matter – is all potentially dangerous. Other pollutants that must also be considered are discarded pyrotechnics (e.g. ships' flares and distress rockets), as well as drugs, and chemicals leaked from the hulls of ships.

For years the sea has been used as a cheap and easy waste disposal system on a vast scale. Nine million tonnes of sewage sludge (the by-product of sewage treatment works), 42 million tonnes of dredged spoil – the silt removed from harbours and estuaries to keep them clear for shipping – and over 2 million tonnes of industrial waste, including coal waste and fly ash, are dumped off the UK shore each year. The wastes also contain high levels of chemical contamination with the result that the North Sea, for example, receives over 10 tonnes of mercury, 12 tonnes of cadmium, 1250 tonnes of lead and 200 tonnes of copper each year.

Sources of Pollution

The source of a pollutant may be easy to identify – an outfall pipe or a dump ship deliberately discharging waste into the sea. Waste also enters the sea via rivers, from ships, in land run-off, and from the atmosphere. Some of the sources are easy to locate, others are less easy to define and hence control. An estimated 5 million tonnes of oil enter the sea each year, but only 4% comes from major tanker accidents. The majority is released during routine shipping and oil refining operations. In many cases individual pollution incidents are neither obvious nor devastating to the local area. However, their cumulative effect means that all the trade routes and ocean currents abound with tar balls, many of which will eventually end up on beaches.

The sources of pesticides and other agricultural chemicals which find their way into streams, rivers and eventually the sea, are difficult to locate accurately. These chemicals, particularly the organochlorines like aldrin and dieldrin, are extremely stable and persistent. They accumulate in the sea and have been found in virtually all marine mammals and humans.

The Effects of Pollution

In some cases, the effects of pollution are easy to identify and link to specific causes. Plastics discarded overboard entangle wildlife causing death by drowning or strangulation. It has been estimated that 2 million sea birds and 100,000 marine mammals are killed each year due to marine debris, either by eating it or becoming entangled in it. The death of a marine animal may not be as easily attributed to marine litter if the animal has eaten the refuse and died either because of some poisonous chemical in the waste or starvation due to a permanently full stomach. On the shoreline, where much refuse ends up, it remains a hazard for wildlife and the holiday-maker.

The consequences of oil pollution are not only the obvious oiled sea bird or oil-spotted sands; there are also toxic effects. Water-soluble chemicals in oil are poisonous to animals and plants. The dumping of solid wastes also causes direct physical damage to marine life, smothering animals and plants, but as with many pollution problems there are combined effects. For example, dredged spoil is highly contaminated with chemicals. Dumping wastes offshore not only does physical damage to the environment but the chemicals are released and may poison wildlife, or affect their growth and reproduction.

Thousands of chemicals like mercury (used in the paper and pulp industry), lead from petrol, titanium dioxide (a whitener in the paint industry), polychlorinated biphenols (found in electrical components), pesticides like organochlorines (e.g. DDT) are released into the sea and have been found in all marine life. They have been linked to fish diseases, the disappearance of species, and breeding failure.

In very low concentrations the chemicals may have minimal effect but the danger increases as they become concentrated up the food chain. A single shrimp may have a tolerable amount of a chemical in its body but when a fish eats lots of shrimps it absorbs all the chemicals from each shrimp and the result can be lethal. For example, around Minamata Bay in Japan, 46 people died and 2,000 people suffered from crippling mental and physical deformities. The tragedy was the result of eating shellfish from the bay which had accumulated methyl mercury released into the waters from a local factory.

Sewage is a particular problem that has direct effects on beaches and bathers. Over 300 million gallons (1350 million litres) of sewage are disposed of in our coastal waters each day, most is untreated or receives only primary treatment. It is frequently discharged close to the shore and the raw sewage, often including toilet paper, fat balls and other nuisance solids, is washed back on to the beach with each incoming tide. This is not only very unsightly but also harmful to health. The sewage contains bacteria and viruses that can cause a number of infections so that an upset stomach or bad throat suffered on holiday might have been caused by swimming in polluted water or eating shellfish that had accumulated the bacteria as they filtered the sea water to feed.

The discharge of sewage also has effects on marine life. The decomposition of the sewage requires oxygen, and the reduction in oxygen that occurs as the sewage is broken down can lead to a decline in the number and variety of plants and animals. This can also result from the high nutrient input from sewage, when plankton and vegetation bloom at the expense of less tolerant species. As the algal colonies die, they break up and create foam which is frequently washed ashore.

There has been much debate about the final fate and the effect of the many pollutants that find their way to our seas. Much, however, remains unknown. Are the problems we are seeing now the result of pollution? Are the algal blooms caused by the high nutrient inputs from sewage and agriculture? Where did the seal virus originate? The need for more information about the pollution problems of the sea and better understanding will help us answer these questions and protect the sea.

Pollution Control

There are several international and national agreements which aim to control pollution. The problem with many of these agreements is their successful implementation. For example, the International Agreement on the Prevention of Marine Pollution from Land (the Paris Commission, 1974) lists a series of chemicals that must only be discharged in 'trace amounts'. It is the interpretation of this definition that has caused problems in its implementation. The International Convention for the Prevention of Pollution from Ships (MARPOL 73/78) and its five annexes were originally drawn up in 1973. But they only come into force when enough countries, representing 50% of the world's shipping tonnage, sign each part of the agreement. Until then it could be effectively ignored even by those that had signed. The convention and Annexes 1 and 2 were agreed and became law in 1978. It was not until the end of 1987, ten years later, that the United States signed Annex 5, concerning dumping of refuse from ships. This took the tonnage over the 50% mark making the annex law, 12 months later on December 31st 1988.

As of 1st January 1989 it became illegal to dispose of any plastic from ships at sea. Added to this, other forms of garbage, biodegradable food waste etc, can only be discharged at sea under strictly controlled conditions. The refuse now has to be deposited at special reception facilities which should have been set up at ports and harbours. It is hoped this will improve the colossal problem of marine litter. Unfortunately the law only applies to the countries who have signed the annexe (approximately 75% of the world fleet). How the regulations are to be enforced remains to be seen. Annexes 3 and 4 of the convention are not yet ratified by sufficient countries.

The European Community has also introduced legislation to control pollution. But there have also been problems with the implementation of these regulations. The Directive on Discharges into the Aquatic Environment which attempted to stop dumping, was never introduced because of a UK veto. The Bathing Waters Quality Directive was introduced in 1976 when, after three years and much persuasion, Britain designated its 'bathing beaches'. It designated only 27. France designated 1,498, Italy 3,308 and even Luxembourg, with no coastline, came up with more bathing sites than Britain – 34. Resorts such as Brighton and Blackpool (without a doubt one of the largest bathing resorts in Europe) did not feature within the 27, indicating a lack of commitment to the spirit of the Directive. It was not until 1987, after much criticism, that the Government yielded to pressure and the number was increased to 391.

By 1989, this had risen to 404, but this should not encourage complacency – the Marine Conservation Society has more than three times this many 'bathing beaches' on record. The problem is that of defining and agreeing on terms and such dogma has plagued the Bathing Waters Directive throughout its existence. Even now, there is no standard European interpretation of the directive and thus the results from each EC country are not comparable. Even within our own country, the amount of samples taken, and the range of tests performed on them, varies from region to region.

In the past, pollution control has very much been the implementation of regulations to solve problems as they have been proved to be damaging the environment. Regulations were quickly introduced to ban the use of anti-fouling paints containing tributyl tin once it was proved that the chemical was accumulating in fish and shellfish.

If we are to solve the problems of our seas we must adopt a precautionary approach. This acknowledges that we do not know the effects of all substances that are discharged and that we should therefore err on the side of caution and not discharge these materials, even if there is no scientific evidence that they actually cause damage. Widely accepted throughout Europe, this is only just beginning to be given consideration in the UK. The acceptance of this approach by the second North Sea Ministerial Conference in 1987 was a major step forward in pollution control throughout Europe.

Governments are beginning to realise that the sea is not infinite and we cannot continue to use it as a huge dustbin. International agreements are being reached, often due to the pressure from people like you and me. Industry, bowing to public opinion and legal enforcement, is slowly cleaning up its act. As 1992 and the Single European Market approaches, legislation from Brussels will have an increasing influence in the UK and this too may bring environmental gain. However, there is still a long way to go, and if we are to enter the 21st century with cleaner seas, it is up to everyone who goes down to the shore to keep an eye out for any pollution and to report it to the water authority, environmental health department, local council, MP and the Marine Conservation Society. People and companies that pollute the sea and shore are criminals, offending by intent or neglect. **Don't let anyone get away with it – the more we remain silent, the worse it will become.**

Where Land meets Sea

S. GUBBAY

Marine Site Protection Officer at Marine Conservation Society

The best time for exploring a beach is when the tide is out. It is especially interesting to walk down to the water's edge at low tide where you can get a glimpse of the plants and animals which live permanently submerged by the sea.

At the Edge of the Sea

At the edge of rocky shores you may be able to see the tops of kelp plants bobbing on the surface of the water. These are large brown seaweeds which form underwater forests just beyond the level of the lowest tide down to a depth of 50 feet (15m). Just like an oak tree in a forest on land, kelp plants provide shelter and are a source of food for other animals. They also provide a firm surface on which a variety of seaweeds and animals will attach themselves. The leafy parts of the kelp plant are known as fronds and a close look at these will usually reveal an encrusting layer of delicate, grey-coloured 'sea mats'. These are colonies of very small animals which are an important source of food, particularly for the many snails which wander over the surface of the kelp. The multi-coloured top shells also take advantage of this food so these too can be found in large numbers on the kelp. Another species which can be seen on the fronds is the attractive blue-rayed limpet. It may only be ½ inch (1cm) long but it is quite distinctive because of the iridescent blue stripes along the length of its shell.

Kelps do not have true roots like land plants. Instead they attach themselves to the rock surfaces by means of a 'holdfast'. This provides an ideal shelter for small animals which can live amongst its branches. A closer look will reveal brittle-stars, sponges, and even small shrimp-like animals.

18

Underneath the kelp plants, where less light penetrates, red seaweeds are common. Many have delicate branches and resemble land plants but often the most common, although least obvious, are the encrusting red seaweeds. These species form a thin covering over rock surfaces giving them a pink appearance. They can be widespread, particularly where there are many sea urchins, as the urchins are efficient at grazing away most other species of seaweed.

The common sea urchin is one of the most distinctive animals you might find under the kelp and amongst the red seaweeds. It can be as large as 6 inches (15cm) in diameter which makes it one of the world's largest urchins. The spiky surface is very obvious and some of the spikes have small pincers at the ends to act as additional discouragement for predators. Because of their efficient grazing powers, sea urchins have a considerable influence on the type of kelp forest that develops, so it is particularly important not to collect them.

The water's edge is also a good place to look for fish. One species that comes close inshore to lay its eggs during the summer months is the lumpsucker. This is a large, round-bodied fish with rows of lumps along its side. The male, which has a distinctive bright orange belly during the breeding season, guards the eggs until they hatch, even if they were laid near low water. If you are lucky you might find one on the lower shore. Another fish you are likely to find is the butterfish. It has an eel-like body, up to 8 inches (20cm) long, with distinctive dark spots along the body. These fish depend on camouflage for protection so usually lie very still on the surface of a rock.

The Shore Between the Tides

Further up the beach is the area uncovered by every tide. Animals and plants that live here have to survive extreme conditions. They have to contend with the full force of storm waves breaking on the beach, and the danger of drying out on hot sunny days whilst the tide is out. To cope with this, many of the animals of the intertidal zone are likely to be hiding or tightly closed whilst the tide is out. The best places to find them are the damp areas between rocks, under overhangs and beneath stones and boulders. The shore crab in particular likes to hide in these places, but you might also find starfish, small shrimp-like animals and snails. Remember these animals are in shaded places to stop them drying out so, after having a look, return them to the same area so that they can survive until the tide comes in. Overhangs are the place to look for sponges but don't expect to find them the size of a bath-sponge! They are usually spread like a mat over the rock surface although you can see the pores through which they circulate seawater to feed. One conspicuous animal you are likely to find on a rocky shore is the Beadlet Anemone. It comes in a variety of colours ranging from red to green and yellowy-brown. Its surface is covered with a slimy film to prevent drying out during low tide. The anemone feeds by extending its tentacles which are covered with stinging cells, and catching small animals as they float past.

The animals on the open rock are better able to withstand drying out. Limpets, for example, clamp themselves down tightly against the rock face whilst the tide is out; whereas barnacles, which are permanently attached to the rock, close the valves at the top of their shells. When they are covered with water these valves slide apart and the barnacle, which looks like a shrimp lying on its back, sticks its legs out of the top to catch food. Amongst the barnacles you will probably find Dog Whelks. These are smaller versions of the Edible Whelk and measure up to 1 inch (2.5cm) in height. Dog Whelks feed on barnacles and mussels by boring a hole through their shells and sucking out the contents. Their diet is thought to influence shell colour, so Dog Whelks feeding on barnacles tend to have a light coloured shell, and those feeding mainly on mussels can have a shell with dark bands. Clusters of pale yellow egg cases of the Dog Whelk are easy to find if you look beneath overhangs or damp crevices.

Rock Pools

In some rocky intertidal areas pools of sea water remain after the tide has dropped. These rock pools are some of the most interesting places to look for marine life. They not only contain typical rock pool species but also offshore animals that have been stranded until the next tide.

The variety of life in a rock pool depends on its size. Deep, large pools can be a suitable habitat for some of the kelps but perhaps the seaweed most frequently seen in rock pools is the Coralweed. This small, tufty, red seaweed has a chalky skeleton and grows around the edge of the rock pool along with encrusting red seaweeds which make the rock surface appear pink. Rock pools are well-known haunts of shrimps but you can also find small fish like the blenny and goby, along with starfish, mussels and sea anemones.

Sandy Beaches

The sandy shores we head for when looking for a good beach can be very hostile areas for marine life. Areas of coarse sand dry out quickly and do not contain much organic material for food. As the sand grains get finer, the sandy shores become more hospitable to marine life. These conditions limit the variety of animals which live on sandy beaches and those that do usually bury themselves into the sand whilst the tide is out. Despite this it is possible to find the hiding places of the animals by the clues they leave behind.

The Sand Mason Worm is a frequent inhabitant of many sandy beaches and can be found near the low water mark. It lives in a tube which it builds from coarse sand and fragments of shells. This projects above the beach surface as a ragged edged tube. On some beaches large areas of the lower shore are covered by these tubes with perhaps more than 25 in a square metre. The Lug Worm also leaves a clue of its whereabouts on the surface of the sand. These worms live in burrows and leave a conspicuous cast on the surface around the hole. A more obvious worm which can be found on sandy beaches where there are outcrops of rock is the Honeycomb Worm found on southern and western coasts of Britain. Each worm forms a tube of coarse sand on the rock surface which can build up as 'reefs' many metres across.

One of the larger animals which lives buried in the sand is the Sea Potato or Heart Urchin. This hairy, sandy coloured ball is a sea urchin but unlike the Common Sea Urchin of rocky areas it has a distinctive head and tail end. The Sea Potato tunnels its way through the sand feeding on small particles of organic matter. At the same time it maintains a channel to the surface through which water is drawn for respiration. The Masked Crab has a somewhat similar lifestyle. It also lives buried in sand and uses its two long antennae to form a tube to the surface, bringing down sea water from which it can extract oxygen.

Some of the more muddy beaches are colonised by 'beds' of Sea Grasses. These are flowering plants just like those found on land, which are able to survive when totally submerged by the tide. They produce small flowers during spring and summer, and it is also possible to find the seeds attached. Sea Grass beds provide shelter for a variety of juvenile fish and Cuttlefish eggs, and small Stalked Jellyfish can be found attached to the leaves. These areas can be damaged by trampling so do try to walk around the edges of any Sea Grass beds.

The Strand Line

The strand line is a popular haunt for beachcombers because something new is brought in with every high tide. It is a particularly interesting area to explore after stormy weather because seaweeds and animals found in deeper waters are washed ashore. One of the more common types of animals found in this area are jellyfish. Often swarms are washed up on the beach, and here, without the support of the seawater, they lose all shape and look like a lump of jelly. Some jellyfish can still sting when dead so don't touch them with bare hands. These, along with other dead animals, are soon cleaned away by gulls, crabs and even small snails, leaving only the empty shells and egg cases on the shore.

The Sand Hopper is an animal commonly found near the strand line. It lives in burrows or under seaweeds and emerges at night to feed on any debris which has been brought in with the tide. It gets its name from its habit of springing away when disturbed.

Nature Conservation on the Coast

The coast around the British Isles is under continual pressure from urban, industrial and recreational uses. The sea and shore are also sources of food and minerals, and are often used for waste disposal. These competing demands have made it necessary to ensure that areas which have special features are not lost or damaged. This can only be achieved by proper management of the coastal zone. There is a network of protected and designated areas to help achieve this.

There are 38 stretches of undeveloped coastline of high scenic quality in England and Wales, totalling 785 miles (1263km), which have been designated as Heritage Coasts by the Countryside Commission. The Scottish Development Department have defined 22 Preferred Conservation Zones: coastline considered to be of environmental, scenic or ecological importance. Often these areas are also designated as Areas of Outstanding Natural Beauty in England, Wales and Northern Ireland or National Scenic Areas in Scotland. These various designations do not give specific protection but there are management plans drawn up which are referred to when local developments are being considered.

In addition, numerous Sites of Special Scientific Interest have been identified because of their flora, fauna, geology or physiography. They are not managed reserves but any development by the private landowner should be reported to the Nature Conservancy Council and potentially damaging operations can be restricted. There is also a wide range of reserves with coastal sections which are managed to protect their environment. For example National Nature Reserves, County Conservation Trust, Royal Society for the Protection of Birds, and local authority reserves.

However, all these designated conservation sites are for the management and protection of features above the tide line. The area below high water is owned by the Crown and managed by the Crown Estates Commission. Until recently even the most outstanding sites for marine life had no legal protection.

One method being used to afford some protection to the marine environment is the establishment of Voluntary Marine Conservation Areas. These are areas where some form of consultative/ management group has been set up to bring together organisations and individuals involved with the sea, whether for work or recreation. Their aim is to promote harmonious use of the area, whilst preventing deterioration of the quality of the marine environment and the life it supports. There are nine of these Voluntary Marine Conservation Areas; five in England – Helford River, Roseland, Wembury, Purbeck and the Seven Sisters; two in Wales – Bardsey Island, Skomer Island; one in Scotland – St. Abb's Head; and one in Northern Ireland – Strangford Lough.

Since 1981 it has been possible to set up legally protected Marine Nature Reserves. The first one was declared in November 1986, around the island of Lundy which lies off the coast of Devon, an area which is particularly rich and varied in its marine life. At least six more Marine Nature Reserves are planned around the country. These are likely to be at special places along our coast but we still have a responsibility to be thoughtful when we explore the beach wherever we are. The Marine Conservation Society's 'Seashore Code' is a useful guide to help you enjoy exploring the coast while keeping it intact for those who follow you.

Coastal Paths

DR CAROLYN HEEPS
Conservation Officer

Walking is the best way to appreciate the seascape and rich diversity of plant and animal life around the coastline of the British Isles. Parts of Britain's 7,000 miles (11,000) km of coastline are owned or managed by conservation bodies such as the National Trust, RSPB and County Wildlife Trusts whilst other areas, although in private ownership, are within designated National Parks, Areas of Outstanding Natural Beauty and Heritage Coasts. Most allow access via a network of public footpaths and bridleways, many of which follow long stretches of the coastline. It is worth getting away from the hustle and bustle of the main tourist resorts in order to explore and appreciate breathtakingly beautiful scenery and the rich and varied wildlife – linger awhile on a prominent headland, look out to sea, and you may be rewarded with a glimpse of dolphins or basking sharks.

Planning and Preparation

Footwear is vitally important – don't be tempted to walk any distance in beach sandals: a good pair of trainers may be adequate for a stroll along a well-used path, but for more serious walking over more rugged terrain a pair of well-fitting, comfortable walking boots is essential.

Invest in a map of the area: the Ordnance Survey produce a range of maps suitable for recreational and leisure purposes with footpaths and bridleways clearly marked, or purchase a good local guidebook which details walks of varying distance over a range of terrains. Other essentials include a small rucksack for carrying food and drink, a first-aid kit and lightweight waterproofs – we all know how unpredictable the British weather can be! A pair of binoculars and a camera are useful if you have them – they enable you to get a good view of animal wildlife without disturbing them, and photographs are a good reminder of an enjoyable walk. It is wise to plan your walk in advance – the local Tourist Board, National Trust office or any nearby nature reserve information centre will be able to give advice and details of local walks. They may also advertise guided walks in the company of an expert: guided walks are a good way of learning a lot about a specific site in a limited amount of time.

For those who enjoy walking holidays, many long-distance footpaths have coastal sections; indeed, some of Britain's finest footpaths are completely coastal.* These paths are clearly marked on Ordnance Survey maps and are well signposted on the ground.

Above all, enjoy your walk, whether it is a short, leisurely amble along a deserted beach or a hike along the rocky slopes of our wildest stretches of coastline. Remember the Seashore and the Country Codes and take time to enjoy the wonders of the marine environment.

* The major coastal paths of the British Isles are marked on the maps in the regional sections.

Seashore Code

* SHOW RESPECT FOR SEA CREATURES
* TAKE YOUR RUBBISH HOME WITH YOU
* TAKE PHOTOS, NOT LIVING ANIMALS
* DRIVE ON ROADS, NOT BEACHES
* BE CAREFUL NEAR CLIFFS
* AVOID DISTURBING WILDLIFE

Key to the Entries

The Golden List

This edition of the Good Beach Guide is the first to include *The Golden List*, a publication first compiled in 1960 by the Coastal Anti-Pollution League. Their work has now been incorporated into that of the Marine Conservation Society and so the two publications can be joined together into one definitive guide.

The Golden List gives at-a-glance information on any beach which is designated by the EC as a bathing water, any undesignated beach which is monitored by the local National Rivers Authority (NRA) unit, or any beach where a sewage outfall is present. Where an outfall is present, details of the treatment method, the population that the outfall serves and the location of the pipe itself is listed. *The Golden List* for each area is given at the beginning of the relevant section.

Water Quality

The 1976 European Bathing Waters Quality Directive specifies that designated bathing beaches in each EC country must be monitored throughout the bathing season (usually taken to be May–September) and their compliance to the Directive published. The UK government has chosen to base compliance of beaches on the levels of total coliform bacteria and faecal coliform bacteria found in the samples. These bacterial levels give a good indication of the level of human sewage in the water. For a beach to pass, the imperative (I) (or minimum standards) must be met. Guideline (G) standards also exist, which are twenty times stricter than the (I) values.

When the government releases the annual bathing water results for the UK, each beach is simply listed as pass or fail. This will tell you whether a beach met minimum standards during the season, but will not tell you just *how* well (or how badly) a beach passed or failed. We have therefore devised a grading system to help further distinguish the quality of bathing water.

There are many criteria listed in the directive (such as viral levels and the presence of salmonella) which the Marine Conservation Society would like to see considered in the monitoring of beaches, but as the government only bases its results on two sets of criteria, we can only do the same. However, we have decided to make more use of the guideline (G) values for total/faecal coliform bacteria – and grade beaches in relation to these values, too. This has been done by allocating star ratings to each monitored beach where:

★★★★ has met *all* (I) and (G) values. These waters are of a very high quality.

★★★ has met all (I) values but not all (G) values. These waters are of good quality.

★★ has not met either all (I) or (G) values. ★★ is the border area for pass or fail and so some will be marked **f**★★ if they failed in 1989.

The ★★ band is a very broad one: it runs from generally clean beaches, where one exceptional sample has not met the (I) values, to others where the (I) values have been exceeded in several samples. Certainly beaches which passed but only have a ★★ value should not be considered a cause for great concern.

★ beaches *are* a cause for concern. All fail the minimum EC standard for clean bathing water, have exceeded the (I) values in more than a third of the samples taken and have failed.

Star gradings divided by a line are those where there was insufficient data to further distinguish water quality.

Sewage Treatment

Details of sewage discharge are given in both *The Golden List* at the start of each regional chapter and with the entries in the guide itself. Entries in the text show the type of treatment given and these are explained below.

Raw sewage
Sewage that goes straight from the toilet or sink to the sea.

Screening
A wire mesh (usually with a pore size of less than 6mm) sieves out any large non-biodegradable solids such as plastics or rock.

Maceration
The sewage is mashed (or comminuted) to aid the breakdown of the organic material after sea disposal. Its value is now under question: not only may its acceleratory effect be overestimated but other wastes, such as plastic strips from sanitary towels, tend to be chopped up too and land up as plastic 'confetti' on the beach. (If people stopped putting plastics down the toilet altogether this would be a great help.)

Tidal tank
If the waters off a beach are shallow, a tidal tank may be used. The sewage, treated or untreated, is stored in a tank and is only released as the tide is going out. The aim is to achieve maximum dilution and prevent the sewage washing back on to the beach.

Primary treatment
Sewage is passed through settlement tanks. Large solids settle out and are disposed of as a sludge, either by dumping on land or at sea.

Secondary treatment
After primary settlement, the sewage passes to an activated sludge plant where it is mixed to increase the oxygen content and hence increase bacterial activity which breaks it down. The effluent is then passed slowly through a final treatment pond, where the bacterial numbers fall before the treated effluent is discharged. Alternatively, after initial treatment, the sewage is trickled through a gravel bed before disposal through a pond. There is bacterial growth on the large surface area of the gravel and this ensures the breakdown of the sewage.

Other treatments
A large number of different chemical treatments can be used to disinfect and sterilize sewage effluent before discharge: for example, hydrogen peroxide, chlorine or ozone. An alternative to disinfection is flocculation – a process in which a lime-based chemical slurry is combined with the sewage in a single stage upward flow treatment tank. This makes the suspended solids combine with the slurry to form a sludge that can be removed from the tank.

KEY TO GOLDEN LIST

Beaches in **bold** are EC designated beaches which have been monitored between May and September. Beaches in light type are not EC designated beaches.

LSO   Long Sea Outfall
SSO   Storm Sewer Overflow
STW   Sewage Treatment Works

LWM   Low Water Mark
HWM   High Water Mark

Other entries

Litter

Where possible, we have tried to include details of any significant litter problems reported and any cleaning undertaken on a regular basis.

Dogs

We have tried to indicate where dogs are not permitted on beaches. In most cases, local by-laws have been introduced to restrict access of dogs to the beach, with provisions for their control on the surrounding land – promenades, paths, gardens etc. In some areas, laws regarding the removal of canine faeces have also been applied and owners are required to clean up any mess their pet makes on the beach or surrounding area. At some beaches 'poop scoops' are available.

Bathing Safety

Reported conditions that make bathing dangerous are indicated, but always remember to take great care wherever you enter the water.

f = failed to meet EC standard for clean bathing water in 1989.
Numbered beaches are included in the following chapter.

Long distance coastal paths
South West Coast Path
562 miles (904km), but made up of four main sections:
(1) Minehead to Padstow 131 miles (211km).
(2) Padstow to Falmouth 158 miles (254km).
(3) Falmouth to Exmouth 174 miles (280km).
(4) Exmouth to Poole 99 miles (159km).

Isle of Wight Coastal Path
A circuit of the island 60 miles (97km).

Solent Way
Milford on Sea to Portsmouth 60 miles (97km).

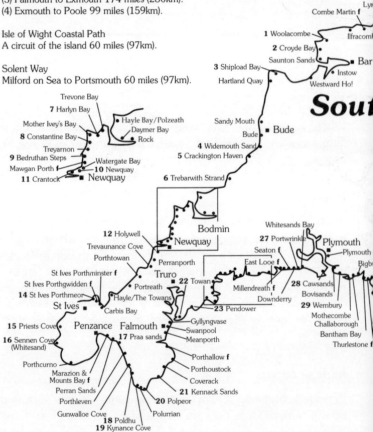

■ Bristol

Clevedon **f**
Sandy Bay
Weston-Super-Mare ● ■ Weston-Super-Mare
Brean ●
Weir ●
Berrow **f** ●
Minehead **f** ● Burnham on Sea **f**
■ Blue Anchor
ad ●
Dunster **f**

■ Taunton

est England

Southampton

Avon Beach **f**
Mudeford Sandbanks   **52** Highcliffe
Hengistbury Head   Castle
51 Bournemouth   Cowes **f**
Lyme Regis **f** Charmouth   **50** Poole
Seaton **41** Seatown   Dorchester   Ryde **f**
                 ■   **45** Durdle Door   Seagrove **f**
Branscombe   Church Ope Cove Shell Bay Gurnard St Helens **f**
         Eypemouth Lodmoor   **46** Lulworth Cove Colwell
         West Bay   **49** Studland Totland Ventnor **f**
Beer   **48** Swanage **56** Compton
39 Sidmouth   **47** Kimmeridge   Bay
Ladram Bay   **42** Burton Bradstock   Shanklin
38 Budleigh Salterton **43** Weymouth **44** Ringstead Bay   **53** Sandown
                                      Bowleaze Cove   Whitecliffe Bay **f**
Sandy Bay   Portland Sandfoot Castle   Bembridge **f**
              Portland Castle Cove

                                          37 Dawlish Warren
                                  Teignmouth ● ● Dawlish
                        Maidencombe ●   Shaldon
                        Babbacombe ●   Ness Cove
Par and Spit **f**   Torquay ■   Watcombe
Crinnis **f** Readymoney Cove   **33** Torre Abbey **36** Oddicombe
Charlestown **f** **25** Lantic Bay Hollicombe ● **35** Ansteys/Redgate Cove
Porthpean   Lantivet Bay Paignton ●   Beacon Cove
Pentewan **f**   Lansallos Bay Goodrington ● **34** Meadfoot
Portmellon   Talland Bay   **32** Broadsands Shoalstone
         Polkerris   St Mary's Bay
Porthluney Polstreath
         Gorran Haven
24 Vault or Bow

31 Blackpool Sands
and Sugary Cove
30 Slapton Sands
rth **f**

Dartmouth Castle

South-West England

There are hundreds of kilometres of glorious coastline along the South-West Peninsula. Long sweeping bays and small secluded coves are separated by rugged headlands. There are spectacular rocky cliffs to contrast with smooth turfed slopes where wild flowers abound. Some of Britain's loveliest unspoilt scenery is to be found along this coast. But the area is not completely free of problems. Various forms of pollution affect the beaches; untreated sewage discharged close inshore is washed back on to the sands at several places. A number of beaches are affected by industrial pollution. The china clay industry has covered some sands with a film of white dust and the Cornish tin mining industry discharges waste either directly into the sea or into rivers flowing to the sea, for instance the beautiful beaches on the eastern side of St Ives Bay are affected by a 'red' river. The river, containing suspended mining waste, flows across the sand, turns the waves pink and the waste is washed back on to the shore.

Large numbers of tourists flocking to the beaches during the summer can cause problems. Long queues of traffic develop on the narrow lanes and the picturesque Cornish fishing villages become congested. The beaches become crowded and this can lead to damage, for example the erosion of dunes is a particular problem. Careless visitors leaving rubbish will ruin an otherwise lovely beach. To avoid some of these problems a visit in spring or autumn is recommended and in winter you can have miles of golden sands to yourself.

Beaches receiving the European Blue Flag in 1989:

Porthmeor – St Ives, Sennen Cove, Crinnis (Carlyon Bay), Blackpool Sands, Torre Abbey Sands (Corbyn), Ansteys Cove, Oddicombe, Quaywest (Goodrington), Exmouth, Sidmouth, Jacob's Ladder (Sidmouth), Weymouth Central, Poole Shore Road, Swanage, Bournemouth Pier and Lee on Solent.

Beaches receiving Clean Beach Awards from the Tidy Britain Group in 1989:

Hayle Gwithian Towans (St Ives Bay), Praa Sands, Towan Beach, Porthpean, Gyllyngvase, Holywell Bay, Pendower, Poldhu, Portreath, Dawlish Main Beach, Dawlish Warren, Teignmouth, Poole (Sandbanks to Branksome Dene Chine), Brixham Breakwater, Abbey Sands Torquay, Paignton.

The Golden List   *See page 26 for further details*

Beach No on Map	Rating. The more stars the better. f=failed	Resort	Sewage outlets	Population Discharging from outlet	Type of treatment	Discharge point relative to low water mark, unless otherwise stated. Distance given in metres	Remarks
AVON							
	f ★	**Clevedon**	5	1,800	Raw	Above LWM	Rocks and mud. £1 million improvement scheme.
	★★ ★★ ★★★	**Weston-Super-Mare**	1	75,000	Maceration/ other	400m below HWM	Chlorination treatment at present. £13 milion improvement scheme.
SOMERSET							
	f ★★	**Berrow**					Sandy.
	★★	**Brean**					Sandy.
	f ★★	**Burnham-on-Sea**					Improvement work undertaken.
		East Quantoxhead	1	800	Macerated	At LWM	Rocks and sand.
		Doniford	1	5,000	Raw	100 above LWM	Sand and mud.
		Watchet	1	4,500	Raw	100 below LWM	Sand and mud.
	★★	**Blue Anchor**	2	2,500	Tidal tank	100 below LWM	Sand and shingle.
				1,500	Raw	400 above LWM	
	f ★	**Dunster**	1	2,000	Raw	400 above	Sand and shingle.
	f ★	**Minehead**	2	16,000	Macerated	At LWM	Sandy. STW near completion.
				6,000	Raw	At LWM	
	★★★	**Porlock Bay**	3	850 1,200 450	Raw Raw Raw	At LWM At LWM At LWM	Pebbles.
	f ★★	**Lynmouth**	1	4,700	Raw	110 below	Pebbles. New LSO planned.
	f ★★	**Combe Martin**	1	3,900	Raw	65 below	Pebbles and sand. New LSO planned.
	★★ ★★★	**Ilfracombe: Hele Beach Capstone Beach**	2	24,800 1,102	Raw Raw	235 below 30 below	Sandy. Bathing safe.

Beach No on Map	Rating. The more stars the better. f=failed	Resort	Sewage outlets	Population Discharging from outlet	Type of treatment	Discharge point relative to low water mark, unless otherwise stated. Distance given in metres	Remarks
1	★★★★ ★★★	Woolacombe: Putsborough Village	1	11,000	Secondary	100 below	Sandy. New plant gives full treatment.
2	★★★	Croyde Bay	1	6,800	Maceration	At LWM	Sandy. Surf bathing. Strong undertow at all times. Lifeguards.
	★★★	Saunton Sands					Sand. Safe bathing except near river mouth. Lifeguards.
	★★	Instow					Polluted by River Taw and Torridge. £62.4m LSO and STW scheme.
	★★★	Westward Ho!	1	12,534	Raw	10 below	Sand and pebbles. Surf bathing.
		Clovelly	1	254	Raw	At LWM	Sand at low tide only.
	★★	Hartland Quay					Rocks and pebbles.

CORNWALL

	★★★	Sandy Mouth					Sandy. Swimming dangerous at low tide. Surf bathing. Lifeguards.
	★★ ★★★	Bude Summerleaze Bude Crooklets	1	18,000	Tidal tank	75 below	Sandy. Surf bathing. Scheme to resite outfall and screen sewage.
4	★★★	Widemouth Sand					Sandy. Bathing dangerous at low tide. Lifeguards.
		Boscastle	1	585	Raw	At LWM	Harbour outfall inaccessible.
		Tintagel	2	270 625	Raw Raw	At LWM At LWM	Shingle.
		Port Isaac	1	2,425	Secondary	At LWM	Fishing port.
	★★	Polzeath	1	366	Primary	At LWM	Sandy. Bathing can be dangerous at low water. Lifeguards.
	★★★	Daymer Bay					Sandy, Safe swimming.

Beach No on Map	Rating. The more stars the better. f=failed	Resort	Sewage outlets	Population Discharging from outlet	Type of treatment	Discharge point relative to low water mark, unless otherwise stated. Distance given in metres	Remarks
	★★★	**Rock**					Sandy. Good sailing. Swimmers beware currents.
		Padstow	1	4,500	Raw		Small harbour. No swimming.
	★★	**Trevone Bay**	1	1,875	Raw	At LWM	Sandy. Bathing can be dangerous. Lifeguards.
7	★★★	**Harlyn Bay**	1	3,202	Secondary (summer)	At LWM	Sandy. Safe bathing. Lifeguards.
	★★★	**Mother Ivey's Bay**					Sandy. Safe bathing. Pedestrian access.
8	★★★	**Constantine Bay**					Sandy. Bathing dangerous.
	★★★	**Treyarnon Beach**					Sandy. Surfing dangerous at low tide.
	f ★★	**Magwan Porth**					Sandy. Surfing dangerous at low tide.
	★★	**Watergate Bay**					Sandy.
10	★★★	**Newquay Bay**	1	60,000	Maceration/ screens	75 below	Sandy. Surfing. Lifeguards.
	★★★	**Fistral Bay**					Sandy. Strong currents when rough.
11	★★★	**Crantock**					Sandy. Surfing. Swimming dangerous at low water and near Gannel estuary.
12	★★★	**Holywell Bay**					Sandy. Surfing dangerous at low tide. Lifeguards.
	★★★ ★★★	**Perranporth: Penhale Village**	1	3,000	Maceration	At LWM	Sandy. Good surfing. Dangerous at low tide. Lifeguards.
	★★★	**Trevaunance Cove**	1	4,650	Maceration	At LWM	Sandy. Powerful surf. New £2.3 million improvement scheme.
	★★★	**Porthtowan**					Sandy. Surfing dangerous at low water. Lifeguards.

Beach No on Map	Rating. The more stars the better. f=failed	Resort	Sewage outlets	Population Discharging from outlet	Type of treatment	Discharge point relative to low water mark, unless otherwise stated. Distance given in metres	Remarks
	★★★	**Portreath**	1	25,000	Raw	At LWM	Sandy. Surfing. Swimming dangerous near pier. Lifeguards.
		Deadman's Cove	1	25,000	Raw	At LWM	Sand and rocks.
13	★★★ ★★	**The Towans – Hayle** **The Towans – Godrevy**					Sandy. Surfing. Swimming dangerous at low water. Lifeguards.
	★★★	**Carbis Bay**					Sandy and sheltered.
	f ★★	**St Ives Porthminster**	1	50	Raw	At LWM	Sandy. Sheltered. Safe swimming.
	f ★★	**Porthgwidden**	1	42,000	Raw	20 below	Sandy beach. Outfall to be linked to the new £48.7m Marazion sewage scheme.
14	★★★	**St Ives Porthmeor**					Sandy. Surfing.
16	★★★	**Sennen Cove**	1	2,160	Raw	At LWM	Sandy. Surfing north of beach is dangerous. Lifeguards.
		Porthgwarra	2	30 500	Tidal tank Tidal tank	At LWM At LWM	Sandy at low tide.
	★★	**Porthcurno**	1	252	Macerated	At LWM	Sandy.
		Lamorna Cove	1		Tidal tank	At LWM	Sand and rocks.
		Mousehole	2	4,160 25	Raw Raw	At LWM At LWM	Fishing port
	f ★ f ★★ f ★★ ★★★	**Marazion and Mounts Bay**	12	37,585	Raw	11 at LWM 1 at 50 below	Sand and shingle. New £48.7m sewage disposal scheme proposed for Newlyn and Penzance for completion in 1995.
	★★★	**Perran Sands**	1	1,615	Raw	At LWM	Sandy. Good swimming.
17	★★★	**Praa Sands**					Sandy. Surfing. Lifeguards.
	★★	**Porthleven West**	1	4,000	Raw	At HWM	Flint and pebbles. Bathing dangerous. £3.2 million improvement scheme.

Beach No on Map	Rating. The more stars the better. f=failed	Resort	Sewage outlets	Population Discharging from outlet	Type of treatment	Discharge point relative to low water mark, unless otherwise stated. Distance given in metres	Remarks
	★★★	**Gunwalloe Cove**					Swimming dangerous in rough weather. Lifeguards.
18	★★★	**Poldhu Cove**					Sandy. Bathing dangerous at low tide. Lifeguards.
	★★★	**Polurrian Cove**	1	2,000	Macerated	At LWM	Sandy. Weekend lifeguards.
		Church Cove	1	1,700	Macerated	500 below	Rocky fishing cove.
21	★★★	**Kennack Sands**					Silver sands. Safe swimming in calm weather.
	★★	**Coverack**					Sand and shingle.
	★★★★	**Porthoustock**					Shingle with sand at low tide.
f	★★	**Porthallow**					Grey stones.
	★★	**Maen Porth**					Sand and shingle. Safe swimming except when rough. Lifeguards.
	★★★	**Swanpool Beach**	1	31,156	Macerated	At LWM	Sand and shingle. £14.5m improvement scheme planned.
	★★★	**Gyllyngvase (Falmouth)**					Sandy. Safe swimming. Lifeguards.
		St Mawes	1	3,500	Other		Sandy. Safe swimming.
		Portscatho	2	2,400 25	Raw Raw	At LWM At LWM	Sand and rock.
23	★★★	**Pendower Beach**					Sand and rock. Safe bathing.
		Portloe	1	375	Maceration/ screens	At LWM	Sand and rock. Fishing village.
	★★	**Porthluney Cove**					Sandy. Safe swimming.
	★★★	**Gorran Haven**	1	3,128	Raw	At LWM	Sandy. Safe swimming. Improvement scheme planned for completion in 1997.
	★★	**Portmellon**					

THE GOOD BEACH GUIDE

Beach No on Map	Rating. The more stars the better. f=failed	Resort	Sewage outlets	Population Discharging from outlet	Type of treatment	Discharge point relative to low water mark, unless otherwise stated. Distance given in metres	Remarks
		Mevagissey	1	6,930	Raw	At LWM	Fishing harbour. No beach.
	★★★	**Polstreath**					Contaminated by the Mevagissey sewage outfall – improvements planned.
	f ★★	**Pentewan**					Sandy. STW planned.
	★★★	**Porthpean**	1	45	Raw	At LWM	Sandy.
	f ★★	**Charlestown & Duporth**	1	7,703	Raw	At LWM	Sandy. Leisure complex.
	f ★★	**Crinnis Beach (Carlyon Bay)**					Sandy. Swimming dangerous near stream.
	f ★★	**Par Sands (Spit Point)**	1	23,263	Primary	60 below	Sandy. Dominated by china clay factory.
	★★★	**Polkerris**	1	72	Raw	5 below	Sandy.
	★★★	**Readymoney Cove (Fowey)**	1	36	Raw	At LWM	Sandy.
		Polperro	1	3,466	Macerated	At LWM	Pebbles.
	f ★★	**East Looe**					Sandy. Safe bathing.
	f ★★	**Millendreath**					Sandy.
	f ★★	**Seaton Beach**	1	685	Raw	At LWM	Grey sand and pebbles. Improvement scheme planned.
	★★★	**Downderry**	1	1,035	Raw	At LWM	Silvery sand.
27	★★★	**Portwrinkle**	1	785	Macerated	At LWM	Grey sand.
28		Cawsand Bay	2	185 55	Raw Raw	At LWM 50 below	Pebbles and rocks.

DEVONSHIRE SOUTH

Beach No on Map	Rating. The more stars the better. f=failed	Resort	Sewage outlets	Population Discharging from outlet	Type of treatment	Discharge point relative to low water mark, unless otherwise stated. Distance given in metres	Remarks
		Kingsands Bay	2	1,000	Raw	5 & 12 below	
	f ★★ ★★	**Plymouth Hoe**	3	49,000	Primary		£37.6 million improvement scheme.
				368 2,300	Raw Raw		

38

Beach No on Map	Rating. The more stars the better. **f**=failed	Resort	Sewage outlets	Population Discharging from outlet	Type of treatment	Discharge point relative to low water mark, unless otherwise stated. Distance given in metres	Remarks
	★★	**Bovisands Bay**					Sand and rocks. Polluted by untreated sewage from Plymouth outfalls.
29	★★★	**Wembury**	1	2,823	Primary	100 below	Silvery sand and rocks.
	★★★	**Mothecombe**					Sandy. Bathing safe only on incoming tide.
	★★	**Challaborough**					Sandy and rocky. Bathing dangerous at low tide.
	★★	**Bigbury-on-Sea**	1	1,780	Primary/other	At LWM	Sandy. Swimming dangerous near river mouth.
	★★	**Bantham**					Sand and mud. Bathing dangerous.
	f ★★	**Thurlestone North**	1	1,207	Raw	At LWM	Red sand. Sheltered swimming. Improvement scheme.
	★★★	**Thurlestone South**					
	★★	**Hope Cove**	1	1,152	Primary	At LWM	Sandy.
	f ★★	**Salcombe North**	1	132	Raw	50 below	Sandy.
	★★★	**Salcombe South**	1	222	Raw	7 below	Improvement scheme.
	★★★	**Mill Bay**					Sandy.
		Torcross	1	980	Raw	At LWM	Fishing port.
30	★★★★	**Slapton Sands**	1	280	Raw	30 below	Tiny red pebbles.
31	★★★	**Blackpool Sands**					White sand. Shelves steeply.
		Leonard's Cove	2	240 1,750	Raw Raw	At LWM At LWM	Shingle.
	★★★	**Dartmouth Castle & Sugary Cove**					Shingle.
	★★	**St Mary's Bay**	1	90,000	Screened	220 below	Sand and pebbles. Improvement scheme.
	★★★	**Shoalstone Beach**					Pebbles.

Beach No on Map	Rating. The more stars the better. f=failed	Resort	Sewage outlets	Population	Discharging from outlet	Type of treatment	Discharge point relative to low water mark, unless otherwise stated. Distance given in metres	Remarks
32	***	Broadsands Beach						Muddy sands and pebbles.
	***	Goodrington Sands	1			Screened	At LWM	Sand and pebbles. Storm water overflow.
	**	Paignton Sands	1			Screened	200 below	Red sands.
	***	Preston Sands	1			Screened	At LWM	Red sands. Stormwater overflows.
	***	Hollicombe						
33	***	Torre Abbey Sands						Safe bathing.
	***	Beacon Cove						
34	***	Meadfoot Beach						Sandy at low tide.
35	***	Anstey's Cove						Shingle.
	***	Redgate Beach	1	89,000		Screened	At LWM	Sand and shingle. Outfall off Hope's Nose; improvements planned.
	**	Babbacombe	1	1,000		Raw	5 below	Shingle.
36	***	Oddicombe						Shingle.
	***	Watcombe Beach						Sandy.
	***	Maidencombe						Red Sand.
	**	Ness Cove						
	***	Shaldon	1	1,721		Raw	At LWM	Sandy.
	***	Teignmouth	2	14,350		Screens/tidal tank	At LWM	Sandy.
	f **	Holcombe	1	2,500		Raw	At LWM	Rocky.
	***	Dawlish	2	22,948		Macerated	At LWM/330 below	Red sand/shingle.
37	***	Dawlish Warren						Sand and dunes. Bathing dangerous near river.
	***	Exmouth	1	45,153		Primary	166 below	Sandy. Improvement scheme.

Beach No on Map	Rating. The more stars the better. f=failed	Resort	Sewage outlets	Population Discharging from outlet	Type of treatment	Discharge point relative to low water mark, unless otherwise stated. Distance given in metres	Remarks
	★★★	**Sandy Bay**					Red sand.
38	★★★	**Budleigh Salterton**	1	5,000	Raw	50 below HWM	Pebbles sloping steeply.
	★★★	**Ladram Bay**	1	3,055	Primary	At LWM	Pebbles.
39	★★★	**Sidmouth**	1	15,562	Macerated/ screens	400 below	Pebbles with sand.
	★★★	**Sidmouth: Jacob's Ladder**					
	★★	**Beer**	1	3,280	Raw	At LWM	Pebbles. Steep beach.
	★★★	**Seaton**					Pebbles. Steep beach. Improvement scheme.

DORSET

Beach No on Map	Rating	Resort	Sewage outlets	Population	Type of treatment	Discharge point	Remarks
f	★★	**Lyme Regis**	2	4,500	Raw	10 below	Sandy. £8.7 million improvement scheme.
				5,400	Raw	15 below	
	★★★	**Charmouth**					Sand and shingle. £2.7 mllion improvement scheme.
41	★★★	**Seatown**					Pebbles.
	★★★	**Eypemouth**					Pebbles.
	★★★	**West Bay**	1	30,000	Maceration/ screens	1500 below	Shingle; steep beach.
		Chesil Beach	1	86,000	Maceration/ screens	1300 below	Pebbles. Swimming very dangerous.
	★★★★	**Church Ope Cove**					
		Portland Harbour:					
	★★★	**Sandsfoot**					Sandy.
	★★★	**Castle Cove**					Sandy.
43	★★★ ★★★	**Weymouth**					Sandy.
	★★★	**Bowleaze**					Fine shingle and sand.
44	★★★	**Ringstead Bay**					Shingle and pebbles.

Beach No on Map	Rating. The more stars the better. f=failed	Resort	Sewage outlets	Population Discharging from outlet	Type of treatment	Discharge point relative to low water mark, unless otherwise stated. Distance given in metres	Remarks
45	★★★★	**Durdle Door**					Sand and pebbles.
46	★★★	**Lulworth Cove**	1	2,000	Macerated/ screens	below LWM	Shingle. Discharge is outside the cove.
47	★★★	**Kimmeridge Bay**					Rocky.
48	★★★	**Swanage**	1	20,000	Maceration	100 below	Sandy. Outfall off headland.
49	★★★	**Studland Bay**					White sand.
	★★★	**Shell Bay**					Sandy. Strong currents.
		Poole:					
	★★★	**Rockley Sands**					Sand and shingle.
	★★★	**Lake**					Muddy at low tide.
	f ★★	**Harbour**					Sand and mud.
50	★★★★	**Sandbanks/ Shore Road**					Sand.
51	★★★ ★★★	**Bournemouth**					Sandy.
	★★ f ★★ ★★★	**Christchurch Harbour**					Sailing harbour. Shingle and mud. Rivers Avon and Stour contain treated sewage giving a high bacterial count in the harbour.
52	★★★	**Highcliffe**					Shingle.

ISLE OF WIGHT

	★★★	**Totland**	1	2,000	Maceration	300 below	Shingle.
	★★	**Colwell Bay**					Shingle.
		Yarmouth	2	15,000	Raw	170 below	Sailing harbour. Shingle beach.
					Maceration	230 below	Sandy.
	★★★	**Gurnard Bay**	2	1,500	Maceration	250 below	Shingle. Safe bathing.
			2	4,300	Raw	150 below	
	f ★★	**Cowes**	15	15,000	Raw	Varies	Sailing centre. £5 million improvement scheme.
	f ★★	**Ryde**	2	17,000	Maceration	3km below LWM	Sandy. Safe swimming. New outfall completed.

Beach No on Map	Rating. The more stars the better. f=failed	Resort	Sewage outlets	Population Discharging from outlet	Type of treatment	Discharge point relative to low water mark, unless otherwise stated. Distance given in metres	Remarks
		Seaview	4	4,000	Raw	200 below	Sandy and rocks. Bathing safe.
	f **	**Bembridge**	1	7,000	Maceration/ tidal tank	800 below	Sailing centre.
	f **	**Whitecliffe Bay**					Sandy. Safe bathing.
		Yaverland	1	50,000	Primary	250 below	Sandy. Safe bathing.
53	***	**Sandown**					Sandy. Safe bathing in calm weather.
	**	**Shanklin**					Sandy. Safe bathing.
	f **	**Ventnor**	2	5,300	Maceration	At LWM	Sandy. Safe bathing.
	**	**Compton Bay**					Pebbles.
	f **	**St Helens**	1	1,500	Raw		Sandy.
	f **	**Seagrove Bay**	1	500	Raw		Sandy.

1 Woolacombe Sand, Woolacombe, Devon   OS Ref: SS4500

Two rugged headlands, Morte Point and Baggy Point, bound this long, straight, west-facing beach. 2 miles (3.3km) of lovely flat sands extend south from the rocky shore at Woolacombe to the sandstone cliffs of Baggy Point at Putsborough. This end of the beach was one of a few in the UK to achieve a ★★★★ Good Beach Guide grade for its water quality. The 380 yard (350m) wide sands are backed by extensive dunes behind which the shrub-covered slopes of Woolacombe Down rise. The beach is popular with surfers because of the crashing waves that wash the shore and with families wanting to relax on the beach. After building sand castles and exploring the rock pools, you can escape from the crowds by taking a stroll on the headlands at either end of the bay. On the northern side of Woolacombe is a pocket-sized beach, in complete contrast to the long sweeping sands to the south. The small sandy Barricane beach nestles within the rocky shore stretching to Morte Point and is overlooked by the hotels and guesthouses of Woolacombe.

Water quality Beach monitored by the NRA and found to meet the EC standard for clean bathing water in 1989. One outfall serving 5,000 people discharges fully treated sewage 22 yards (20m) below low water, north of the beach.

Bathing safety It is dangerous to swim near the rocks or at low tide due to undertow currents. Lifeguards patrol the beach from Whitsun to the second week in September.

Access A turning off the approach road to Woolacombe from the B3231 leads to car parks behind the beach. There are paths through the dunes to the sands.

Parking There are several car parks behind the dunes which provide over 1,000 spaces. National Trust car park close to Baggy Point.

Toilets There are toilets in the car park behind the dunes and at the Putsborough end of the beach.

Food Cafés and shops at Woolacombe end of the beach; shop at Putsborough car park.

Seaside activities Swimming, surfing, windsurfing, diving, sailing and fishing. Surfboards are available for hire. Hang gliding from Woolacombe Down.

Wildlife and walks The North Devon Coast Path leads in both directions from Morte Bay. To the south, the gorse-clad Baggy Point affords excellent views across the bay, as does the jagged slate headland of Morte Point. On a clear day you can see Lundy Island lying 15 miles (24km) away in the Bristol Channel. The island is a Marine Nature Reserve, renowned for the rich marine wildlife around its rocky shores. The steep cliffs that soar 130 yards (120m) above the sea are the haunt of numerous sea birds. Trips to the island to explore its superb shore in greater detail are available from Ilfracombe harbour.

2 Croyde Bay, Croyde, Devon   OS Ref: SS4439

A good flat scenic beach of soft sand. The mile (1.6km) of sand is separated from the picturesque village of Croyde by sand dunes. The pale sandstone cliffs of Baggy Point stretch away at right angles from the northern end of the beach. The southern side of the beach is flanked by a grassy headland which is the seaward end of Saunton Down. The rocky shore below the cliffs at either side of the bay contains rock pools perfect for exploring. The beach is noted for the variety of shells that are washed up. It is popular with surfers, and a surfing centre in the village caters for their needs. There is some marine litter.

Water quality Beach monitored by the NRA and found to meet the EC standard for clean bathing water in 1989. One outfall serving 6,800 people discharges macerated raw sewage at low water mark on the southern side of Baggy Point.

Bathing safety Strong undertows make bathing unsafe particularly at low tide; the beach is patrolled by lifeguards from Whitsun to the second week in September.

Access Croyde Bay signposted from Croyde village. Road leads to car park from which beach is signposted. A path leads through dunes to the beach.

Parking Holiday park behind dunes has a car park with 100 spaces open to the public.

Toilets At beach entrance.

Food Shop, beach club and café on path through dunes.

Seaside activities Swimming, surfing, windsurfing, diving, sailing, fishing. There is a surf centre in the village from which boards may be hired.

Wet weather alternatives The Croyde Rock and Gem Museum.

Wildlife and walks Baggy Point provides excellent walks from this beach; there are numerous flowers to be seen and the steep cliffs are home to many types of sea bird. The point provides excellent views south across the extensive sands of Bideford Bay. The path skirts the headland leading north to Morte Bay and Woolacombe.

3 Shipload Bay, Hartland, Devon   OS Ref: SS2428

Far removed from the seaside resort or the quaint tourist attraction, this is a small unspoilt cove on the northern side of Hartland Point. The 330 foot (100m) cliffs rise sharply above the half moon of shingle and low tide sand. There are rocky reefs at either side of the beach below the grassy covered cliffs. The steps down to this sheltered beach are steep and quite difficult.

Water quality No sewage is discharged in the vicinity of this beach.

Bathing safety Safe bathing from the centre of the beach but beware of currents that may cause problems.

Access From Hartland take the road signposted to Hartland Point lighthouse. The bay lies just off the road a mile before the point; there are steps down the steep cliffs.

Parking There is a National Trust car park on the cliff top.

Toilets None.

Food None.

Seaside activities Swimming.

Wildlife and walks The North Devon Coast Path leads along the cliff path to Hartland Point. The strenuous walk is rewarded with excellent views along the rocky shore to the south and to Lundy Island on the far horizon. From the point, you look down on to the lighthouse standing on a lower promontory (the lighthouse is not open to the public).

4 Widemouth Sand, Widemouth Bay, Cornwall   OS Ref: SS2002

In contrast to a lot of beaches in North Cornwall, the flat sands at Widemouth Bay are backed by low cliffs and undulating grassy fields which stretch down to the beach from the whitewashed houses of Widemouth village. Flat rocks, which can be too hot to lie on, stretch away in either direction from this popular surfing beach. A grassy slope leads down to this safe, sandy beach. The easy access, which is so important if you do not wish to negotiate steep cliff paths, unfortunately often means that in summer the beach becomes very congested. The cliffs that rise on either side of the beach provide walks away from the busy sands.

Water quality Beach monitored by the NRA and found to meet the EC standard for clean bathing water in 1989. No sewage is discharged in the vicinity of the beach.

Litter There are reports of bottles and containers being washed up on the beach. The beach is cleaned by the local authority.

Bathing safety Surf bathing is dangerous at low tide, and beware of currents near the rocks at each side of the beach. Lifeguards patrol the beach during the summer.

Access Widemouth Bay is signposted from the A39 south of Bude. Sandy slopes and steps lead from the car parks on to the beach.

Parking There are two car parks behind the beach, at either end of the bay, with space for approximately 200 cars in each.

Toilets At the car parks.

Food A café at the southern car park and a beach shop at the northern car park.

Seaside activities Swimming, surfing, windsurfing and fishing. Surfboards are available for hire.

Wildlife and walks The coast path leads off the road south of the beach, climbing Penhalt cliff towards Dizzard Point. There are superb views looking back along the straight coastline stretching north of Bude.

5 Crackington Haven, Cornwall   OS Ref: SX1496

A steep-sided valley opens to the coast at Crackington Haven. At its mouth is a small 'V' shaped sandy beach, flanked on either side by sheer, dark cliffs. Those of Pencarrow Point on the north-eastern side of the beach rise 400 feet (120m) above the sands, which are edged with rocky outcrops. Surfers ride the waves that wash this beach, although anyone swimming or surfing should steer well clear of the rocks on either side of the bay. A perfect little beach for the family wishing to spend a day on a beach with a lovely setting; there are superb walks along the coast path for those that tire of the sand and surf. Unfortunately the village can be rather congested in summer. Dogs banned from the beach between Easter Sunday and 1st October.

Water quality No sewage is discharged in the vicinity of this beach.

Bathing safety Bathing is safe in the centre of the bay, but the rocks on the southern shore are very dangerous. Lifeguards patrol the beach in summer.

Access Signposted from the A39, steep lanes lead down to the village where there is a small car park; it is a short walk to the sands. A road runs parallel with the beach, and grass slopes and rocky outcrops edge the beach.

Parking There is a car park in the village which fills very quickly in summer. A Parish Council car park, with picnic facilities, is situated close to the beach.

Toilets There are public toilets in the village.

Food There is a shop, café and two pubs in the village.

Seaside activities Swimming, surfing and fishing.

Wildlife and walks The stretch of coast that lies both north and south of this bay must be one of the wildest and most magnificent in the country. The coast path follows the grass slope which rises south of the bay: the path leads to High Cliff – a stretch of extremely rugged shale cliffs that rise 731 feet (222m) above the waves. As its name suggests, this is one of the highest cliffs in England. Below is a sandy beach known as The Strangles because of the numerous boats that have found their final resting place on this shore. The rock-studded sands can be reached down an extremely steep and rough path, which is not to be recommended. Bathing from the beach is very dangerous. There are superb views all along the coast path from Crackington to Boscastle; the path can be reached from the National Trust car park south of Trevigne. There is also an information point at this site.

6 Trebarwith Strand, Treknow, Cornwall OS Ref: SX0587

The lane through a deep wooded valley ends at what can appear to be a tiny rocky cove with cliffs framing an attractive view to Gull Rock. But as the tide recedes, an expanse of sand stretching north below steep cliffs is revealed. From the lane end smooth rocks must be crossed to reach the rock-studded sand. A most impressive beach but one on which great care must be taken as the rising tide can cut off the unwary visitor; signs at the entrance to the beach warn of the dangers.

Water quality No sewage is discharged in the vicinity of this beach. There are, however, concerns about the quality of the stream which flows across the sands.

Bathing safety Swimming can be dangerous at low water and close to rocks. Great care must be taken when surfing. The beach is patrolled by lifeguards during the summer months.

Access Trebarwith Strand is signposted from the B3236, Camelford to Tintagel road. The road ends at the shore, with smooth rocks leading down on to the sand.

Parking There are two car parks off the road with about 140 spaces; it is a 2 minute walk down to the beach.

Toilets At the entrance to the beach.

Food There is a café, hotel, restaurant and pub at the beach entrance.

Seaside activities Swimming and surfing. There is a surf school based on the strand.

Wildlife and walks From the coast path which follows the cliffs there are good views of the rocky cliffs, beach and the Gull Rock (in appearance, a small version of the Ailsa Craig rock on the Clyde coast). North, the path leads to Tintagel with its clifftop castle, the legendary seat of King Arthur. In the village the Old Post Office and King Arthur's Hall can also be visited. Tintagel is a honey pot for visitors and becomes very congested in summer. The Heritage Coast Mobile Visitor Centre comes to the area regularly in the summer.

7 Harlyn Bay, Harlyn, Cornwall OS Ref: SW8776

A wide bite into the cliffs on the sheltered eastern side of Trevose Head contains the sandy arc of Harlyn Bay, ⅔ mile (1km) in length. A bank of soft sand overlaid with a scattering of pebbles gives way to gently shelving surf-washed sand. Backed by the dunes of Harlyn Warren which are themselves bounded by the dark grey and brown-flecked cliffs towards Cataclews Point. There is a small indent in the cliffs, forming Big Guns Cove. Access to the beach is from the south eastern corner at Harlyn Village, where a stream flows on to the beach and curves to St Cadoc's Point. The remains of an Iron Age cemetery were found below the sands behind the beach.

Water quality Beach monitored by the NRA and found to meet the EC standard for clean bathing water in 1989. One outfall serving 3,000 people discharges secondary treated sewage at low water mark east of Cataclews Point. In winter, sewage only undergoes maceration.

Litter Some sea borne litter is washed on to the shore. The beach is cleaned by the local authority.

Bathing safety Safe bathing. The beach is patrolled by lifeguards during the summer.

Access The road from the B3276 to Harlyn runs along the south-eastern corner of the beach. There is a footpath from the car park to the sand.

Parking There is a car park off the road directly behind the beach.

Toilets At the car park.

Food Refreshments available close to the beach.

Seaside activities Swimming, surfing and fishing.

Wildlife and walks The walk along the cliffs north east of the bay skirts Mother Ivey's Bay; a lifeboat house stands on the northern shore of this rocky cove. The footpath continues along the cliffs to the point of Trevose Head where a lighthouse stands sentinel. There are superb sea views towards Pentire Head in the north-east and south towards Newquay, with several small, rocky islands lying just east of the head.

8 Constantine Bay, Treyarnon, Cornwall   OS Ref: SW8575

This wide, sweeping arc of gently shelving soft pale sands, backed by large marram-covered dunes and bounded on either side by low headlands with rocky outcrops stretching seawards, is a picture to behold. There is very limited parking and there are few facilities available at the beach.

Water quality Beach monitored by the NRA and found to meet the EC standard for clean bathing water in 1989. No sewage is discharged in the vicinity of this beach.

Bathing safety Bathing is dangerous near the rocks.

Access A road off the B3276 at St Merryn is signposted for Constantine Bay. The road ends behind the dunes.

Parking A private car park with space for 200 cars is located two minutes from the beach.

Toilets At the entrance to the beach.

Food None.

Seaside activities Swimming, surfing.

Wildlife and walks The dunes behind the beach are under restoration, with marram grass being planted to stabilise the sands. There are interesting rock pools to explore. The coast path skirts the bay but the low cliffs do not provide the spectacular views that can be found elsewhere on this coastline.

9 Bedruthan Steps, Trenance, Cornwall   OS Ref: SW8469

The beach that lies below the towering grey cliffs is a visual marvel, best appreciated from the cliff-top. The steep slopes of the granite cliffs are reflected in the many islands and rock stacks that have been left isolated by the retreating cliff line. At low tide the rock stacks which punctuate the beach are separated by golden sands. At high tide the beach completely disappears and the rocks are pounded by the waves that have created this wonderful scenery. From Carnewas Island the sands stretch 1¼ miles (2km) north to Park Head. Steep steps lead down the cliff to the beach. Visitors should note that swimming from the beach is dangerous and that there are areas of the beach that are quickly cut off by the rising tide. Legend says that the rocks were used by a giant, Bedruthan, as stepping stones and this gives the beach its name. The National Trust owns this section of coastline and they have provided good facilities for the numerous visitors that come to view the lovely scenery.

Water quality No sewage is discharged in the vicinity of this beach.

Bathing safety Bathing is dangerous, particularly at low tide.

Access Signposted from B3276 north of Trenance, the road ends at the car park. A path from the car park leads to steep steps down the cliff.

Parking There is a National Trust car park on the cliff-top with space for approximately 100 cars.

Toilets Public toilets at car park.

Food There is a National Trust shop and a café near the car park.

Seaside activities Swimming.

Wet weather alternatives There is a National Trust Information Centre close to the beach.

Wildlife and walks The Cornwall North Coast Path provides good walking north and south of the beach, with fine views along this beautiful rocky coastline.

10 Newquay, Cornwall   OS Ref: SW8262

Originally a fishing port with a busy harbour, Newquay is now one of the foremost holiday resorts in Cornwall with all the facilities of a good holiday centre. Newquay boasts several lovely, safe, sandy beaches that are famous for their booming surf. The excellent surf conditions have made Newquay the surfing capital of Britain, and the World Championships are regularly held here. On the eastern side of Towan Head lies Newquay Bay with its four sandy beaches which merge at low tide to give a long sweep of sand below the steep encircling cliffs. Adjacent to the harbour is the sheltered Towan Beach. A promenade at the base of the cliffs is reached by steps from the town above. This beach is bounded to the east by an island, linked to the cliffs by a bridge. Beyond the island, on the south-eastern side of the bay, are the Great Western and Tolcarne beaches; both are popular for surfing and are separated by Tolcarne Point. Lusty Glaze beach is beyond Barrowfield, an area of open grassland. The final beach which faces Newquay is Porth beach. As its name suggests, this is a 'porth' type beach with a long, narrow beach located at the mouth of a valley. Cliffs rise on either side of the sands but in contrast to the other beaches there is level access and soft sands which remain exposed at high water. On the western side of Towan Head lies the ⅔ mile (1km) sweep of Fistral Bay; it is backed by low dunes and a golf course. It is particularly good for surfing as it is exposed to the full force of the Atlantic. Dogs are banned from Porth beach between Easter and 1st October.

Water quality Towan and Fistral beaches are designated bathing waters monitored by the NRA. Both met the EC standard in 1989. One outfall serving 60,000 people discharges macerated sewage at low water mark off Towan Head.

Litter Newquay's beaches are cleared daily during the summer.

Bathing safety Safe bathing from all beaches, unless red flag is flying. The beach is patrolled by lifeguards from mid-May to the end of September.

Access Beaches are signposted from Newquay and there are ramps and steps down the cliffs to the sand.

Parking For Newquay Bay beaches there are car parks at Narrowcliff, Manor Road, Dane Road and Headland Road. There is a large car park off the road behind Porth beach. For the Fistral beach there is a car park at the end of the Headland Road, adjacent to the Headland Hotel.

Toilets There are toilets at the North and South piers of the harbour, at Fore Street (with disabled facilities), and at Narrowcliff and Trebarwith Crescent.

Food Snacks are available on the beach and in the town there is a full range of catering outlets to suit every taste and pocket.

Seaside activities Swimming, surfing, sailing, diving and fishing. There are sea angling trips available from the harbour. Trenance Gardens pitch and putt, a golf driving range, and a boating lake.

Wet weather alternatives Sports centre, aquarium, Dairyland and Lappa Valley, Huers Hut, Trenance Cottages Museum and Tunnels through Time. Trenance Leisure Park and Zoo, including Water World – a water centre with fun pool, toddlers' pool and 28 yard (25m) lane pool. Water World will be incorporated into the new Blue Lagoon Leisure Complex during 1990 and this will add water rides and social areas to the attractions listed above.

Wildlife and walks There are some pleasant walks only a short distance from Newquay. Taking the coast path north of the town, the path climbs on to a headland which overlooks the Whipsderry, a small cove walled by high cliffs. On the headland, there are two Bronze Age burial mounds and the remains of a fortress. Continuing along the coast there are excellent views back across Newquay Bay and Watergate Bay. There are also walks south on to Towan Head where you are rewarded with excellent views north along the coast. The coast path continues along Fistral Beach to Pentire Head East which overlooks Crantock Beach.

11 Crantock, Cornwall   OS Ref: SW7761

An excellent sandy beach nestles between the twin headlands of Pentire Point East and Pentire Point West. The beach is backed by high dunes and Rushy Green, an area of undulating grassland behind the dunes. The tidal channel of the River Gannel bounds the northern side of the beach, below Pentire Point East. There is a deep inlet in the low cliffs on the south side of the bay, Vugga Cove, which can only be reached at low tide. There are also a number of caves; the one closest inshore – Piper's Hole – can be explored at low tide. There are many signs of man's activities around the bay; two slipways are cut into the rocks of Vugga Cove, a poem is carved on a rock in Piper's Hole and there is evidence along the Gannel of its past use as a natural harbour.

Water quality Beach monitored by the NRA and found to meet the EC standard for clean bathing water in 1989. There is no sewage discharged in the vicinity of this beach.

Bathing safety Bathing is dangerous at low tide and near the Gannel. Flags indicate where and when it is safe to swim. The beach is patrolled by lifeguards between mid-May and mid-September.

Access Crantock is signposted from the A3075 south of Newquay. A lane from Crantock leads to a car park behind the dunes. There is a path through the dunes to the beach. The beach can also be reached from West Pentire; a path leads from the village to steps down the cliffs. The Gannel can be crossed from Newquay by either ferry or tidal bridge at Fern Pit or Trethellan.

Parking There is a National Trust car park behind the dunes and another in West Pentire.

Toilets There are toilets at both car parks.

Food There are cafés, shops and pubs in Crantock and West Pentire.

Seaside activities Swimming, surfing and fishing.

Wildlife and walks There is a network of paths south of the beach providing pleasant circular walks. The footpath which follows the cliffs on the southern side of the beach passes Piper's Hole, a deep crevice in the cliffs where fulmars may be seen nesting. The path continues to the end of the headland where there is a collapsed cave and beautiful views to be enjoyed. Tucked below the headland is a tiny unspoilt cove, Porth Joke. The walker can either continue around the next headland, Kelsey Head, toward Holywell beach or make the return journey across Cubert Common.

12 Holywell Bay, Holywell, Cornwall   OS Ref: SW7559

Holywell Bay gets its name from 2 wells in the area said to contain waters with healing powers. ⅔ mile (1km) of lovely sands sweep south from the low cliffs of Kelsey Head to Penhale Point. The beach is backed by dunes that rise to 200 feet (60m). At the southern end a stream flows through the dunes and across the sands. A narrow cave entrance in the cliffs, at the northern end of the bay, can be explored at low tide. It contains one of the holy wells.

Water quality Beach monitored by the NRA and found to meet the EC standard for clean bathing water in 1989. No sewage is discharged in the vicinity of this beach.

Bathing safety Bathing is only safe between the orange and red flags. Surfing is dangerous at low tide. Lifeguards patrol the beach during the summer months.

Access Holywell is signposted from the A3075 south of Newquay. A path leads from Holywell village along the side of the stream to the beach.

Parking There is a car park in Holywell village.

Toilets There are toilets in Holywell.

Food There are shops and pubs in Holywell.

Seaside activities Swimming and surfing.

Wet weather alternatives Holywell Bay Leisure Park on the approach road to the village.

Wildlife and walks There is a path north along the beach, it follows the cliffs on to Kelsey Head, where the scant remains of a castle can be seen. From the headland there are excellent views back across the beach, north to the adjacent Pentire Point West and also over 'The Chick', a small rocky island offshore. Seals may often be seen around the island. To the south of the bay the path leads to Penhale Sands, an extensive area of sand hills stretching to Perranporth 3½ miles (5.5km) away. Unfortunately the path is sometimes closed because parts of the dunes are used by the Ministry of Defence as a range. A red flag indicates when access is restricted.

13 Hayle, St Ives, Cornwall   OS Ref: SW5639

St Ives Bay has a magnificent necklace of golden beaches, backed on its southern edge by high dunes and some rocky outcrops. The approach to the beach at Hayle is uninspiring; there has been a lot of development on the landward side of the dunes which is rather unattractive and an army of telegraph poles marches across the scene. However, once down on these lovely sands, all is forgotten – the 3 miles (5km) of rippled, pale golden sands remain untouched by the development behind. From the mouth of the River Hayle the sands, fringed by magnificent dunes and rocky outcrops, stretch north towards Godrevy Point where Godrevy lighthouse stands on an island just offshore. Hayle residents have voted in favour of a £200 million development scheme for the area proposed by Mr Peter de Savary. If the scheme progresses, over 1,000 new holiday units will be created. Dogs are banned from Easter to 1st October at Hayle and Godrevy.

Water quality Beach monitored by the NRA and found to meet the EC standard for clean bathing water in 1989. No sewage is discharged in the vicinity of this beach, an outfall is to be constructed at Gwithian to discharge St Ives and Penzance sewage.

Litter The beach is cleaned regularly and was awarded a Clean Beach award by the Tidy Britain Group in 1989.

Bathing safety There are strong currents around the river mouth which make bathing dangerous.

Access The beach is signposted from the A30 through Hayle. The road leads up to the car parks behind the dunes and the sands are less than 5 minutes walk away.

Parking Car parks behind the dunes provide plenty of spaces.

Toilets At the car parks.

Food Beach shop and café at the car parks. A hotel provides snacks and meals.

Seaside activities Swimming and surfing. Surfboards are available for hire.

Wet weather alternatives Hayle Paradise Park and West Cornwall Leisure and Bowling Club.

Wildlife and walks Following the beach north brings you to the rocky shore towards Godrevy Point where the coast path leads along the cliffs to Navax Point. There are lovely views back across St Ives Bay and numerous sea birds can be seen nesting on the cliffs.

14 Porthmeor, St Ives, Cornwall   OS Ref: SW5241

The delightful old buildings which are crowded together on the narrow streets around the harbour spill directly on to the beach at Porthmeor. A row of stone houses faces on to the sands but they in no way spoil this most attractive of beaches. Below St Ives Head, also known as The Island, ⅔ mile (1km) of soft sand backed by low cliffs stretches west. Unlike the more sheltered beaches on the other side of the headland. Porthmeor is a surfer's beach, with the waves from the Atlantic rolling on to the shore. A promenade at the foot of the cliffs provides all the facilities needed for a day on this lovely beach which was awarded a Blue Flag in 1989. St Ives is famous for its quality of light and this has made it popular with artists, a fact reflected in the numerous art galleries and craft workshops to be found in the town. Dogs are banned from Easter until 1st October.

Water quality Beach monitored by the NRA and found to meet the EC standard for clean bathing water in 1989. No sewage is discharged in the vicinity of this beach. An outfall off Porthminster beach on the St Ives Bay side of the headland discharges untreated sewage through a tidal tank. There have been complaints that this can wash back into the bay.

Litter The beach is cleaned daily in the summer.

Bathing safety Care must be taken. The beach is patrolled by lifeguards in the summer. An area for use of surfboards is marked with buoys.

Access The beach is signposted within the town but it is best to use the large car park above the town and walk down to the beach. There are steps and a lane down on to the sands.

Parking The main car park for the town is signposted on the approach roads. There are car parks at either end of the beach, each has space for about 40 cars.

Toilets At the car parks.

Food Beach shop and café on the promenade.

Seaside activities Swimming and surfing. Deck chairs, surfboards and beach huts are available for hire. Boat trips around St Ives Bay are available from the harbour.

Wet weather alternatives Art galleries, craft workshops, Barbara Hepworth Museum, St Ives Museum, St Ives Leisure and Squash Club.

Wildlife and walks From the beach a coastal path leads west along the low rocky cliffs to a series of sandy and rocky coves.

15 Priest's Cove, St Just, Cornwall OS Ref: SW3532

Cape Cornwall was recently presented to the National Trust by Heinz, as part of their Guardians of the Countryside programme with the World Wide Fund for Nature. The headland and surroundings remain unspoilt having escaped the commercialisation of Land's End. A tall chimney stands sentinel on the domed headland, a disused ventilation shaft for the mines far below. The rocky Priest's Cove shelters on the southern side of the Cape, its 200 feet (60m) of shingle ringed by low rugged cliffs. There are numerous quiet and unspoilt coves around the toe of Cornwall; rocky shores with a small fishing boat or two drawn up on to the pebbles. A good starting point to enjoy this rugged windswept coastline and explore the shore where marine life is plentiful.

Water quality No sewage is discharged in the vicinity of this beach.

Bathing safety Bathing can be unsafe due to the rocky nature of the shore and the large swell that develops.

Access A narrow lane from St Just leads to a car park behind the beach. There is a path and concrete ramp to the shore.

Parking Car park with about 70 spaces behind the beach.

Toilets At the car park.

Food Occasionally an ice cream van at the car park.

Seaside activities Swimming and fishing.

Wet weather alternatives North of St Just at Trewellard is Geevor Mine and Mining Museum and at Pendeen a mineral and mining museum.

Wildlife and walks There is a pleasant walk on to the Cape with good views along the coast towards Land's End and out to the Brison Rocks where seals can be seen. The coast path provides good walking both north and south along the rugged granite cliffs which are dotted with the remains of mines.

16 Whitesand Bay, Sennen Cove, Cornwall OS Ref: SW3626

On the rugged Land's End Peninsula the splendid sweep of Whitesand Bay is in sharp contrast to the many rocky coves that indent the cliffs. From the picturesque little harbour of Sennen Cove the beach stretches north 1 mile (1.6km) to Aire Point, with steep cliffs ringing the northern section. The southern end of this moderately shelving beach is good for swimming and surfing, being sheltered by offshore reefs. The northern end is open to the full force of the Atlantic and conditions can be wild and dangerous. The beach gained Blue Flag status in 1989. Dogs are banned from the beach between Easter and 1st October.

Water quality Beach monitored by the NRA and found to meet the EC standard for clean bathing water in 1989. One outfall serving 2,100 people discharges untreated sewage at low water mark by the harbour. There have been some complaints of sewage slicks in the bay.

Bathing safety Bathing and surfing are safe at the southern end of the bay. Lifeguards patrol the beach during the summer months.

Access A road from the A30 to Land's End leads steeply down to Sennen Cove. There is easy access to the beach.

Parking There is a car park in Sennen Cove and another on the approach road.

Toilets There are toilets in the village.

Food There are shops, cafés and a pub in the village.

Seaside activities Swimming, surfing and angling. Fishing trips are available from the harbour. Surfboards can be hired.

Wildlife and walks The granite cliffs south from Sennen Cove to Land's End are owned by the National Trust. The coast path follows the cliff top which can be wild and windswept. It is probably the best way to approach Land's End avoiding the severe summer congestion of the most westerly tip of Britain, which has been rather spoilt by uncontrolled development.

17 Praa Sands, Ashton, Helston, Cornwall   OS Ref: GR5827

This fine, attractive sweep of sand between rocky headlands is a popular beach for the family. Sheltered by Hoe Point cliffs to the west, the 1 mile (1.6km) sandy strip edged by high dunes stretches east to Lesceave Cliff and the granite Rinsey Headland. At low water 110 yards (100m) of gently sloping sand is exposed, with rockpools at either end containing an interesting variety of marine life. There is a car park on the headland and a path leads down to the quiet sandy cove of Porthcew. The beach received a Tidy Britain Group Clean Beach Award in 1989. Caravan parks close by make the beach busy.

Water quality Beach monitored by the NRA and found to meet the EC standard for clean bathing water in 1989. No sewage is discharged in the vicinity of this beach.

Litter Although the beach is cleaned regularly by the National Trust, sea borne litter is frequently washed ashore.

Bathing safety A rip current makes bathing at low tide very unsafe; the beach is patrolled by lifeguards during the summer season.

Access Praa Sands is signposted from the A394 between Helston and Penzance. From the car park that is a short walk down a sloping path to the beach. From the car park further up the hill there are steps and a steeper path to the beach.

Parking On the road down to the beach is a car park with 100 spaces. At the bottom of the hill, adjacent to the beach entrance, is another small car park.

Toilets At the entrance to the beach.

Food Cafés/takeaways and a pub/restaurant at the beach entrance.

Seaside activities Swimming, diving, surfing, windsurfing, sailing, raft racing and fishing.

Wildlife and walks The coast path from the eastern end of the beach leads away from the often crowded sands up Lesceave Cliff and on to Rinsey Head. Wheal Prosper, the engine house of an old copper mine, stands on the headland; the property and surrounding land is owned by the National Trust. The mine shaft has been capped and the building restored. A mile (1.6km) further east the ruin of another mine stands on Trewavas Head. To the west of Praa Sands the coast path rises over the cliffs at Hoe Point, passing Kenneggy Sands and Prussia Cove before reaching Cudden Point.

18 Poldhu Cove, Mullion, Cornwall   OS Ref: GR6620

A stream crosses this sheltered, sandy cove backed by dunes and bordered by steep, turf-covered slopes. At high tide there is a fair-sized beach, and the falling tide reveals wide, gently sloping sands, washed by clear green seas. This cove is easily accessible, making it popular and often busy. It can be a good starting point for reaching coves north and south which are quieter. The South Cornwall coast path leads south to the Marconi Memorial ¾ mile (1.2km) away, and north to Church and Dollar Coves. Both are fine, sandy coves framed by low, rocky cliffs, but they are unsafe for swimming at low tide. On the rocks of Church Cove stands the 15th-century church of St Winwaloe.

Water quality Beach monitored by the NRA and found to meet the EC standard for clean bathing water in 1989. There is no sewage discharged into Poldhu Cove.

Bathing safety Signs warn that it is unsafe to swim for one hour either side of low tide. The beach is patrolled by lifeguards during the summer season.

Access A lane north-west of Mullion, signposted to Poldhu, leads to the car park behind the beach. There is a path to the sands.

Parking There is a car park with 100 spaces close to the beach. There is another car park behind Church Cove.

Toilets There are toilets on the beach.

Food There is a beach shop/café.

Seaside activities Swimming, surfing, windsurfing, and fishing from the beach, but no hiring facilities for boards, etc.

Wildlife and walks There are pools among the rocks that fringe the beach, with plenty of marine life to be examined.

19 Kynance Cove, The Lizard, Cornwall   OS Ref: GR6912

A classic Cornish cove which is extremely well known for its magnificent cliff scenery and is therefore popular with visitors. 200 feet (60m) cliffs shadow the golden sands which are revealed at low tide. Softer layers of rock between the richly coloured serpentine have been eroded to form some spectacular cliff formations, impressive isolated stacks, arches and caves. This includes 'The Devil's Bellows' stacks which tower as high as the cliffs and are surrounded by the sands of the cove at low tide. The beach completely disappears at high tide, so take great care to avoid being cut off by the rising tide.

Water quality No sewage is discharged in the vicinity of this beach.

Bathing safety Safe bathing away from the rocks.

Access A toll road from the A3083 north of The Lizard leads to a car park on the cliff top. It is a 5 minute walk to the cove down a valley path to the north of the car park.

Parking There is a National Trust car park on the cliff top.

Toilets In the car park.

Food Beach café. Seasonal refreshments in the car park.

Seaside activities Swimming.

Wildlife and walks There is good walking on the coast path along the cliffs from which views of the sea birds nesting on the cliffs and stacks can be best appreciated. There are caves that can be explored at low tide.

20 Polpeor, the Lizard, Cornwall OS Ref: SW7012

The Lizard Peninsula is beautiful and remote, with much of interest for the naturalist. Unfortunately, in the summer it is overwhelmed by visitors and the narrow roads become congested with traffic. If you want to appreciate the lovely coves around the headland, make your visit early or late in the season to avoid some of the crowds. Polpeor is a small rock and shingle cove at the southernmost tip of the Lizard, framed by the cliffs of the Lizard Head and the Lizard Point, a rocky promontory that shelters the beach. The 110 yard (100m) wide beach disappears at high water. A former lifeboat house and slipway adjoin the beach on to which a few boats are still drawn. The turning of the local marble-like serpentine rock has become a small local industry with many of the items sold locally.

Water quality No sewage is discharged from this beach.

Bathing safety Safe bathing.

Access There is a path from the car park 500 yards (450m) from the beach.

Parking There are 2 car parks with 100+ spaces.

Toilets On the beach.

Food Cafés close to the beach.

Seaside activities Swimming and fishing.

Wet weather alternatives Museum of Cornish History in the village, lighthouse and lifeboat house open to the public.

Wildlife and walks Several rare plant species flourish in the mild climate of the Lizard Peninsula, particularly those of the maritime heathland which is a feature of the headland.

21 Kennack Sands, Kuggar, Cornwall OS Ref: SW7316

Probably the best swimming beach on the Lizard. Two separate 550 yard (500m) beaches merge at low tide to form one wide, gently sloping sandy beach. The pale sands, on the sheltered eastern side of the Lizard Peninsula, are fringed by dunes. At either end of the bay the sand gives way to shingle, which is bounded landwards by cliffs. This is a popular family beach.

Water quality Beach monitored by the NRA and found to meet the EC standard for clean bathing water in 1989. No sewage is discharged in the vicinity of this beach.

Bathing safety Safe bathing.

Access A road from Kuggar village signposted for Kennack ends behind the beach; there is a short walk through dunes to the sands.

Parking There is a car park at the beach entrance with 250 spaces.

Toilets There is a toilet in the car park.

Food Cafés at the entrance to the beach.

Seaside activities Swimming, surfing, diving, windsurfing and fishing. Surf boards are available for hire adjacent to the beach.

Wildlife and walks The Cornwall South Coast Path proceeds east from the beach along the cliff tops towards Black Head where you can enjoy good sea views.

22 Towan Beach, Portscatho, Cornwall   OS Ref: SW8733

A safe and sandy beach south of the fishing village of Portscatho. 550 yards (500m) of sand and pebbles are encircled by low shale cliffs on which wild flowers abound. St Anthony Head, south-east of the beach, guards the entrance to Carrick Roads.

Water quality No sewage is discharged in the vicinity of this beach.

Litter Fishing materials and plastics are regularly washed up on the beach although the beach is cleaned by the owners, the National Trust.

Bathing safety Safe bathing.

Access From Portscatho take the road to St Anthony Head. The car park is off this road. There is a 330 yard (300m) level walk from the car park behind the beach to the sands.

Parking There is a National Trust car park behind the beach at Porth Farm with 200 spaces.

Toilets There are toilets, including disabled facilities, 275 yards (250m) from beach.

Food None.

Seaside activities Swimming, windsurfing, diving and fishing.

Wildlife and walks The beach lies on the Cornwall South Coast Path, which can be followed in either direction. There is a 6 mile (9.6km) circular route starting at the beach; follow the path inland along the Froe Creek, turning east along the Percuil to Carricknath Point and beach. From there continue to the lighthouse on St Anthony Head, where there is a super panorama of Falmouth Bay and the Black Rock. The path returns to Towan beach along the cliff top.

23 Pendower Beach, Veryan, Cornwall   OS Ref: SW9038

A lovely, unspoilt beach with an attractive setting facing Gerrans Bay; there are good views from the beach towards the gorse-covered cliffs of Nare Head. There is a ⅔ mile (1km) strip of coarse sand fringed by dunes which have suffered from erosion. In order to repair the damage, access is restricted with areas fenced off. Further west the sand gives way to the rocky outcrops and sand of Carne Beach. There are rocky platforms below the steeply sloping cliffs towards Nare Head. A good family beach with easy access and a winner of a Tidy Britain Group Clean Beach Award in 1989.

Water quality Beach monitored by the NRA and found to meet the EC standard for clean bathing water in 1989. No sewage is discharged in the vicinity of the beach.

Bathing safety Safe bathing.

Access A turning off the A3078 leads to the car park behind the beach. Do not take cars right to the end of the road as there is only parking for hotel patrons. There are board walks across the dunes suitable for wheelchairs.

Parking A National Trust car park behind the dunes has about 200 spaces.

Toilets There are toilets in the car park.

Food The Pendower House Hotel overlooks the beach; it has a café which serves refreshments.

Seaside activities Swimming, windsurfing, diving, sailing, canoeing, waterskiing and fishing.

Wet weather alternatives Veryan Sports Club.

Wildlife and walks There is abundant marine life to be found in the rock pools along the shore. The coast path follows the cliffs that rise to the south east of the beach. There are excellent views from Nare Head and from Carne Beacon. The panorama along the coast stretches from Zone Point in the west to Dodman Point in the east.

24 Bow or Vault Beach, Gorran Haven, Cornwall   OS Ref: SX0141

Sheltered on the eastern side of Dodman Point is the superb Vault Beach. A sweep of sand and shingle below steep bracken and heather-clad cliffs. From Maenease Point the beach curves for ⅔ mile (1km) to the rock outcrop of Penover Point. The cliffs rise beyond to the impressive 370 foot (110m) bulk of Dodman Point.

Water quality One outfall servicing 3,000 people discharges untreated sewage at low water mark on the north side of Maenease Point.

Litter There is only a very small amount of litter on this beach.

Bathing safety Bathing is safe with care.

Access The coast path must be followed south from Gorran Haven to reach a steep path down the cliffs. Alternatively, there is a path down from Lamledra Farm.

Parking There is a National Trust car park at Lamledra Farm, above the beach.

Toilets None.

Food None.

Seaside activities Swimming.

Wildlife and walks The coast path along the cliff-top leads on to Dodman Point – there is evidence of an Iron Age fort with a ditch and bank. At the point, a granite cross stands as a memorial to all the ships that have been wrecked around the point. There are superb views along much of the Cornish coast.

25 Lantic Bay, Polruan, Cornwall   OS Ref: SX1451

A superb sandy cove framed by high turf and shrub-covered cliffs which can only be reached by a 10 minute walk from the nearest road. The shingle and sand beach shelves steeply. The undulating land approaches and the smooth profiled cliffs give the area an impression of gentleness in comparison to the jagged outlines of the cliffs to the east. This is a fine bathing beach owned by the National Trust, but much care is needed when swimming due to a strong undertow.

Water quality No sewage is discharged in the vicinity of this beach.

Litter A lot of plastic bottles, caps and rope are regularly washed up on to the beach which is cleaned by the National Trust.

Bathing safety Strong undertow.

Access From the car park off the Polruan to Polperro road there is a 10 minute walk along the coast path towards Pencarrow Head to reach a very steep path down to the cove. This path can be dangerous when wet.

Parking There is National Trust car park on the cliff-top road east of Polruan.

Toilets None.

Food None.

Seaside activities Swimming.

Wildlife and walks The 400 foot (120m) Pencarrow Head rises east of the beach and from its summit you can see from Devon to the Lizard on a clear day. The coast path that skirts the headland leads to the adjoining Lansallos Bay. To the west of Lantic Bay the coast path follows the cliffs to St Saviour's Point and Polruan at the mouth of the Fowey. Grey seals may often be seen in the bay.

26 Lansallos Bay, Cornwall   OS Ref: SX1651

This lovely small sandy cove owned by the National Trust is completely unspoilt. This cove, shadowed by high cliffs, is reached by a 15 minute walk from Lansallos and this ensures that it remains relatively secluded even during high summer. The grass-topped cliffs slope gently to the rock-studded beach below. There are many rock pools full of interesting marine life, and seals are a common sight offshore.

Water quality No sewage is discharged in the vicinity of this beach.

Bathing safety Safe bathing.

Access From the A387 north of Polperro there is a side road to Lansallos. It is approximately 15 minutes' walk from the village down the valley path to the cove.

Parking There is a National Trust car park in Lansallos Barton.

Toilets None.

Food Cream teas available in Lansallos Barton.

Seaside activities Swimming and fishing.

Wildlife and walks. The coastal path east of the beach leads to Pencarrow Head, a 400 foot (120m) high headland which provides magnificent views of the Cornish coast. East of the beach the path leads along the cliffs to Polperro some 4 miles (6.4km) away.

27 Whitsand Bay, Freathy, Cornwall   OS Ref: SX4052

A 3 mile (5km) sweep of sand backed by 250 foot (75m) cliffs stretches from Portwrinkle south-east to Rame Head. The rugged slate cliffs slope gently down to the beach where rocky outcrops dot the pale grey sands. Portwrinkle, with its tiny harbour, overlooks the rocky shore at the eastern end of the bay. Once a pilchard fishing village, it is now given over to the holiday industry with holiday development spreading over the cliff top. Further west the beach remains unspoilt by development. There are not many access points to this long stretch of beach. There are paths down the cliffs at Tregantle and Freathy. The former provides the easiest route down, but the beach lies below the Tregantle Fort which is used as a firing range. There have also been reports that this section of beach suffers considerably from marine litter washed on to the shore. At Freathy the path is steeper but the reward is a superb clean and quiet beach. There are excellent views along the bay to Rame Head, its seaward pointing finger ends in a knoll topped by a small chapel. On a calm day the water may look very inviting, but beware of strong rip currents.

Water quality Portwrinkle monitored by the NRA and found to meet the EC standard for clean bathing water in 1989. One outfall serving 800 people discharges macerated sewage at low water mark. A £0.9 million scheme for a long sea outfall should be completed in 1995.

Litter There is a problem in some parts of the bay, with marine litter being washed onto the beach. There is a considerable amount of plastic including bottles, old buckets and packaging.

Bathing safety Bathing is unsafe; the beach is valleyed which causes a tidal race and undertow. Two lifesaving clubs patrol the beach at weekends.

Access Whitesand is signposted from the B3247. There are paths down the cliffs at Portwrinkle, Tregonhawke, Tregantle and Freathy. The area around Tregantle Barracks is use by the army as a firing range and a red flag indicates when access is prohibited.

Parking There are cliff-top car parks at the access points; there are 150 spaces at Freathy.

Toilets There are public toilets on the beach at Freathy.

Food At Freathy there is one café on the cliff top and another at the base of the cliff.

Seaside activities Swimming, surfing and fishing.

Wildlife and walks Tregantle Cliffs and Rame Head are owned by the National Trust and provide good walks over the scrub headland with fine sea views.

28 Cawsand Bay, Cawsand, Cornwall   OS Ref: SX4451

Cawsand Bay is at the approaches to Plymouth Sound, the largest of the series of rias (drowned river valleys) along the south coast. The bay overlooks the Plymouth breakwater, built in the 19th century to provide a safe and sheltered anchorage. There is a continually changing scene of traffic, naval and civilian, plying in and out of the Sound. The bay curves 3 miles (5km) from Picklecombe Point to Penlee Point. The two villages of Cawsand and Kingsand fringe the southern end of the bay. Their colourful houses overlook the sand and shingle beach which is sheltered by the Rame Head peninsula to the south. The beach is a series of moderately shelving sandy pockets between rocky outcrops. At either end of the beach the sand gives way to rocky foreshore backed by wooded slate cliffs.

Water quality Two outfalls serving 240 people discharge untreated sewage, one at low water mark and the other 55 yards (50m) below. Three other outfalls exist in the bay, but they appear to be redundant or negligible in their discharges.

Bathing safety Bathing is safe except when there are south-east winds.

Access A launching ramp leads from the village to the beach.

Parking There is a car park in the village with 100 spaces.

Toilets There are public toilets adjacent to the beach.

Food There is a beach shop, and there are hotels and cafés in the village.

Seaside activities Swimming, windsurfing, sailing, diving and fishing. There are boats available for hire.

Wet weather alternatives Cremyll and Rame Churches, Mount Edgcumbe House and Country Park.

Wildlife and walks 2 miles (3km) north along the coast path lies the Mount Edgcumbe Country Park, 800 acres of wooded park land with superb views of Drake Island and Plymouth Sound. The park contains the original Tudor house and a deer park. South of the beach the coastal path follows the wooded slopes to Penlee Point and continues westwards along the cliffs to Rame Head.

29 Wembury, Devon   OS Ref: SX5248

Wembury is a marine protected area set up to maintain its diverse marine wildlife. It is a particularly attractive and unspoilt bay. A valley opens to the back of the beach where the only development is a car park and a small shop and café. Flanked on either side by low cliffs, a narrow strip of sand curves round the bay. Low tide reveals a series of sandy pockets between rocky reefs which contain numerous pools. This area is of significant marine biological interest and, while beach users should take the opportunity to investigate the shore life, a great deal of consideration is required to ensure the area remains unspoilt. The disturbance or collection of marine life should be avoided, as should littering, or any other type of damage to the beach and its surroundings. The view from the beach is dominated by the Great Mew Stone just offshore. There is excellent snorkelling in the area.

Water quality Beach monitored by the NRA and found to meet the EC standard for clean bathing water in 1989. One outfall serving 2,800 people discharges primary treated sewage 10 feet (3m) below low water mark west of the bay. A £100,000 scheme for a sewage treatment works is due for completion in 1992.

Litter A small amount of marine litter, including plastic and metal containers, is washed up onto the beach.

Bathing safety Safe bathing but beware of rocks offshore.

Access Wembury is signposted from the A379. A lane from the village leads to the car park behind the beach, and a path approaches the beach about 33 yards (30m) away.

Parking National Trust car park behind the beach.

Toilets There are toilets at the car park.

Food National Trust café and shop adjacent to beach.

Seaside activities Swimming, windsurfing, diving, sailing and fishing.

Wildlife and walks The South-West Peninsula Coast Path skirts the bay, but the path to Wembury Point is frequently closed when the firing range around the point is in use.

30 Slapton Sands, Devon   OS Ref: SX8445

A 2.5 mile (4.5km) stretch of shingle beach extending from Pilchard Cove in the north to Torcross in the south. The main road from Dartmouth to Kingsbridge runs along the edge of the beach, with a large, reed-rimmed freshwater lake (Slapton Ley) on the other side. The village of Slapton itself is about 1 mile (1.6km) inland. The beach was used in 1943-44 as a practice area for the D-day landings and all the local villages were evacuated while the US army took over the area. A Sherman tank has been salvaged from the sea and is on display in Torcross as a memorial, and opposite the lane to Slapton there is a stone obelisk put up by the US army as a 'thank-you' to the local people. As can be expected on such a long, open beach, it is often very windy but the views all round Start Bay are spectacular. At low tide it is possible to walk round the headland from Torcross to Beesands, the next cove along, but if you get cut off there is an arduous walk back on the cliff path.

Water quality Beach monitored by the NRA and found to meet the EC standard for clean bathing water in 1989. Two outfalls discharge untreated sewage, one at low tide and the other 33 yards (30m) below low water mark.

Bathing safety Safe bathing but beach shelves steeply – beware of the undertow.

Access The A379 runs along the edge of the beach; access is easy.

Parking There are car parks at Strete Gate, Torcross and approximately half-way down the length of the beach.

Toilets In Torcross and at the car parks.

Food Shops, cafés and pubs in Torcross.

Seaside activities Swimming, fishing, and a children's play area at Strete Gate.

Wet weather alternatives Field Study Centre at Slapton Ley.

Wildlife and walks The area is rich in differing habitats and the Slapton Ley Field Centre organise guided walks throughout the summer. On the edges of the beach itself, the unusual Yellow Horned Poppy can be found, which should be admired, not picked. Slapton Ley itself is the largest body of fresh water in the south-west of England and as a result is a mecca for many species of wildfowl and other animals. At Torcross there is a hide (with disabled access) to allow panoramic observation across the Ley and also a corner where children can feed the ducks and swans.

31 Blackpool Sands, Stoke Fleming, Devon OS Ref: SY8747

Blackpool Sands is a complete contrast to its Lancashire cousin. The only development of this beach, an unspoilt cove at the northern end of Start Bay, comprises a car park, restaurant and toilet block. A crescent of coarse pink sand and pebbles ⅔ mile (1km) long is flanked by steep wooded cliffs. On the southern side of the cove below Matthew's Point, a valley opens to the shore, from which a stream, the Gara, flows across the moderately shelving sands. This lovely beach with a most attractive setting was awarded a Blue Flag in 1989. Easy access and safe bathing make it very popular. Dogs are banned between May and September.

Water quality Beach monitored by the NRA and found to meet the EC standard for clean bathing water in 1989. No sewage is discharged in the vicinity of the beach.

Bathing safety Safe bathing but care is required because the beach shelves steeply.

Access The A379 south of Stoke Fleming leads to Blackpool Sands. A side road leads to the car parks where there is a promenade to the sands.

Parking There are three car parks adjacent to the beach.

Toilets There are toilets at the car park.

Food Licensed restaurant, takeaway and beach barbecue.

Seaside activities Swimming, windsurfing, sailing, fishing and diving. Windsurf boards and canoes are available for hire. Windsurfing school with RYA instructors. Beach shop hiring deckchairs etc.

Wildlife and walks North of the beach the South Devon Coast Path can be followed north, passing Leonard's Cove and Redlap Cove to the entrance to the Dart Estuary. South, the footpath leads to Forest and Pilchard Cove at the northern end of Start Bay which sweeps 5 miles (8km) south, fringed by shingle beaches.

32 Broadsands, Torbay, Devon OS Ref: SY9057

On the southern side of Tor Bay, this wide arc of gently shelving red sand has been awarded a Blue Flag for the past three years. The beach is set among pleasant scenery; on the northern flank, green fields slope steeply down to the shore and to the south there are the gentle grass slopes of Elberry Down. A concrete promenade, with good facilities, backs the sands which disappear at high tide. The steam trains of the Dart Valley Railway can be seen on the viaduct which crosses the valley behind the beach. Dogs are banned from the beach between May and September.

Water quality Beach monitored by the NRA and found to meet the EC standard for clean bathing water in 1989. No sewage is discharged in the vicinity of this beach. Broadsands will be linked into the proposed £19.6 million sewage scheme at St Mary's Bay.

Litter Easterly winds can bring a lot of litter on to the beach. It is cleaned daily from April to October by the local authority.

Bathing safety Safe bathing.

Access Broadsands beach is signposted from the A3022 between Paignton and Brixham. The road leads down to the car park behind the beach. There are ramps from the promenade to the sands.

Parking Car park with nearly 1,000 spaces behind the beach.

Toilets On the promenade.

Food Café and beach shop on the promenade.

Seaside activities Swimming, windsurfing, sailing and fishing. Boats are available for hire. Pitch and putt course on Elberry Down.

Wildlife and walks There is a pleasant walk over Elberry Down to Elberry Cove, with good views out across Tor Bay. To the north lies another Blue Flag winning beach for 1989, Goodrington Sands (Quaywest).

33 Torre Abbey Sands, Torquay, Devon OS Ref: SY9263

Torbay is referred to as the English Riviera on account of the mild climate that the bay enjoys. The palm-filled gardens, the white hotels and the new marina all contribute to the riviera atmosphere which is particularly evident on Torre Abbey Sands. The beach gets its name from the abbey ruins which stand in gardens of the same name close by. The main A379 linking Torquay and Paignton runs directly alongside the sands separating the beach and gardens. A wide concrete promenade edging the sands is popular for sun bathing at high tide when the beach disappears. As the tide recedes, fine red sands typical of most of Torbay's beaches are revealed, stretching from the harbour/marina south to the rocky outcrops at Corbyn's Head. In Torbay, entertainments are provided throughout the summer and should keep anyone looking for sun, sea and fun happily occupied. Awarded a Blue Flag in 1989. Dogs are banned from May to September.

Water quality Beach monitored by the NRA and found to meet the EC standard for clean bathing water in 1989. There are three stormwater overflow pipes at the harbour; sewage is discharged off Hope's Nose at the north end of the bay.

Bathing safety Safe bathing.

Access The A379 runs parallel with the beach. There are steps and a slipway from the promenade to the sands.

Parking Car parks are signposted close to the beach.

Toilets At either end of the beach and in Torre Abbey Gardens.

Food Ice cream and snacks are available at the beach; the hotel overlooking the beach has a restaurant and bar open to non-residents.

Seaside activities Swimming, windsurfing and sailing. In August there is a children's week: throughout the week, entertainment competitions and games are provided for the younger members of the family. During the summer there is also the Paignton regatta, the Torbay Carnival and regular firework displays.

Wet weather alternatives English Riviera Centre (with swimming pool), aquarium.

34 Meadfoot, Torquay, Devon OS Ref: SY9463

A past Blue Flag winner, this beach has an attractive natural setting below steep shrub-covered slopes on the southern side of Hope's Nose headland. 880 yards (800m) of moderately shelving fine sand and shingle is backed by a sea wall and road which makes access very easy. The wooded Ilsham valley opens to the northern end of the shore with the cliffs towards Hope's Nose rising beyond. From the cliff tops there are panoramic views across Tor Bay and the Thatcher Rock standing just offshore. The beach is cleaned daily during the season and dogs are banned between May and September.

Water quality Beach monitored by the NRA and found to meet the EC standard for clean bathing water in 1989. One outfall serving 89,000 people discharges untreated sewage at low water mark off Hope's Nose. A £19.5 million sewage improvement scheme is planned for completion in 1998.

Litter The beach is cleaned daily during the season.

Bathing safety Safe bathing.

Access Marine Drive, which turns off the Torquay to Babbacombe road close to the harbour, leads to, and runs alongside, the beach. There are ramps on to the sands.

Parking There is some car parking along the road and a car park on the cliff top.

Toilets At the southern end of the beach.

Food Café and beach shop.

Seaside activities Swimming, windsurfing. Beach huts are available for hire.

Wet weather alternatives English Riviera Centre.

Wildlife and walks There are good cliff walks on Hope's Nose, with excellent sea views and sites for observing sea birds. The path continues north passing through the woods which fringe Anstey's Cove.

35 Anstey's Cove, Torquay, Devon   OS Ref: SY9465

Another in the chain of Blue Flag winning beaches in this area. A path winds down a steep wooded slope to a short walkway which leads round the rocky Devil's Point to a short promenade overlooking this most picturesque of coves. The small shingle beach nestles below towering limestone cliffs. On the western side of the cove, the shingle is flanked by large boulders strewn at the base of the cliff. Here rock samphire grows in profusion in the crevices and on the slopes above. Redgate Cove shares the same bay and the small sandy beach is reached by a footbridge. On either side of the bay the rugged cliffs extend seawards, falling sheer to the water, their mellow colour perfectly complementing the blue of the sea. The cove is a sun-trap and the soft shingle is often too hot to walk on. Dogs are banned between May and September in both Anstey's Cove and Redgate Cove.

Water quality Beach monitored by the NRA and found to meet EC standard for clean bathing water in 1989. One outfall serving 89,000 people discharges untreated sewage at low water mark off Hope's Nose. A £19.5 million improvement scheme is due for completion in 1998.

Litter Cleaned daily from April to October.

Bathing safety Safe bathing.

Access The beach is signposted off the Torquay to Babbacombe road. A steep concrete path opposite the car park leads down to the beach.

Parking Car park at cliff top with 60 spaces.

Toilets On the promenade.

Food Refreshment kiosk.

Seaside activities Swimming, diving and fishing. Deck chairs and beach cabins for hire.

Wet weather alternatives Kent's Caverns, a network of show caves open to the public, are close to the beach.

Wildlife and walks On the cliff top there is a series of walks through the woods on the southern side of the bay. The paths provide pleasant walks onto Black Head and Hope's Nose.

36 Oddicombe Beach, Torquay, Devon   OS Ref: SX9366

One of a series of sheltered coves north of Torquay, Oddicombe has been awarded a Blue Flag for the past three years as part of the 'Foundation for Environmental Education in Europe' programme of awards for good beaches (cleanliness and facilities), conducted in Britain by the Tidy Britain

Group. It is a busy beach but it remains relatively natural in comparison to the beaches that face Tor Bay itself. Oddicombe's 550 yards (500m) of pink shingle is ringed by steep cliffs. The dark green of their wooded slopes contrasts with exposed dark red sandstone outcrops and makes an attractive setting for the beach. A cliff railway descends to the beach giving easy access to the promenade at the cliff base where there is a café and beach shop. The beach is bounded to the north by the rocky Petit Tor Point and stretches to Half Tide Rock at the centre of the bay. This separates it from Babbacombe Beach – a short shingle beach stretching south to a stone pier below the cliffs, which is popular with fishermen. Oddicombe Beach loses the sun in the late afternoon because of the high cliffs. The beach is cleaned daily from April to October. Dogs are banned from May to September.

Water quality Beach monitored by the NRA and found to meet the EC standard for clean bathing water for 1989. No sewage is discharged in the vicinity of this beach.

Bathing safety The beach shelves steeply and care is required when bathing.

Access The beach is signposted from Torquay and Babbacombe. A steep lane meanders down the cliffs to the beach, and there is also a cliff railway to the beach.

Parking There is parking along the roads on the cliff top.

Toilets Public toilets on the promenade.

Food Café and beach shop on the promenade.

Seaside activities Swimming, sailing and fishing. Boats, pedalos, deck chairs and beach cabins are available for hire. Boat trips to Torquay and around Lyme Bay are available. There is a model village in Babbacombe.

Wildlife and walks There are walks across Babbacombe Down, open grassland on the cliff top. This is part of the Tor Bay Coast Path which extends from Maidencombe in the north to Elberry Cove in the south.

37 Dawlish Warren, Devon   OS Ref: SX9778

From the Langstone rock a 220 yard (200m) wide sandy beach extends 1.2 miles (1.6km) north-east and forms the seaward facing edge of a double sand spit at the mouth of the River Exe. The south-west end of the beach is backed by a promenade with shops, cafés, amusements and a grassy picnic area. This contrasts sharply with the main body of the beach. This forms part of the Dawlish Warren nature reserve which includes the dunes that lie behind the beach and the mudflats on the estuary side of the spit. There are good views across the mouth of the Exe to Exmouth and the red sandstone cliffs beyond. This beach provides something of interest for everyone, from swimming, surfing and family fun, to beachcombing and birdwatching. Great care must be taken to ensure that the dunes and sand spit are not damaged. Dogs are banned between 1st May and 30th September.

Water quality Beach monitored by the NRA and found to meet the EC standard for clean bathing water in 1989. No sewage is discharged at Dawlish Warren but there are water quality problems at Exmouth on the other side of the Estuary.

Litter Waste paper and plastic left by tourists is a regular problem although the beach is cleaned regularly and received a Tidy Britain Group Clean Beach award in 1989.

Bathing safety Currents from the mouth of the Exe affect parts of the beach; signs indicate where it is safe to swim. The beach is patrolled by lifeguards from May to September.

Access Dawlish Warren is signposted from the A379 north of Dawlish and the beach is signposted from the village. There is a short walk from the car parks to the beach; steps and a ramp lead from the promenade.

Parking Four car parks close to the beach provide 1,700 spaces.

Toilets There are toilets behind the promenade and at the car park entrance.

Food A selection of cafés, snack-bars and ice cream stalls behind the promenade.

Seaside activities Swimming and surfing. Windsurfers and surf canoes available for hire.

Wet weather alternatives Amusement arcade. Dawlish has all the usual facilities of a seaside town.

Wildlife and walks Dawlish Warren nature reserve is a Site of Special Scientific Interest owned by the Teignbridge District Council and Devon Trust for Nature Conservation. It covers 505 acres on the spit at the mouth of the Exe and includes a wide variety of habitats: sandy shore, mud-flats, salt-marsh and dunes. Together these provide diverse flora and fauna. Over 180 types of birds can be seen annually at the reserve, with thousands of waders, geese and ducks over-wintering on the mud-flats. There are 778 species of plant and fungi, including some rare ones. The reserve is also a bird sanctuary, and a hide overlooks the mud-flats. Guided walks of the reserve begin at the visitors' centre, signposted from the north-east end of the promenade.

38 Budleigh Salterton, Devon   OS Ref: SY0782

The beach and sea wall have changed little since Millais painted 'The Boyhood of Raleigh' here. The town remains a quiet resort. From the mouth of the River Otter, the wide red shingle beach extends 3 miles (5km) westwards past the promenade to the sandstone cliffs of West Down Beacon, known as the Floors. Small boats are winched up on to the flat pebbles, of which several hundred metres remain exposed at high tide.

Water quality Beach monitored by the NRA and found to meet the EC standard for clean bathing water in 1989. One outfall serving 5,000 people discharges untreated sewage 55 yards (50m) below high water mark.

Bathing safety Safe bathing.

Access From the promenade.

Parking There is a large car park at the Otter Mouth and a smaller one in the town centre 3 minutes walk from the beach.

Toilets Blocks at each end of the promenade.

Food One refreshment kiosk with some chairs outside, by the Otter Mouth car park, and another at the Steamer steps at the west end of the beach. One small café on Marine Parade.

Seaside activities Swimming, diving, windsurfing and fishing from the beach. Indoor and outdoor bowling. East Devon golf course.

Wet weather alternatives Otterton Mill – a water-powered mill still used to grind flour. Bicton Park two miles from Budleigh Salterton towards Otterton includes narrow gauge railway, countryside museum and other facilities.

Wildlife and walks Budleigh Salterton lies on the South Devon Coast Path. This can be followed west along the sandstone cliffs known as the Floors towards Exmouth. This route, offering excellent views, passes Littleham and Otter Coves before reaching Sandy Bay, which, as the name suggests, is a good sandy beach. East from Budleigh Salterton the coastal path leads to Ladram Bay. Here, the crumbling sandstone cliffs have been eroded into some spectacular shapes with huge blocks isolated by the waves. There are also several walks in the Otter Valley, part of which is a conservation area with good bird life. A guide to twelve walks in the Otter Valley is available from the local tourist office.

39 Sidmouth, Devon   OS Ref: SY1287

An elegant Regency seaside resort overlooking Lyme Bay which has escaped over-commercialisation. Sidmouth has two beaches: the town beach and Jacob's Ladder beach to the west. The commitment of the local authority towards the maintenance of their beaches is illustrated in the fact that both these sites were awarded Blue Flags in 1989. Even when the antiquated outfall started to malfunction during the long, hot summer of 1989, all the relevant local bodies were quick to act. The town sits in an open hollow between impressive sandstone cliffs facing a ⅔ mile (1km) long pebble beach. To the west are the West Chit Rocks and the Connaught Gardens, which give access to the 1 mile (2km) shingle and sand beach of Jacob's Ladder backed by the 500ft (160m) west cliff. Sidmouth has all the amenities one may require of a quiet resort and is an ideal place for relaxing on the beach or walking in the surrounding countryside, but not a spot for those seeking bright lights and amusements. However, the town comes alive during the first week of August when it hosts an International Folk Festival. Dogs are banned between 1st May and 30th September.

Water quality Beach monitored by the NRA and found to meet the EC standard for clean bathing water in 1989. One outfall serving 16,000 discharges screened and macerated sewage through a tidal tank 440 yards (400m) offshore.

Litter Generally a clean and litter-free beach, cleaned by local authority.

Bathing safety Safe bathing. The beach is patrolled at weekends by the Sidmouth Inshore Rescue Club.

Access Steps and slope from the promenade lead on to the town beach; a sloping ramp gives access to Jacob's Ladder beach.

Parking Ham, Manor and Bedford car parks close by in the town.

Toilets In the Connaught Gardens and Port Royal.

Food Cafés and kiosks at the town beach and a kiosk at the Jacob's Ladder beach.

Seaside activities Swimming, windsurfing, sailing and fishing. There are paddle floats, windsurfboards, and deckchairs available for hire. Putting course. Golf course.

Wet weather alternatives Sports centre, museum and theatre.

Wildlife and walks There are some good walks on the surrounding hills and cliffs; the prospect of Sidmouth, and the Heritage Coast from Peak Hill, Fire Beacon and Salcombe Hill are excellent.

40 Branscombe, Devon   OS Ref: SY2188

A quiet undeveloped 3 mile (5km) pebble beach stretching from Beer Head to Weston Mouth. A wide valley opens to the coast at Branscombe Mouth with grassland stretching down to the edge of the beach. The cliffs and crags to the east are chalk, whereas to the west there are steep red sandstone cliffs. At Weston Mouth, a stream flows down a steep grassy valley to the beach which is more secluded due to the restricted access (pedestrian only).

Water quality No sewage is discharged in the vicinity of this beach.

Litter A clean beach normally free of litter.

Bathing safety Safe bathing.

Access Branscombe is signposted off the A3052 between Sidmouth and Seaton. At Branscombe Mouth there is a short, level walk from the car park to the beach.

Parking There is a car park adjacent to Branscombe beach with 400 spaces; limited parking in Weston village (20 spaces).

Toilets Public conveniences.

Food Café on beach.

Seaside activities Swimming, windsurfing, sailing, diving, and fishing. Boats available for hire. Snorkelling and fishing competitions.

Wet weather alternatives Roman camp, pottery, forge and bakery all open to the public.

Wildlife and walks East of Branscombe, walks along the Hooken Cliffs take you to Beer Head. In the other direction the South West Way follows the cliffs to Weston, Sidmouth and beyond. The area is geologically very interesting with landslips, deep cut valleys and fossils. There is a varied and interesting flora and rock pools on the shore abound with marine life.

41 Seatown, Bridport, Dorset   OS Ref: SY4292

This is an undeveloped and completely unspoilt beach in a most attractive setting. The green and lush Winniford valley opens to the coast at Seatown, where a lovely shingle beach shelves steeply to some sand at low tide. Steep sandstone cliffs rise on either side of the valley, the mellow coloured sandstone making a pleasing contrast to the green grassland above. The cliffs show the distinctive signs of the sea's continual attack, sheer exposed rock at their summit with rock slumped at their base. To the west lies Golden Cap, the highest point on the southern coast, where the cliffs rise 626 feet (190m) above the shore. The beach is very popular with fishermen.

Water quality Beach monitored by the NRA and found to meet the EC standard for clean bathing water in 1989. No sewage is discharged in the vicinity of the beach.

Bathing safety The beach shelves steeply and great care is required when bathing.

Access A narrow lane from Chideock on the A35 leads to the shore.

Parking Car park behind the beach.

Toilets In the car park.

Food The pub overlooking the beach serves food.

Seaside activities Swimming and fishing.

Wildlife and walks On either side of the beach the rugged sandstone and shale cliffs rise and fall steeply where river valleys cut through to the sea. To the west of the beach the Dorset coast path climbs on to the Golden Cap, and from its flat table summit there are terrific views along the coastline and inland over the undulating patchwork of fields. To the east is Thorncombe Beacon, where a fire used to be lit to warn of potential invasion.

42 Burton Bradstock, Dorset   OS Ref: SY4890

Chesil Beach officially begins here and runs the whole length of the coast until Portland. The shingle beach is backed by dramatic sandstone cliffs which are owned by the National Trust. At low tide a band of sand is revealed. The highly picturesque village of Burton Bradstock is worth exploring, too, with its thatched, stone-built cottages set around a 15th-century church.

Water quality No sewage discharged in the vicinity of this beach. To the west lies West Bay, which was monitored by the NRA and found to meet the EC standard for clean bathing water in 1989.

Bathing safety The beach shelves steeply and there is a strong undertow which can make bathing dangerous.

Access The beach is signposted off the B3157 in Burton Bradstock, 3 miles (5km) east of Bridport.

Parking There is a 500-space car park close to the beach.

Toilets Public toilets with disabled facilities.

Food Beach café.

Seaside activities Swimming.

Wildlife and walks The coast path follows the cliff with fine views over Lyme Bay. As with most stretches of the Dorset coast, there are good geological exposures to be admired.

43 Weymouth, Dorset   OS Ref: SY6779

The wide sweep of soft sand overlooked by the elegant Georgian houses of the esplanade makes this a very popular beach. To the north of the town, the beach is backed by the Lodmoor Country Park which extends round the bay to Overcombe and Bowleaze Cove. To the south lies Weymouth harbour which combines the old and the new; the modern berths used by cross-channel ferries and luxury yachts contrast with the picturesque 17th-century fishing harbour. This is set in the old town which provides a pleasantly different atmosphere to the busy sea-front. Through the lift bridge in the old town lies a marina for 1,000 craft, beyond which lies the Radipole Lake. There are views from the beach of the Isle of Portland and Portland Harbour. A Blue Flag winner in 1989, with a reputation for sand highly suitable for building sand castles. Dogs are banned from the main beach areas. Dogs on a lead are permitted in a designated area near the Weymouth Pavilion Complex. Poop scoops are available free.

Water quality Beach monitored by the NRA and found to meet the EC standard for clean bathing water in 1989. No sewage is discharged in the vicinity of this beach. Screened and macerated sewage is discharged through an outfall 1,378 yards (1,300m) off Chesil Beach.

Bathing safety Very safe swimming from all of the beach, which is patrolled by lifeguards throughout the holiday season, April to October. There is a lost children's hut on the beach near the King's statue. From March to October there is a full-time Beach Supervisor and staff equipped with two-way radios.

Access There are steps and ramps from the promenade to the sand. There is an hourly open-top bus service along the esplanade to Overcombe and Bowleaze Cove, and also to Portland.

Parking There are car parks at Swannery: 800 spaces, Lodmoor: 1000 spaces and Pavilion: 300 spaces.

Toilets Men/Women (with disabled facilities) at three points along the beach.

Food Cafés all along the esplanade.

First aid St John's Ambulance post on the beach near the King's statue.

Seaside activities Swimming and boating from the beach, with rowing and motor boats available for hire. There are organised sailing and windsurfing regattas throughout the season. Sand sculpture, Punch and Judy, merry-go-rounds, swings, bumper boats and a free children's beach club provide traditional entertainment. The Weymouth country park at Lodmoor provides a number of seaside attractions including mini golf, model world miniature railway, and leisure ranch.

Wet weather alternatives Pavilion Theatre and complex. Swimming pool, Diving and Shipwreck Centre, Nothe Forte museums, sea life centre, butterfly farm, Portland Bill lighthouse and open days at Portland navy base.

Wildlife and walks Radipole Lake and swannery is a nature reserve with a wide variety of habitats from freshwater lagoon to grassland and scrub. There are many walks through the reserve where numerous types of birds can be seen, including the bearded tit and cetti warbler. There are conducted tours from the RSPB visitors' centre. The Lodmoor Country Park also contains a nature reserve with walks providing views across Weymouth Bay. There are cliff-top walks on Portland which provide excellent views across the bay. Other paths allow access on to the Ridgeway and to the White Horse.

44 Ringstead Bay, Dorset OS Ref: SY760814F

Chalk cliffs and undercliffs produced by landslips surround Ringstead Bay, and at their foot, a pebble beach with scattered rock pools curves 1¼ miles (2km) round the bay. 'Burning Cliff' to the east of the beach is so named because oil shale smouldered for several years in the early 19th century. There are magnificent views from White Nothe Undercliff Nature Reserve at the eastern side of the bay.

Water quality Beach monitored by the NRA and found to meet the EC standard for clean bathing water in 1989. No sewage is discharged in the vicinity of this beach.

Bathing safety Care is required when swimming as the beach shelves steeply.

Access Ringstead is signposted off the A353 3 miles (5km) east of Weymouth. The road leads to a National Trust car park on the crest of the down or alternatively, a toll road can be taken to the car park in Ringstead.

Parking There are 2 car parks with approximately 400 spaces.

Toilets Public conveniences in the village.

Food Small café and shop.

Seaside activities Swimming, windsurfing, sailing, diving and fishing.

Wildlife and walks The area is of interest for its geology, fossils and the vegetation and wildlife of the undercliffs, particularly invertebrates. The White Nothe Undercliff Nature Reserve is run by the Dorset Trust for Nature Conservation. The Dorset Coast Path skirts the cliff top. To the east, Durdle Door and Lulworth Cove are reached and westwards the path leads past the medieval village site towards Bowleaze and Weymouth, 5 miles (8km) away.

45 Durdle Door, Dorset   OS Ref: SY8280

This beach is famous for Durdle Door Arch, formed by the great erosive power of the sea and probably the most photographed view along the Dorset coast. The eastern end of the beach (Durdle Door Cove) is protected by the arch while the rest of the beach is partially protected by a submerged offshore reef that dries in places along its length. The beach is a steep, narrow strand of mixed shingle, gravel and sand which makes a strenuous ⅔ mile (1km) walk to the western end where Bats Head, a chalk headland, forms an attractive boundary to the beach itself. All the cliffs backing the beach are steep and prone to occasional rockfalls – thus climbing or sheltering underneath them is not advised.

Water quality Beach monitored by the NRA and found to meet the EC standard for clean bathing water in 1989. No sewage is discharged in the vicinity of the beach, and gained a ★★★★ Good Beach Guide grade for water quality by meeting both imperative and guideline standards for coliform levels.

Litter A small amount of marine litter, including plastic, rope and wood is washed up in Durdle Door Cove.

Bathing safety Care required as with most shingle and gravel beaches there can be sudden steep slopes underwater. The western end of the beach may be cut off under certain tide and wave conditions.

Access Beach approached by steep 880 yard (800m) footpath from cliff top car park. Access on to the eastern end of the beach down a steep flight of steps cut into the clay cliff can be slippery in wet weather.

Parking Large cliff top car park at Durdle Door Caravan Camping Park (with excellent views across Weymouth Bay to the Isle of Portland).

Toilets At the caravan park.

Food Café and store in the caravan park.

Seaside activities Swimming, diving, snorkelling and fishing. The steep access to the beach means that heavy equipment, including picnic tables, should not be carried down.

Wildlife and walks The undulating cliffs form a challenging section of the Dorset Coast Path. To the east lies Lulworth Cove and the Isle of Purbeck, to the west White Nothe headland. However, the reward for tackling this stretch of Heritage Coast is a fine view across Weymouth Bay and to the glorious beaches below. The chalk habitat creates picturesque downland with its accompanying flora and fauna.

46 Lulworth Cove, West Lulworth, Dorset   OS Ref: SY8380

The spectacular scenery along the Dorset coast attracts large numbers of visitors and this is particularly true of Lulworth Cove. The diamatic cliffs and rock formations are famous among geologists. There is a series of layers of different rock types parallel to the shore; the band on the seaward edge is hard Purbeck Limestone which is very resistant to erosion. At Lulworth this hard rock has been breached and the invading sea has eroded the softer clay behind to form the impressive cove. A narrow shingle beach margins the round bay which is ringed by rugged cliffs. The eastern edge of the cove marks the edge of the Lulworth Army Firing Range. The sound of firing can often be heard. Access to the range is restricted to weekends and August. Local notices indicate when it is safe to enter.

Water quality Beach monitored by the NRA and found to meet the EC standard for clean water in 1989. One outfall serving 2,000 people discharges screened and macerated sewage several metres below low water mark just outside the cove. There have been reports that the waste is sometimes visible and washed back into the cove. A £11.9 million improvement scheme should rectify the problem.

Bathing safety Bathing is only safe close inshore because of strong currents and rocks within the cove.

Access The road from West Lulworth leads down to the shore.

Parking There is a privately owned car park (Weld Estate) on the cliff-top with about 1,300 spaces.

Toilets Public toilets including disabled facilities.

Food Beach café, several cafés, restaurants and hotels in West Lulworth.

Seaside activities Swimming, windsurfing, diving, sailing, canoeing, rowing and fishing. There are rowing boats available for hire and boat trips along the coast to Durdle Door.

Wildlife and walks Rock pools abound below the cliff and contain a wealth of marine life – between 20 and 30 different types of animals and plants can be seen. The surrounding area is also rich in wildlife, for a wide variety of flowers, butterflies and birds complement the unique geological features. There is a series of circular walks starting at the main car park. Clearly marked paths lead west over Hambury Tout to Durdle Door, a magnificent rock arch. There is a short walk from the car park to Stair Hole, a second cove in the early stages of development. Waves break through a series of arches in the hard limestone and are eroding the softer rock lying behind. There are some excellent rock folds and faults exposed in the hole. When the Lulworth Army Range is open, marked paths can be followed east to Mupe Bay. It is worth stopping at Pepler Point to view the superb prospect across the cove from its narrow entrance. After entering the range, a short detour leads to the remains of a fossil forest. Steps lead down the cliff where fossilised remains of trees can be seen in the cliff. In the range it is dangerous to leave the marked paths. Leaflets which describe the walks in detail are available at the information centre close to the beach.

47 Kimmeridge, Nr. Wareham, Dorset   OS Ref: SY9078

The beach has no sand and is formed of cobbles and stones sheltered below crumbling shale cliffs. It is a good spot for combining a coastal walk with explorations of the excellent rock pools. Better for older children than the young. The bay is part of the Purbeck Marine Wildlife Reserve, and a wealth of marine life abounds on the shore and in the shallow waters. On the eastern headland of this square bay stands the Clavell Tower, which was built as a folly and for a time used as a coastguard look-out post. The tower now stands empty overlooking the bay. The opposite side of the bay marks the edge of the army firing range which covers the land between the bay and Lulworth Cove to the west. The shale cliffs around the bay are very unstable and beach users should not climb on the cliffs or sunbathe below them because of the danger of falling rocks. The bay provides some of the best conditions for windsurfing in the south of England.

Water quality Beach monitored by the NRA and found to meet the EC standard for clean bathing water in 1989. No sewage is discharged in the vicinity of this beach.

Litter A lot of plastic rubbish is frequently washed up on to the beach; cleaned occasionally.

Bathing safety Bathers must beware of submerged rocks that can make swimming dangerous. There are, however, no strong currents or dangerous tides. A coastguard's hut is manned by auxiliary coastguards at weekends and sometimes in rough weather during the summer.

Access A toll road from Kimmeridge village leads to the bay, and a track leads from the car park to the beach.

Parking There are two car parks on the cliff top with about 700 spaces.

Toilets There are two toilet blocks near the beach and a toilet for the disabled in Kimmeridge village, 1 mile (1.6km) from the beach.

Food Ice cream kiosk. There is a shop/restaurant in Kimmeridge village.

Seaside activities Swimming, diving, surfing, windsurfing and fishing. There are two slipways for launching small boats from the beach.

Wildlife and walks There is an information centre at the eastern end of the bay run by the Dorset Trust for Nature Conservation who sponsor the Purbeck Marine Wildlife Reserve. The centre can provide information on the numerous animals and plants to be found around the bay. In addition, they produce a leaflet describing a nature trail which is laid out in the area. There are well marked walks across the firing range to the west, which are open at weekends, for a few days at Christmas, the two public holidays in May and for the whole of August. Information about opening days can be obtained by ringing the Range office on Bindon Abbey 462721.

48 Swanage, Dorset   OS Ref: SZ0379

Swanage Beach has frequently received Blue Flags for its high standard of cleanliness and facilities. The safe sheltered bay is flanked by magnificent chalk headlands on either side: Ballard Point in the north and Peveril Point to the south of the bay The gently sloping sands form a good 1¼ mile (2km) family beach with a promenade providing all the facilities of a small seaside resort. The development has not spoilt the seafront. Swanage is an ideal spot for a holiday combining days on the beach with explorations of the superb Dorset coastline. The beach is very popular and there can be major traffic problems at the height of the summer. Dogs banned from beach between 1st May and 30th September.

Water quality Beach monitored by the NRA and found to meet the EC standard for clean bathing water in 1989. One outfall serving 20,000 people discharges screened and macerated sewage 110 yards (100m) below low water mark off Peveril Point.

Litter A clean beach with only a small amount of litter left by visitors; the beach is cleaned daily. There are reports that marine litter can be a problem after an east wind.

Bathing safety Safe bathing. No lifeguard, but a beach inspector patrols the beach during the summer. There is a first aid post on the promenade adjacent to the tourist information centre.

Access Steps and ramps from the promenade lead to the sand.

Parking There are car parks at Broad Road, De Moulham Road, Victoria Avenue and one in the town centre.

Toilets Public toilets with facilities for the disabled at several points along the promenade.

Food Numerous cafés, restaurants and take-aways within easy reach of the beach.

Seaside activities Swimming, windsurfing, diving, sailing and fishing. There are pedalos and motor boats for hire. Fishing and boat trips are available from the quay, where there is also a diving school.

Wet weather alternatives Tithe Barn Museum and Arts Centre, Railway Station Steam Museum, Harrow House Sports Centre, indoor bowling complex. The lifeboat house is open to visitors.

Wildlife and walks The Dorset Coast Path extends in both directions from Swanage Bay, passing through beautiful countryside along this section of coast. To the north of the beach Ballard Cliff rises onto Ballard Down, and the path follows the cliffs round to Handfast Point, which provides excellent views of Old Harry Rocks lying just offshore, and across Poole Bay. South of Peveril Point above Durlston Bay and Head is the Durlston Country Park. There is parking within the park and an information centre provides details of a series of walks in the area. The long distance coast path follows the cliffs beyond Anvil Point Lighthouse, passing the Dancing Ledge, Seacombe Cliff and continuing to St Aldhelm's Head and beyond. There are a series of shorter circular routes starting from the country park that explore both the coast and the beautiful scenery inland. A leaflet produced by the Dorset Heritage Coast Projects describes the various walks.

49 Studland, Dorset   OS Ref: SZ0483

A lovely clean beach that has been designated an Area of Outstanding Natural Beauty. 3 miles (5km) of excellent sandy beach is backed by unspoilt dunes. The beach sweeps south from the entrance to Poole harbour to the splendid chalk cliffs of Handfast Point, once connected to the Needles of the Isle of Wight, which are visible on the horizon most days. The beach can be divided into three areas, south beach, middle beach and the north, or Knoll beach. There is separate access to all three areas with facilities at each. Behind the Knoll beach there is a brackish lake and marsh area which forms the Studland Heath National Nature Reserve. Visitors should note that a section of the beach is used by naturists. Byelaws require that dogs are kept on leads and all faeces must be removed from the beach by the owners.

Water quality Beach monitored by the NRA and found to meet the EC standard for clean bathing water in 1989. No sewage is discharged in the vicinity of this beach.

Litter This is a very clean beach due to the excellent efforts of the National Trust. In summer, 4–5 tons of litter are removed daily from litter bins and sands.

Bathing safety Safe bathing off the main beach; strong currents at the entrance to Poole harbour make bathing at the northern end of the beach unsafe. The beach is patrolled by National Trust Wardens from Easter to September.

Access Each section of the beach is signposted from Studland. It is a short walk from the car parks to the sands. There is a wheelchair ramp at Knoll beach.

Parking 4 car parks provide space for 2,500 cars.

Toilets 5 blocks. New toilets at middle and Knoll beach have disabled facilities, with provision for nursing mothers at Knoll beach.

Food Cafés and kiosks.

Seaside activities Swimming, surfing, windsurfing, diving, sailing, water-skiing and fishing. Windsurfboards are available for hire.

Wildlife and walks The Studland Heath National Nature Reserve containing the brackish lagoon, Little Sea, lies on the landward side of the beach. The reserve cannot be reached from the beach but must be entered from the road which bounds its western edge. There is a wide variety of wildlife including the rare smooth snake and adders. Walkers are advised to wear stout shoes and stick to the marked paths. A leaflet describing 7 local walks is available from National Trust information centre at Knoll beach. A leaflet, which describes local wildlife and guided walks in the area, is produced by the Dorset Heritage Trust and Dorset Trust for Nature Conservation and is available locally. The Dorset Coast Path starts, or alternatively finishes, at the entrance to Poole Harbour. It follows the bay south and on to the Foreland. There are splendid views of the cliffs and the chalk pillars, Harry and Old Harry's Wife, isolated from the adjacent headland by the ever eroding waves. The path continues south towards Ballard Point where there are fine views of Swanage Bay.

50 Sandbanks, Poole, Dorset OS Ref: SZ0487

The sole beach in the UK to achieve a Blue Flag and ★★★★ Good Beach Guide water quality grade in 1989. From North Haven Point at the end of the Sandbank spit, the fringe of golden sand stretches 3 miles (5km) north-east to merge with the beaches of Bournemouth. The pedestrian promenade is backed by the steep pine- and shrub-covered Canford Cliffs. Flaghead Chine, Cranford Chine and Branksome Chine cut through the cliffs to the beach. South-west, the cliffs give way to the low lying Sandbanks peninsula at the mouth of Poole harbour. Here the beach is edged by dunes and overlooked by holiday development and the Sandbanks Pavilion and recreation area. The whole of Poole Harbour is a centre for sailing and water sports, and there is an everchanging boating scene at the harbour entrance. However, there has been a spate of complaints from watersports enthusiasts about the water quality in the harbour area as several people have come up in boils and rashes after water contact. There are excellent views across the harbour and of Brownsea Island from Evenning Hill off the western shore road. A removal of canine faeces by-law has been introduced.

Water quality Beach monitored by the NRA and found to meet the EC standard for clean bathing water in 1989. No sewage is discharged in the vicinity of this beach.

Bathing safety Safe bathing except at extreme western end of the beach near the harbour entrance. Warning signs indicate where not to swim. There is a boat-free zone marked by buoys which is reserved for the exclusive use of bathers. Beach is patrolled by lifeguards at weekends and on bank holidays from May to September. A first-aid post manned by St John Ambulance at weekends.

Access There is easy access along the length of the beach; paths lead down the cliffs to the promenade.

Parking There are 7 car parks along the length of the beach with 1,400 spaces. There is also parking available on adjacent streets.

Toilets There are toilets (with disabled facilities) along the beach.

Food There are cafés and kiosks close to the beach.

Seaside activities Swimming, windsurfing, sailing and fishing. There are windsurfboards and boats for hire. Poole harbour has several windsurfing and sailing schools. There is also a putting green, crazy golf and a variety of children's amusements.

Wet weather alternatives in Poole Sports centre, swimming pool, aquarium, Guildhall Museum, Archeological Museum, Royal National Lifeboat Museum, Maritime Museum, Waterfront Museum, Arts Centre and Poole Pottery.

Wildlife and walks There is a car and pedestrian ferry from North Haven Point to Shell Bay where the extensive Studland Heath National Nature Reserve backs an excellent beach. There is also a pedestrian ferry to Brownsea Island. 200 acres of this 500 acre National Trust owned island form a nature reserve run by the Dorset Trust for Nature Conservation. There are many different types of habitat to be found on the island, including heathland, woodland, freshwater lakes, salt-marsh and the seashore. There is a nature trail and guided walks are available during the summer. Further information is available from the National Trust shop on the island's landing quay.

51 Bournemouth, Dorset   OS Ref: SZ4109

Bournemouth is often referred to as 'the garden city by the sea' because of its many parks, including the upper and lower Bourne Gardens. These wind their way through the town centre following the Bourne Valley, and emerge at the sea front. Bournemouth has an excellent family beach which was awarded a Blue Flag in 1989. Throughout the summer the wide promenade, which backs the golden sands, is traffic-free. The steeply sloping shrub-covered cliffs that rise above the promenade are bisected by a series of deep wooded glades, known as chines. These valleys all have their own individual characters and divide the long sea front into distinctive sections. This is not merely a seaside town, but truly a holiday centre. You may just want to enjoy the sun, sea and sand, but you can also take advantage of the resort's numerous facilities. There are two piers, amusements, and a children's beachclub. In addition, there is a full programme of events throughout the summer including carnivals, regattas and competitions. Dogs are not permitted on the beach between Fisherman's Walk and Durley Chine from 1st May to 30th September. Dogs must be kept on a lead on the promenade.

Water quality Beach monitored by the NRA and found to meet EC standard for clean bathing water in 1989. No sewage is discharged in the vicinity of this beach.

Litter Beach cleaned daily.

Bathing safety Hoisted red flags indicate when conditions are unsafe for swimming. Lifeguards, using inflatable safety boats, patrol the beach. All the deckchair attendants are qualified in lifesaving. The Beach Leisure Department survey the beach by closed circuit television during the season.

Access The promenade is reached by zig-zag pathways down the cliff. There is a cliff-lift to the east and west of the pier and at Fisherman's Walk.

Parking There are several car parks close to the beach and in the town, plus spaces along the roads.

Toilets There are 15 public conveniences along the length of the promenade.

Food There are numerous catering outlets along the promenade.

Seaside activities Swimming, surfing, windsurfing, sailing and fishing. Rowing boats and pedalo floats available for hire. There are boat trips from the beach. A land train operates along the promenade between Bournemouth and Boscombe Piers.

Wet weather alternatives Bournemouth International Conference Centre. Leisure centre 110 yards (100m) from the beach with indoor swimming pool. Russell-Cotes Art Museum. Transport Museum and the Shelley Museum. The Pier leisure centre and seafront amusements. The Littledown Centre, with swimming pools, water slides, sports hall and gym.

Wildlife and Walks Stretching east from Bournemouth is the 1¼ mile (2km) long Hengistbury headland which separates Poole Bay and Christchurch Bay, and encloses Christchurch Harbour on its landward side. Most of the headland remains undeveloped and has been designated as a site of Special Scientific Interest because of the wide variety of plant and animal life it supports. The headland is a nature reserve owned by Bournemouth Borough Council. It contains a wide variety of habitats including grassland, heath, woods, salt-marsh, freshwater marsh, dunes, rocky and shingle shore. There is a nature trail on the eastern slopes of the headland. The summit of Warren Hill on the landward end of the headland provides good views of Christchurch Bay, Poole Bay, the Solent and the Isle of Wight beyond. There is a south-facing 1 mile (1.6km) pebble beach below the imposing sandstone cliffs. In sharp contrast to this undeveloped beach is the sand spit stretching north from the headland to the entrance of Christchurch Harbour, where the groyne-ribbed sands are backed by beach huts. A small land train takes passengers from the Hengistbury Head car park to the tip of the headland.

52 Highcliffe Castle, Highcliffe, Dorset   OS Ref: SZ2093

From Highcliffe Castle (which resembles the ruins of an impressive cathedral rather than a castle), steps lead down the gently sloping shrub and tree-covered cliffs directly on to the sand. A lovely, long beach of sand and pebble extends from Mudeford Quay in the west to Milford-on-Sea in the east. It includes Avon beach, Friar's Cliff, Steamer Point, Highcliffe Castle and Highcliffe Crow's Nest beaches along its length. This is a clean, unspoilt beach which is ideal for a day relaxing in the sunshine. Between 1st May and 30th September, dogs are not permitted on Avon, Friar's Cliff or Highcliffe Crow's Nest beaches. On the promenade, cliff paths and adjacent car park, dogs must be kept on a lead. Owners are asked to clean up after their dogs and receptacles are provided.

Water quality Beach monitored by the NRA and found to meet the EC standard for clean bathing water in 1989. No sewage is discharged in the vicinity of this beach. One sampling point at Christchurch harbour failed to meet the EC standard; there have been complaints about the quality of this beach.

Litter There have been some complaints about litter and debris washed on to shore. During the summer the local authority employs a team of litter pickers to clean the beaches and surrounding area.

Bathing safety Safe bathing but care is required because the beach shelves quite quickly. The beach is patrolled by lifeguards and a patrol boat daily from mid-July to early September. This stretch of coast has separate designated areas for swimming and windsurfing, which are signposted on the beach. There is a slight problem with weaver fish.

Access From the A337 through Highcliffe a side road leads to Highcliffe Castle. There are steps and a path down the cliff. The steps are quite gentle but access may be difficult for the elderly and the disabled, particularly the walk back up.

Parking Car park at Highcliffe Castle with 100 spaces, 110 yards (100m) walk to the beach. Car park at Steamer Point with 172 spaces, 330 yards (300m) walk to the beach and car park at Highcliffe top with 600 spaces, 440 yards (400m) walk to the beach.

Toilets In Highcliffe Castle grounds, Friar's Cliff promenade and Highcliffe Crow's Nest.

Food Shop/café in the grounds of Highcliffe Castle. During the summer there is often someone selling ices along the beach from a cool box.

Seaside activities Swimming and windsurfing; the latter is restricted to Highcliffe Crow's Nest, Steamer Point and Avon beach; swimming is confined to Highcliffe Castle and Friar's Cliff. Fishing.

Wildlife and walks There are woodland and nature walks on the cliffs at Steamer Point, where an information centre can provide details of the flora and fauna to be seen in the area.

53 Sandown Bay, Isle of Wight OS Ref: SZ5984

The twin resorts of Sandown and Shanklin face Sandown Bay, the largest bay on the Isle of Wight. From Shanklin Chine, a deep wooded cleft cutting through the cliffs, a safe and sandy beach curves gently northwards to Sandown and the white cliffs of Culver Down beyond. Almost two miles (3km) of unbroken sands separate these busy holiday resorts made popular by the Victorians, and now traditional resorts for a family stay by the sea. Houses and hotels perch on the cliffs and downs which ring the bay, sloping down to the esplanades which edge the beach. There are pleasant walks at each end of the bay, and the old village of Shanklin itself can be explored.

Water quality Beach monitored by the NRA and found to meet the EC standard for clean bathing water in 1989. One outfall serving 50,000 people discharges secondary treated effluent.

Litter The beach is cleaned by the local authority and licensed beach operators.

Bathing safety Safe bathing.

Access Steps and ramps from the esplanade in both Sandown and Shanklin. There is a lift down the cliff to the esplanade in Shanklin.

Parking In Shanklin two car parks off the esplanade. In Sandown several car parks off the High Street.

Toilets At either end of the esplanade in both resorts.

Food Shops, cafés, pubs and restaurants along the esplanades.

Seaside activities Swimming, windsurfing, and fishing. Beach huts, boats and deck chairs for hire.

Wet weather alternatives Pier and amusements, Sandown Leisure Complex, zoo and museum. Putting and crazy golf, tennis courts. In Brading, just outside Sandown, a wax museum, doll's museum, animal world and Roman villa.

Wildlife and walks The Shanklin Chine provides a pleasantly contrasting walk away from the sea front. A footpath south of Shanklin leads along the cliffs to Luccombe. Here another chine gives access to Luccombe Bay – a small and undeveloped beach. North of Sandown the cliffs can be followed on to Cuver Down. There are excellent sea views back across the bay and along the cliffs.

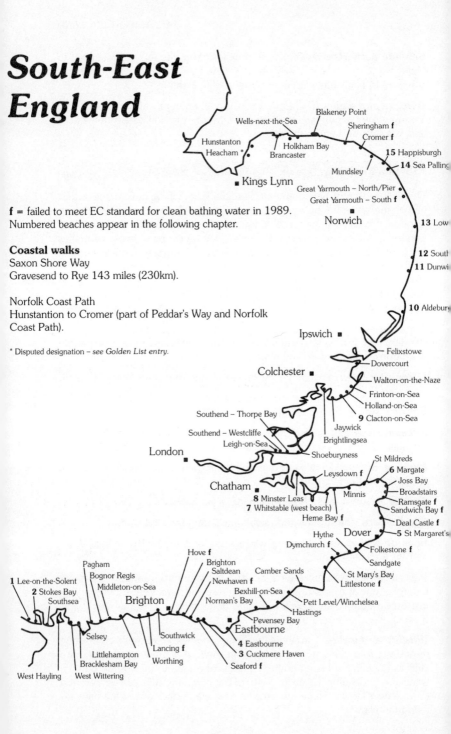

South-East England

f = failed to meet EC standard for clean bathing water in 1989.
Numbered beaches appear in the following chapter.

Coastal walks
Saxon Shore Way
Gravesend to Rye 143 miles (230km).

Norfolk Coast Path
Hunstantion to Cromer (part of Peddar's Way and Norfolk
Coast Path).

* Disputed designation – see Golden List entry.

Blakeney Point
Wells-next-the-Sea
Sheringham **f**
Cromer **f**
Hunstanton
Heacham *
Holkham Bay
Brancaster
15 Happisburgh
14 Sea Palling
Mundsley
Kings Lynn
Great Yarmouth – North/Pier
Great Yarmouth – South **f**
Norwich
13 Low
12 South
11 Dunwi
10 Aldebur
Ipswich
Felixstowe
Dovercourt
Colchester
Walton-on-the-Naze
Frinton-on-Sea
Holland-on-Sea
9 Clacton-on-Sea
Southend – Thorpe Bay
Jaywick
Brightlingsea
Southend – Westcliffe
Leigh-on-Sea
Shoeburyness
St Mildreds
London
6 Margate
Leysdown **f**
Joss Bay
Broadstairs
Chatham
Minnis
Ramsgate **f**
8 Minster Leas
Sandwich Bay **f**
7 Whitstable (west beach)
Heme Bay **f**
Deal Castle **f**
5 St Margaret's
Hythe
Dover
Dymchurch **f**
Folkestone **f**
Hove **f**
Sandgate
Pagham
Brighton
St Mary's Bay
Bognor Regis
Saltdean
Camber Sands
Littlestone **f**
1 Lee-on-the-Solent
Middleton-on-Sea
Newhaven **f**
2 Stokes Bay
Bexhill-on-Sea
Southsea
Brighton
Norman's Bay
Pett Level/Winchelsea
Hastings
Selsey
Southwick
Pevensey Bay
Lancing **f**
4 Eastbourne
Littlehampton
Worthing
3 Cuckmere Haven
Bracklesham Bay
Seaford **f**
West Hayling
West Wittering

South-East England

The south-east of England is rich in sharp coastal contrasts. There are long shingle banks, sand dunes, salt marshes and the wide open skies of Norfolk. Low clay cliffs predominate in Suffolk, powerless to resist the forces of the invading sea. The creeks and mud flats of Essex and the Thames Estuary provide yet another different coastline, while the striking white cliffs of the south coast form an impressive backdrop to many busy holiday resorts and ferry terminals that are the gateway to Europe. Long empty sands and crowded promenades are all to be found.

The south-east has some of the most heavily developed coastal regions and with people and popularity come problems. The heavy traffic in the Channel creates a continual problem with marine litter and oil being washed up on to the beaches. Extensive stretches of the coastline suffer from pollution by sewage. Sludge dumping off the Thames Estuary, nuclear and industrial discharges are all causes for concern. The disturbance around Shakespeare Cliff from the construction of the Channel Tunnel will have a severe long term impact on marine and coastal life. On a coastline under pressure from every type of human activity, tourism, industry, and residential development, continual effort is needed to ensure that those areas left unspoilt will remain so for future generations.

Beaches receiving European Blue Flags in 1989:

Lee-on-the-Solent, Eastbourne, Bexhill, West Beach Clacton, South Beach Lowestoft.

Beaches receiving Clean Beach Awards from the Tidy Britain Group in 1989:

Southsea, Bracklesham Bay, Selsey, Felpham, Bognor, Littlehampton, Pett Level/Winchelsea, Ryde and Appley/Hillhead Beach, Dymchurch Beach, St Mary's, Viking Bay, Marine Sands, Camber Sands, Greatstone-on-Sea, Ramsgate, Sheerness, Leysdown, Minster Leas, Hunstanton, Southwold, Thorpe Bay, Westcliff/Chalkwell, East Beach Shoeburyness.

The Golden List See page 26 for further details

Beach No on Map	Rating. The more stars the better. f=failed	Resort	Sewage outlets	Population Discharging from outlet	Type of treatment	Discharge point relative to low water mark, unless otherwise stated. Distance given in metres	Remarks
HAMPSHIRE							
	★★★	**Barton-on-Sea**	1	17,400	Primary	At LWM	Pebbles and shingle.
	f ★★	**Milford-on-Sea**					Pebbles.
	★★★	**Lepe**					Sand and shingle.
	★★★	**Calshot**	1	448	Maceration/ tidal tank		Mud. Improvement scheme.
1	★★★	**Lee-on-the-Solent**	1	200,000	Primary	1100 below	Sand and shingle. Improvement scheme.
2	★★★	**Stokes Bay**					As above.
	★★	**Southsea**					Shingle.
	★★	**Eastney**	1	200,000	Maceration/ screens/tidal tank	At LWM	Shingle. Sewage discharged into channel between Eastney and Hayling.
	★★	**Eaststoke**					Sandy.
	★★★	**West Hayling**					Sandy.
WEST SUSSEX							
	★★★	**West Wittering**					Sandy. Safe bathing.
	★★★	**Bracklesham Bay**					Sandy.
	★★	**Selsey Bill**					Shingle. Bathing unsafe.
	★★★	**Pagham**					Shingle.
	★★★	**Bognor Regis**	1	71,500	Maceration/ screens	3km below LWM	Sandy. Safe bathing.
	★★★	**Middleton-on-Sea**					Sand and shingle.
	★★★	**Littlehampton**	1	53,000	Maceration/ screens	2.5km below LWM	Sandy. Safe bathing.
		Goring-by-Sea	1	39,000	Primary	At LWM	Sand and shingle. Safe bathing.
	★★	**Worthing**	1	75,000	Primary	335 below LWM	Shingle and sand.

Beach No on Map	Rating. The more stars the better. **f**=failed	Resort	Sewage outlets	Population Discharging from outlet	Type of treatment	Discharge point relative to low water mark, unless otherwise stated. Distance given in metres	Remarks
	f ★★	**Lancing**					Shingle and sand. £29 million improvement scheme.

EAST SUSSEX

		Shoreham-by-Sea	1	52,000	Tidal tank	600 below	Commercial port.
	f ★★	**Hove**					Pebbles and sand. £42 million improvement scheme.
	★★	**Brighton**	5				All storm water overflows.
	★★★	**Saltdean**					Rocky with some sand.
		Portobello	1	300,000	Maceration/ screens	1900 below	New long sea outfall.
	f ★★	**Newhaven**					Sandy beach within break-water. Improvement scheme.
	f ★	**Seaford**	1	18,000	Tidal tank	At LWM	Shingle beach is steep.
4	★★★	**Eastbourne**	1	87,000	Maceration/ screens	650 below	Shingle with sand. £16.7 million improvement scheme.
	★★	**Pevensey Bay**	1	9,590	Maceration/ tidal tank	360 below	Shingle with sand.
	★★★	**Normans Bay**					Shingle with sand at low water.
		Cooden Beach	2			150 above	Shingle with sand at low tide. Storm water overflows.
	★★★	**Bexhill**	3	32,500	Maceration/ tidal tank	400 below	Sand and shingle. Beware sand holes.
		St Leonards	2	23,000	Maceration/ screens	2000 below	Shingle sand and rocks.
	★★★	**Hastings**	4	68,000	Screens/ maceration tank	140 below	Shingle and sand.
	★★★	**Winchelsea**					Shingle. Bathing only safe in calm weather.

Beach No on Map	Rating. The more stars the better. f=failed	Resort	Sewage outlets	Population Discharging from outlet	Type of treatment	Discharge point relative to low water mark, unless otherwise stated. Distance given in metres	Remarks
	★★	**Camber Sands**					Sand dunes. Ridges in sand can be a danger.
		Broomhill Sands	1	9,500	Secondary	300 above	Sandy and coarse shingle.
KENT							
	f ★★	**Littlestone-on-Sea**					Sandy.
	★★★	**St Marys Bay**					Sandy.
	f ★	**Dymchurch**	1	20,800	Secondary	Between HWM & LWM	Shingle and sand.
		Dymchurch Redoubt	1	3,000	Primary	At LWM	Pebbles and sand.
	★★	**Hythe**					Shingle and sand.
	★★★	**Sandgate**					Shingle. £14.5 million improvement scheme.
	f ★★	**Folkestone**	1		Screens	At HWM	Shingle.
		The Warren	1	20,000	Raw	584 below	Danger from falling rocks.
		Shakespeare Cliff	1	30,000	Macerated	635 below	Sand and shingle. Start of Channel tunnel.
5	★★★	**St Margaret's Bay**					Shingle and rocks.
	f ★	**Deal Castle**	3	10,000	Screens maceration tank	731 below	Steep shingle. Improvement scheme.
	f ★	**Sandwich Bay**					Sandy. Improvement scheme.
	f ★★	**Ramsgate**	3	20,000	Screens/ maceration	150 below	Sandy. Improvement scheme.
	★★	**Broadstairs**					Sandy. Improvement scheme.
	★★★	**Joss Bay**	1	12,000	Screens/ maceration	100 below	Sandy.
		Botany Bay	1	40,000	Screens/ maceration tank	100 below	Sandy.

Beach No on Map	Rating. The more stars the better. f=failed	Resort	Sewage outlets	Population Discharging from outlet	Type of treatment	Discharge point relative to low water mark, unless otherwise stated. Distance given in metres	Remarks
6	*** ***	**Margate**	3		Screens	At LWM	Sandy. Improvement scheme.
	**	**St Mildreds Bay**					Sandy.
	***	**Minnis Bay**					Sandy and rocks.
	f **	**Herne Bay**	1	10,000	Screens	460 below	Pebbles and sand. Improvement scheme.
7	***	**Whitstable**	1	10,000	Screens maceration	1500 below	Shingle.
	f **	**Leysdown-on-Sea**					Sandy. Shingle and mud.

ESSEX

Beach No on Map	Rating. The more stars the better. f=failed	Resort	Sewage outlets	Population Discharging from outlet	Type of treatment	Discharge point relative to low water mark, unless otherwise stated. Distance given in metres	Remarks
		Canvey Island	1	56,000	Secondary	At LWM	Muddy sand.
	**	**Southend-on-Sea**	1	205,000	Primary	Over 1km below HWM	Sand, shingle and mud.
	**	**Westcliff**					
	**	**Thorpe Bay**					
	****/ ***	**Shoeburyness**					Sand and shingle.
	**	**Brightlingsea**					Muddy sand. Bathing dangerous.
	***	**Jaywick**	1	29,000	Primary	650 below LWM	Sandy.
9	***	Clacton-on-Sea	2			300 below LWM 50 below LWM	Sandy. Stormwater outfalls only.
	***	**Holland-on-Sea**	1	40,000	Primary	750 below LWM	Sandy. Safe bathing.
	***	**Frinton-on-Sea**	2		Raw	50 below	Sandy. Safe bathing.
	**	**Walton-on-the-Naze**	1	21,000	Secondary	50 below LWM	Sandy. Safe bathing.
	**	**Dovercourt**	1	11,000	Primary	At LWM	Sandy. Safe bathing.

Beach No on Map	Rating. The more stars the better. f=failed	Resort	Sewage outlets	Population Discharging from outlet	Type of treatment	Discharge point relative to low water mark, unless otherwise stated. Distance given in metres	Remarks
SUFFOLK							
		Felixstowe:					
	★★★	**South Beach**	1	10,000	Screens/tank	750 below LWM	Red shingle and sand.
	★★★	**North Beach**	2	15,000	Screens/tank	60 below LWM	Improvement scheme for both beaches.
10		Aldeburgh	1	2,500	Maceration	1000 below LWM	Shingle.
13		**Lowestoft:**					
	★★★	**South beach**		70,000	Screens/ maceration	1,200 below LWM	Sandy.
	★★★	**North Beach**				500 below LWM	Improvement scheme for both beaches.
NORFOLK							
		Great Yarmouth:					
	f ★★	**South Beach**					Sandy. Macerated sewage is discharged into the River Yare.
	★★	**Pier**					
	★★★	**North Beach**					
	★★★	**Mundesley**	1	15,000	Secondary/ other	100 below LWM	Sandy.
	f ★★	**Cromer**	1	6,000	Tidal tank	100 below LWM	Sandy.
		East Runton	1	700	Maceration	At HWM	Sandy.
		West Runton	1	500	Maceration	At LWM	Sand and pebbles.
	f ★★	**Sheringham**	1	9,500	Maceration	250 below LWM	Sand and shingle.
	★★	**Wells-next-the-Sea**					Sandy.
	★★	**Hunstanton**	1	12,000	Screens/ maceration	500 below LWM	Sand, stones and shingle.
•	(f) ★★	**Heacham**		7,000	Secondary		Gravel. Private beach.

• *This beach was passed by the DOE, but MCS was disputing this designation at the time of going to press.*

1 Lee-on-the-Solent, Hampshire   OS Ref: SU5700

A long, gently curving ribbon of groyne-ribbed shingle with sand at low tide faces the Solent, with views of Southampton Water and the Isle of Wight. The residential development along Marine Parade overlooks this uncommercialised beach which was awarded a Blue Flag in 1989. Marine Parade West is separated from the beach by the Solent Gardens which slope down to a promenade on two levels edging the shingle. Another promenade and flat lawns separate Marine Parade East from the beach. The steep shingle may not be the most comfortable for sunbathing on but it is popular with the more active beach user. There is a designated area for water skiing, and recommended launching area for windsurfers. There is always something to watch offshore, whether it is the water sports or the continual shipping traffic plying the Solent. Dogs are banned from the central section of the beach. Dogs on the promenade must be kept on a lead and must not foul the footpaths or the adjoining grass verges.

Water quality Beach monitored by the NRA and found to meet the EC standard for clean bathing water in 1989. One outfall serving 200,000 people discharges primary treated sewage ⅔ mile (1km) below low water mark off Peel Common, north of the beach. There is a proposed £0.6 million sewage improvement scheme under discussion, although many residents feel that this will be insufficient to achieve a major improvement in water quality.

Litter The beach is cleaned regularly by the local authority. Heavy usage of the Solent leads to problems on the beaches, with marine debris and oil being washed ashore.

Bathing safety Safe bathing. Water skiers must use the area buoyed near the Daedalus slipway and windsurf boards should be launched from the Hill Head end of the beach.

Access Lee-on-the-Solent is signposted from the A32; the B3385 leads to Marine Parade running parallel with the shore. There is level access and ramps to the promenade from which there are steps and ramps to the shingle.

Parking Two car parks with approximately 250 spaces are signposted off Marine Parade, two other car parks with approximately 150 spaces are located at the Hill Head end of the beach.

Toilets At the Solent Gardens and the Daedalus slipway.

Food There are shops and cafés on Marine Parade opposite the Solent Gardens. There is a café and sheltered terrace garden off the promenade and a pub at Hill Head.

Seaside activities Swimming, water skiing and windsurfing. Hill Head Sailboards is a RYA windsurfing centre.

Wet weather alternatives In Gosport there is a local museum, Fort Brockhurst and the submarine museum.

Wildlife and walks The Solent Way coastal footpath can be followed in either direction from the beach. To the north, it skirts the Titchfield Haven Nature Reserve and continues along the shore to the River Hamble, an extremely popular yachting centre. To the south it can be followed to Stokes Bay. A section of the grassland adjacent to the Daedalus slipway has been set aside as a conservation area.

2 Stokes Bay, Gosport, Hampshire   OS Ref: SZ5998

The arc of Stokes Bay, with its almost manicured shingle, curves from the No 2 Battery Fort south to Fort Gilkicker, fortifications built in 1860 to protect the western approaches to Portsmouth docks. The narrow band of shingle, which shelves quite steeply to some sand at low tide, widens landward towards the south-east of the bay; the long shore drift currents continually move the shingle in this direction and this has led to the build-up of a wide area of flat shingle stretching towards Fort Gilkicker. The beach, overlooking Ryde on the Isle of Wight, has a wide open feel about it. The promenade is level with the shingle and is backed by flat, grassed recreational areas which are in turn bordered by the trees and shrubs of the adjacent park and school. Popular for water sports; windsurfers can be seen dancing across the waves throughout the year. Lying just off the inshore rescue station are the two remaining legs of a pier which once provided a train-to-ferry link with Ryde. Dogs are banned from the beach. Dogs on the promenade must be kept on a lead and should not be allowed to foul.

Water quality Beach monitored by the NRA and found to meet the EC standard for clean bathing water in 1989. One outfall serving 200,000 people discharges primary treated sewage ⅔ mile (1km) below low water mark off Peel Common, to the north of Lee-on-the-Solent.

Litter The beach is cleaned regularly by the local authority. Heavy use of the Solent by shipping leads to problems on the beaches and marine debris is frequently washed ashore.

Bathing safety Safe bathing. Swimming and windsurfing are restricted to specific areas of the beach which are signposted. First aid post near sailing club. Inshore rescue boat station at southern end of the bay.

Access Stokes Bay is signposted from the B3333 between Lee-on-the-Solent and Gosport. There is easy parking off the road behind the beach and level access on to the shingle.

Parking Car parks are signposted at each end of the beach and at its centre, with over 300 spaces. There is also some parking along the promenade.

Toilets At the car park adjacent to the No 2 Battery Fort and on the promenade near the sailing club.

Food Café on the promenade.

Seaside activities Swimming, windsurfing, sailing, canoeing, and diving.

2 public slipways. Children's paddling pool, miniature golf and tennis courts behind the beach.

Wet weather alternatives In Gosport there is a local museum, the submarine museum and Fort Brockhurst.

Wildlife and walks The Solent Way footpath can be followed south-east past Fort Gilkicker towards Portsmouth Harbour or north-west to Lee-on-the Solent and beyond.

3 Cuckmere Haven, Westdean, East Sussex   OS Ref: TV5298

A path from the Seven Sisters Country Park Centre leads through the lovely Cuckmere valley to this quiet pebble beach. The river, which meanders through the valley, disappears below the pebbles. The impressive white chalk cliffs of the Seven Sisters stretch away east to Beachy Head. Below them there are numerous rockpools which abound with marine life. This is an ideal spot for those who want to combine sun bathing with exploring the shore and surrounds. The nature trail, which starts from the lovely restored flint barn which houses the Country Park Interpretative Centre, is well worth following.

Water quality No sewage is discharged in the vicinity of this beach.

Litter A lot of plastic and metal cans and bottles, both washed up and left by visitors.

Bathing safety The swiftness of the incoming tide and associated currents can cause problems.

Access Pedestrian access only; a mile (1.6km) walk on a marked path through the Cuckmere Valley from the Country Park Centre at Exceat on A259 leads to the beach.

Parking Car park at Country Park Centre.

Toilets At Country Park Centre.

Food Pub at Exceat Bridge provides food.

Seaside activities Swimming and diving.

Wet weather alternatives The Country Park Centre and the Living World exhibition of living animals from the countryside and seashore.

Wildlife and walks A 1½ mile (2.5 km) or 3 mile (5 km) circular trail through the country park covers a selection of wildlife habitats, salt marsh, river meadows and the chalk grassland above the cliffs. Leaflets which describe the route are available at the Country Park Centre. The South Downs Way follows the cliffs and cuts through the valley. Survey work by the Marine Conservation Society showed that the shallow seas of this stretch of coast are particularly rich in marine life and the area has been designated as a Voluntary Marine Nature Reserve.

4 Eastbourne, East Sussex   OS Ref: TV6199

A 1989 Blue Flag winning beach consisting of a lower and upper esplanade, separated by a colourful rock garden, are backed by the Marine Parade which is lined by gardens and overlooked by a number of elegant Regency hotels. Steps from the lower esplanade lead down on to the pebble beach which is ribbed with wooden groynes. Bands of pebbles trapped by the groynes give way to sand at low tide. A Martello Tower on a raised promontory bounds the main beach to the west and provides views along the promenade to the pier and to the white chalk cliffs of Beachy Head. To the east of the pier, the beach is less commercialised, curving away past the Redoubt Fort to Langney Point. A by-law banning dogs from the beach between Wish Tower and the Pier from 1st May to 30th September is currently in force. 'Poop Scoop' regulations will also come into force along the promenade between the Wish Tower and the Butterfly Centre, and dogs must be kept on a lead. Dogs will be permitted on other areas of the beach but owners will have to clean up after them.

Water quality Beach monitored by the NRA and found to meet the EC standard for clean bathing water in 1989. One outfall serving 87,000 people discharges macerated and screened sewage 710 yards (650m) below low water off Langney Point. Macerated sewage has been observed off the beach and there have been complaints about smell. A new, £17 million long sea outfall may rectify the problem.

Litter Very little. Beach cleaned regularly.

Bathing safety The beach between groynes 1 to 18 and 20 to 25 is unsuitable for bathing due to the presence of rocks. Otherwise bathing from the beach is safe unless there is a red flag flying.

Access Steps and a ramp lead down from the esplanade to the beach. There are beach wheelchairs available from the bathing station on the lower esplanade.

Parking Pay-and-display car parks at the fishing station, Princes Park and Wish Tower. Free parking on the promenade, restricted in some areas between 20th May and 20th September. Multi-storey car park in Trinity Place off the sea front and Ashford Road in the town centre.

Toilets Adjacent to band stand, pier, Wish Tower, Holywell, Redoubt and the fishing station.

Food Ice cream and refreshment kiosks on esplanade, cafés on pier and in town.

Seaside activities Swimming, sailing, windsurfing and angling. Windsurfing school at the eastern end of the beach. West of the pier a wheeled gangway gives access across the sand to two converted fishing boats providing cruises around Beachy Head with fine views of the Seven Sisters beyond. Sovereign Centre – all weather beach recreation centre. Children's fun theme park, Punch and Judy and the pier provide traditional seaside entertainment. 'Dotto' land train on promenade. The annual pre-Wimbledon Women's Tennis Championship is held in early June in Devonshire Park.

Wet weather alternatives Lifeboat museum, Wishing Tower, Invasion museum, Martello Tower 73 Museum, Redoubt Fortress Regimental Museum and Aquarium, Butterfly Centre, Sovereign Centre, band stand, pier amusements, tea dancing and leisure pool all provide alternatives close to the beach. In the town there are theatres, five-screen cinema, local history museum, arts centre and gallery.

Wildlife and walks To the east of the town rises Eastbourne Down (part of the Sussex Heritage Coast), 5 miles (8km) of coast covering 4,200 acres of unspoilt chalk upland from Eastbourne to Folkington. From Eastbourne you can walk to Beachy Head with its spectacular views back over the town and of the Beachy Head lighthouse and the Seven Sisters. There is a Visitors Centre at Beachy Head.

5 St Margaret's Bay, St Margaret's at Cliffe, Kent OS Ref: TR3644

A picturesque little cove, once home to both Noel Coward and Ian Fleming, sheltered by towering chalk cliffs, which form part of the White Cliffs of Dover. A narrow lane leads past terraces of holiday homes to the promenade which backs the shingle, kept in place by iron groynes. This cove has been the starting point for many of the cross-Channel swims. The Pines, gardens on the slopes above the beach, are near tropical due to the mild climate of the area. A 'dog-free' zone has been established on the beach and the local council regularly clean the beach and empty the litter bins.

Water quality Beach monitored by the NRA and found to meet the EC standard for clean bathing water in 1989. No sewage is discharged in the vicinity of the beach.

Bathing safety Safe bathing except at high tide. Safety equipment on site.

Access St Margaret's at Cliffe is signposted from the A258. From the village, a narrow road twists to the sea, but it is easier to park on the cliff top and walk down the hill.

Parking Large car park behind sea wall and also at Dover Patrol memorial on cliff top.

Toilets Ladies and gents.

Food Public house, ice cream kiosk.

Seaside activities Swimming, diving, and fishing. Dover District Council operate a boat plot with slipway. Beach huts for hire.

Wildlife and walks The cove is on the Saxon Shore Way with cliff top walks to Dover and Kingsdown, but there is restricted access to some areas at times due to a Marines rifle range. There are good views from the cliff top where the rolling heathland is owned by the National Trust.

6 Margate, Kent   OS Ref: TR3571

The Isle of Thanet ('Kent's Leisure Coast') is fringed by a series of sandy bays between low chalk cliffs. The main sands which stretch out west from Margate harbour received a Clean Beach Award from the Tidy Britain Group in 1989. The bright lights of amusement arcades and the funfair along Marine Terrace overlook the promenade which edges the gently sloping crescent of sand. Margate has a long history as a popular seaside resort: it was here that the covered bathing machine was first used in the 18th century and it remains a traditional resort with lots to do both on and off the beach. Dog bins are provided on the promenade and the local council is currently pursuing the introduction of by-laws relating to dogs and dog access.

Water quality Beach monitored by the NRA and found to meet the EC standard for clean bathing water in 1989. A new outfall was commissioned last year.

Litter The beach is cleaned daily by the local authority. The sale of glass bottles is banned.

Bathing safety Safe bathing. The beach is patrolled by lifeguards throughout the summer. Inshore rescue boat, life boat station and coastguard lookout.

Access From the promenade there are several sets of steps and ramps to the beach.

Parking Several pay and display car parks within easy reach of the beach, including those at College Square, Mill Lane and Trinity Square. Short term parking in Marine Parade, opposite the beach.

Toilets On the promenade with facilities for the disabled.

Food There is a wide range of cafés, restaurants and takeaways within easy reach of the beach and several beach cafés.

Seaside activities Swimming, windsurfing, fishing.

Wet weather alternatives Aquarium, show caves, shell grotto, lifeboat house, local history museum, Tudor House, sports and leisure centre with swimming pool. Tourist information points carry details of nearby walks and trails.

7 Whitstable, Kent   OS Ref: TR1166

This is a quiet resort retaining much of its traditional seafaring atmosphere around the harbour and in the narrow streets, alleyways and weather boarded cottages of the old town. Whitstable was famous for its oysters which are still produced and celebrated annually with an oyster week and carnival. Whitstable's main beach lies to the east of the harbour. Undulating grassy slopes lead gently down from Marine Parade to the promenade and sea wall which edge the pebble beach. A long bank of shingle known as The Street extends seawards from the west end of the beach. ⅔ mile (1km) of the bank is exposed at low water and is a good spot for collecting shells, but is dangerous to swim from. From the slopes at Tankerton there are good views east along the curving beach to Swalecliffe and Herne Bay, with excellent sunsets. Swalecliffe at the eastern end of the Tankerton slopes is used by water skiers as a launching area. The sport is very popular in the bay and the World Water Skiing Championships have been held here.

Water quality Beach monitored by the NRA and found to meet the EC standard for clean bathing water in 1989. One outfall serving 10,000 people discharges screened and macerated sewage, 1 mile (1,500m) below low water mark. There have been complaints in the past about problems with overflow of sewage into the local stream.

Bathing safety Bathing is safe except near The Street where there are unpredictable currents. Warning notices indicate where it is unsafe. There is a mobile coastguard lookout.

Access Steps and ramps from promenade.

Parking Free parking on Tankerton Road; car parks in harbour area charge.

Toilets At Priest and Sow Corner (near the Sailing Club), Beach Walk at the end of Tankerton Slopes, the harbour and Island Wall.

Food A wide variety of cafés, restaurants, ice cream kiosks and snack bars in the town within easy reach of the beach.

Seaside activities Swimming, windsurfing, sailing, water skiing and fishing. Bowling green, tennis courts and golf course.

Wet weather alternatives Heritage Museum, sports centre, indoor bowling.

Wildlife and walks The Saxon Shore Way follows the banks of the Swale passing through the South Swale Local Nature Reserve on the edge of Graveney Marshes, just west of Whitstable. It continues through the town, along the shore to Herne Bay and the Bishopstone mud cliffs beyond.

8 Minster Leas, Isle of Sheppey, Kent   OS Ref: TQ9573

This 880 yards (800m) long by 440 yards (400m) wide sand and mud beach is backed by a promenade and received a Tidy Britain Group Clean Beach Award in 1989. Steep clay cliffs to the east stretch as far as Leysdown. To the west the beach extends to Sheerness where the high sea wall provides views of the busy Thames Estuary.

Water quality No sewage is discharged in the vicinity of the beach.

Bathing safety Safe bathing from the beach which is patrolled by volunteer lifeguards at peak periods.

Access Direct from the promenade.

Parking Car park with 50 spaces plus parking on the streets of Minster.

Toilets None.

Food Shops provide general provisions.

Seaside activities Swimming, windsurfing and fishing from beach.

Wet weather alternatives Minster Abbey gateway contains a museum of local history.

Wildlife and walks The vast majority of the Isle of Sheppey is of scientific interest because of its value to migrating birds. The Nature Conservancy Council and the RSPB operate reserves in the southern half of the island. The beach at Minster has rock pools that contain a variety of marine life; fossils can be found on the beach below the clay cliffs.

9 Clacton-on-Sea, Essex   OS Ref: TM1814

Clacton is a bright and popular resort, justly proud of its lovely gardens. Several kilometres of sandy beach extend from Holland-on-Sea to Jaywick and all the facilities of a major resort are to be found; a pier, golf course, watersports facilities and the newly developed Martello Bay area. A carnival is held at the beginning of August. Dogs are banned on the beach from 1st May to 30th September and the beach is regularly cleaned by the local authority. A 1989 Blue Flag winner.

Water quality Beach monitored by the NRA and found to meet the EC standard for clean bathing water in 1989. Two outfalls discharge 300m and 50m below low water mark: they are storm water overflows only.

Bathing safety Safe bathing except in one or two areas which are clearly marked. The beach is patrolled by lifeguards during the summer months; there is a safety patrol boat and beach inspectors.

Access Direct from the promenade.

Parking Free parking along the sea front and car parks in the town.

Toilets Several near the beach.

Food Catering outlets to suit all tastes and pockets.

Seaside activities Swimming, fishing, sailing and windsurfing. Windsurfer hire available.

Wet weather alternatives Pier, amusements, theatre and leisure centre.

Wildlife and walks Two booklets listing varying walks are available free from the Leisure Office just off the sea front.

10 Aldeburgh, Suffolk   OS Ref: TM4757

This long strip of unspoilt shingle beach falls within the Suffolk Coast and Heath Area of Outstanding Natural Beauty and the Suffolk Heritage Coast. A wide sea wall protects the charming town from the continual attack of the North Sea. Colour-washed houses and hotels face this working beach – a considerable number of boats fish from the beach and most of their catch of crabs, lobster and a variety of fish are sold from seafront huts. The local lifeboat can also be seen drawn up on the shingle. The beach has steep shingle ridges with some sand at low tide and stretches 2 miles (3km) north to Thorpeness. This Edwardian holiday village built around a man-made lake, The Meare, is a mixture of traditional weather-boarding combined with Tudor elegance. The working windmill standing on the heathland behind the beach is also the Heritage Coast visitors' centre and it is well worth a visit to find out more about this curious village and adjacent stretch of coast.

Water quality One outfall serving 2,500 people discharges macerated sewage ⅔ mile (1,000m) below low water mark.

Litter The beach is generally very clean, but subject to occasional spotting with tar and oil from passing ships. It is cleaned by the local authority.

Bathing safety The beach shelves quite steeply but evenly except at Thorpeness where some ridges and pits in the sea bed can be dangerous. It is dangerous to swim near the groynes.

Access Level access from the road on to the promenade and across the shingle to the north.

Parking Pay-and-display at each end of town adjacent to the beach, limited free parking on road adjoining the sea wall. Free car park at Thorpeness.

Toilets Public toilets at the Moot Hall and by coastguard station at the southern end of the promenade.

Food Several cafés, shops and pubs overlook the beach. Ice cream vendor on promenade. Tea shop and inn at Thorpeness.

Seaside activities Swimming, diving, windsurfing, sailing and fishing.

Wet weather alternatives Moot Hall Museum, Thorpeness Windmill and House-in-the-Clouds water tower, Heritage Coast Visitors' Centre. Snape Maltings concert hall on the banks of the River Alde, a short distance inland, is the home of the Aldeburgh Festival. Gallery, craft centre, shops and restaurants at the Maltings.

Wildlife and walks A very good map is available from tourist information centre which details the network of paths that covers Aldeburgh and its surrounding area. Aldeburgh lies on the Suffolk Coastal Path which runs from Felixstowe to Lowestoft. From the village of Snape the route follows the banks of the River Alde and joins the Sailors' Path. This crosses Snape Warren and the marshes north of the town to reach Aldeburgh beach, where shingle plants such as sea holly and the sea pea abound. The path continues north along the beach to Thorpeness and beyond. North Warren RSPB reserve includes The Meare at Thorpeness, the remnant heath, with dry reedbeds, scrub and birch woodland which supports a wide variety of birdlife.

11 Dunwich, Saxmundham, Suffolk   OS Ref: TM4770

A stretch of pebble beach that forms part of a long coastal strip that is continually under attack from the waves. Dunwich village, for example, was once a sizeable town but it is progressively falling into the sea. Between Dunwich village and Minsmere, the RSPB reserve to the south, the shingle-ridged beach is backed by low sand cliffs and heathland owned by the National Trust. The heather and heath plants that thrive on the cliffs provide an attractive splash of colour when in full bloom. The steep banks of shingle which give way to sand at low tide curve northwards protecting the low lying meadows behind. Care is needed to ensure that these coastal defences remain undamaged. This is a quiet beach in an area frequented for the wildlife interest rather than for any holiday beach atmosphere.

Water quality No sewage discharged on to the beach.

Litter Some flotsam is washed up on to the beach.

Bathing safety War remains between low and high tide can be dangerous for swimmers.

Access The beach car park is signposted from the village; there is direct access on to the shingle from the car park.

Parking There is a car park adjacent to the beach.

Toilets In the car park.

Food Beach café at the car park.

Seaside activities Swimming, windsurfing and fishing.

Wet weather alternatives Museum of local history in Dunwich. Bird hides in the Minsmere Reserve are open to the public, free of charge. The Coastguard cottages at Dunwich Heath have an exhibition area along with shop, tea rooms and toilets.

Wildlife and walks There is a marked footpath around the edge of Dunwich Heath which gives the visitor a tour of all the various habitats that the 214 acre site contains. South of the heathland the 1,500 acre RSPB reserve includes reedbeds, lagoons, heath and woodland. Over 100 different species have been recorded breeding within the reserve which makes it one of the most important in Great Britain. There is a shop and information centre at the northern end of the reserve.

12 Southwold, Suffolk OS Ref: TM5076

Southwold once had a pier but all that remains is a short skeleton and the buildings on the promenade. But it is still the focal point for this 3 mile (5km) long beach of sand and shingle. To the north rainbow coloured beach huts line the sea wall which edges the groyne-ribbed beach of soft sand. The beach curves northwards below sand cliffs rising to replace the sea wall. South of the pier the groyne-ribbed beach of sand and shingle stretches to the harbour at the mouth of the River Blyth. Wheeled changing huts line the promenade below scrub covered slopes. The attractive town of Southwold sits aloft, built around seven greens, and shadowed by its lighthouse.

Water quality No outfalls discharge in the vicinity of the beach.

Bathing safety Safe bathing except near the groynes and at the river mouth.

Access The seafront is signposted within the town; car parks adjacent to the promenade/sea wall. There are steps and a steep ramp on to the beach.

Parking Three car parks with a total of 300 spaces adjacent to the pier and harbour.

Toilets On the promenade, including facilities for the disabled.

Food Café, bar, shop and takeaway at the pier.

Seaside activities Swimming, surfing, windsurfing, sailing and fishing. Amusement arcade. Boating lake.

Wet weather alternatives St Edmunds Hall and museum.

Wildlife and walks There are walks along the river and across the meadows. The climb to the summit of Gun Hill is well worth the effort for the reward of some good views. The Suffolk Coastal Path runs north towards Lowestoft and south to Dunwich Forest and Minsmere, approximately 3 miles (5km) from Southwold.

13 South Beach, Lowestoft, Suffolk OS Ref: TM5491

Lowestoft is a popular resort and a busy port. It is split in half by the narrow strip of Lake Lothing. The two sides are linked by a bridge which is occasionally raised to admit large merchant ships into the heart of town. South beach is a 5 mile (9km) long pleasure beach, steeped in golden sand and all the normal paraphernalia of piers, stalls and amusements. Cleaned every day by the local authority, it picked up both a Blue Flag and a Tidy Britain Clean Beach Award in 1989.

Water quality Beach monitored by the NRA and found to meet the EC standard for clean bathing water in 1989. Two outfalls serving 70,000 people discharge screened and macerated sewage 1,500 yards (1,200m) below low water mark.

Bathing safety Safe bathing except near the harbour entrance. The beach is patrolled by lifeguards during the summer months.

Access Direct from the promenade.

Parking There are four car parks near the beach with approximately 800 spaces.

Toilets Four sets of toilets including one with disabled facilities. Another set has showers and baby changing areas.

Food There is a full range of catering outlets at a variety of prices.

Seaside activities Swimming, surfing, fishing, windsurfing, sailing. Punch and Judy shows, two piers.

Wet weather alternatives Multi-sports centre, large central library, Maritime Museum, two cinemas and theatres.

Wildlife and walks Guided walking tours of the fishing harbour start from the Tourist Information Centre on the Esplanade. Lowestoft marks the northern end of the Suffolk Coast Path which runs for 50 miles (90km) south to Felixstowe. Lowestoft Ness is Britain's easternmost point.

14 Sea Palling, Norfolk   OS Ref: TG4327

10 miles (16km) of coastline that is undeveloped and not readily accessible. From Sea Palling the fine stretch of sandy beach to Waxham can be reached. A beautiful unspoilt beach; the gentle sloping sands are fringed by substantial marram covered dunes. The beach is ideal for a quiet day by the sea; no facilities, no razzamatazz, just sand, sea and sky. 3 miles (5km) south, the Broads come within a couple of miles of the dunes, the only protection that the flat low lying land has against the sea. The beach is cleaned daily during the season. Oil has been observed on the sand in winter.

Water quality No outfalls in the vicinity of this beach.

Bathing safety Bathing can be dangerous on the ebb tide because of undertow currents.

Access From the village of Sea Palling, on the B1159, a road leads to a concrete ramp over the dunes.

Parking Car park behind dunes provides spaces for 100 cars.

Toilets In Sea Palling village.

Food A tea shop and two pubs in the village serve food.

Seaside activities Swimming, windsurfing and fishing.

Wildlife and walks Fossils have sometimes been found in the area of the beach, also jet and amber. The more remote parts of the beach are popular for bird watching.

15 Happisburgh, Norfolk   OS Ref: TG3831

The stretch of coastline from Happisburgh (pronounced Hapsboro) east to Winterton is one of the cleanest in Norfolk. There is a continuous gently sloping sandy beach backed by clay cliffs and sand dunes. This attractive stretch of coastline remains undeveloped. Happisburgh, dominated by its red and white lighthouse and the 110 foot (33m) spire of St Mary's Church, is a good family beach, offering safe swimming for children between the groynes that hold the sands in place. The village is set back from the beach on the 50 feet (15m) clay cliffs, an advantage in an area where the ravages of the sea are much in evidence.

Water quality No outfalls in the vicinity of this beach.

Bathing safety Safe bathing. Inshore lifeboat. Coastguard's lookout.

Access From the village on the B1159, a side road leads to parking above the beach. A concrete ramp leads past the inshore lifeboat hut to the beach.

Parking 2 car parks with 100 spaces.

Toilets On cliff top includes disabled facilities.

Food Ice cream van.

Seaside activities Swimming, windsurfing, diving, sailing and fishing.

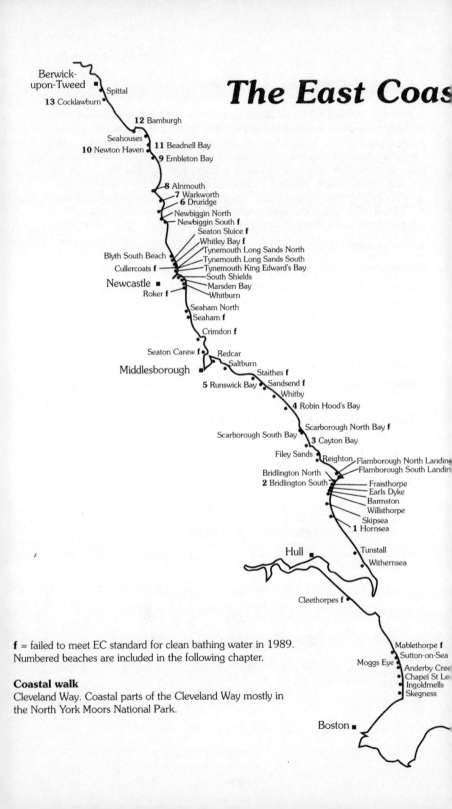

The East Coas

Berwick-upon-Tweed

Spittal

13 Cocklawburn

12 Bamburgh

Seahouses

10 Newton Haven   **11** Beadnell Bay

9 Embleton Bay

8 Alnmouth

7 Warkworth

6 Druridge

Newbiggin North

Newbiggin South **f**

Seaton Sluice **f**

Whitley Bay **f**

Blyth South Beach

Tynemouth Long Sands North

Tynemouth Long Sands South

Cullercoats **f**

Tynemouth King Edward's Bay

South Shields

Newcastle ■

Marsden Bay

Roker **f**

Whitburn

Seaham North

Seaham **f**

Crimdon **f**

Seaton Carew **f**

Redcar

Saltburn

Middlesborough ■

Staithes **f**

5 Runswick Bay

Sandsend **f**

Whitby

4 Robin Hood's Bay

Scarborough North Bay **f**

Scarborough South Bay

3 Cayton Bay

Filey Sands

Reighton

Flamborough North Landing

Flamborough South Landing

Bridlington North

2 Bridlington South

Fraisthorpe

Earls Dyke

Barmston

Willsthorpe

Skipsea

1 Hornsea

Hull ■

Tunstall

Withernsea

Cleethorpes **f**

Mablethorpe **f**

Sutton-on-Sea

Moggs Eye

Anderby Cree

Chapel St Le

Ingoldmells

Skegness

f = failed to meet EC standard for clean bathing water in 1989.
Numbered beaches are included in the following chapter.

Coastal walk

Cleveland Way. Coastal parts of the Cleveland Way mostly in
the North York Moors National Park.

Boston ■

The East Coast

Fabulous, spectacular, dramatic, remote, wild and mysterious have all been used to describe the East Coast. The beautiful sweeping bays of golden sand, unspoilt fishing villages and cliff-top castle ruins of Northumberland; the rugged cliffs and sandy crescents of Yorkshire; the magnificent chalk cliffs of Flamborough with mile upon mile of sand stretching south, backed by the fast retreating mud cliffs of Humberside; the everchanging sand banks of Lincolnshire. Unfortunately, less complimentary terms have also been used to describe parts of this coastline. Industry comes to the shore, with steel works, power stations, oil and chemical works. They discharge a cocktail of toxic chemicals, polluting the coastal waters and their wildlife. Millions of tonnes of dredged spoil, sewage sludge and fly ash dumped offshore add to the problem. Waste from coal mines still blackens the beaches of Tyne and Wear, Durham and Cleveland, although the practice is diminishing. Sewage pollution contaminates many of the bathing waters, particularly around the Tyne and Tees. None of the beaches in the region escape the problem of marine litter.

Beaches receiving Clean Beach Awards from the Tidy Britain Group in 1989:

Saltburn, Withernsea, Hornsea, Bridlington North and South, Scarborough, South, Filey, Seaton Carew, Sandhaven Beach South Shields, Littlehaven Beach South Shields, Marsden and Tynemouth, Ingoldmells, Mablethorpe, Skegness.

Beaches receiving the Blue Flag in 1989:

Cullercoats.

The Golden List See page 26 for further details

Beach No on Map	Rating. The more stars the better. **f**=failed	Resort	Sewage outlets	Population Discharging from outlet	Type of treatment	Discharge point relative to low water mark, unless otherwise stated. Distance given in metres	Remarks
LINCOLNSHIRE							
	★★★	**Skegness**					Sandy. Bathing safe.
	★★	**Ingoldmells**	1	80,000	Primary	2400 below	Sandy. Bathing safe.
	★★★	**Chapel St Leonards**					Sandy. Bathing safe.
	★★	**Anderby Creek**	1	3,000	Secondary	In the creek	Sandy. Bathing safe.
	★★★	**Sutton-on-Sea**					Sandy. Bathing safe.
	f ★★	**Mablethorpe**					Sandy. Bathing safe.
HUMBERSIDE							
	f ★★	**Cleethorpes**	1	80,000	Screens/tank	At LWM	
	★★	**Withernsea Tunstall**	1		Primary	At LWM	Sand and shingle. Sand and pebbles. Safe bathing but not at low tide.
1	★★★	**Hornsea**	2	10,500	Screens/ maceration	1000 below LWM	Sandy.
	★★★	**Skipsea Sands**					
	★★★	**Barmston**					Sand and shingle.
	★★	**Earls Dyke**					Sandy.
	★★	**Friasthorpe**					Sandy.
	★★★	**Willsthorpe**					Sandy.
2	★★	**Bridlington South**	1	50,000	Screens	1600 below	Sandy.
	★★★	**Bridlington North**	2			At LWM	Sandy.
	f ★★	**Flamborough South Landing**					Sewage works discharges into a stream which reaches the sea.

Beach No on Map	Rating. The more stars the better. f=failed	Resort	Sewage outlets	Population Discharging from outlet	Type of treatment	Discharge point relative to low water mark, unless otherwise stated. Distance given in metres	Remarks
	★★★	**Flamborough North Landing**					Sandy. Bathing dangerous.
		Thornwick Bay	1	300	Primary	At LWM	Rocky. Bathing very dangerous.

YORKSHIRE

Beach No on Map	Rating	Resort	Sewage outlets	Population	Type of treatment	Discharge point	Remarks
	★★★	**Reighton Sands**					Sand and boulders.
	★★	**Filey**	2	2,500	Maceration	200 below	Red sand.
3	★★★	**Cayton Bay**					Sandy. Bathing safe.
	★★	**Scarborough: South beach**	2	1,800 29,750	Raw Raw	At LWM	Sandy. Safe bathing. £24.3 million improvement scheme.
	f ★★	**Scarborough: North Beach**	2	55,300 8,700	Raw Raw	At LWM At LWM	Sandy.
4	★★	**Robin Hood's Bay**					Rocky. Swimming dangerous.
	★★★	**Whitby**	1	20,000	Raw	At LWM	Sandy. Swimming safe.
	f ★★	**Sandsend**	1	450	Raw	At LWM	Sand and shingle.
5	★★★	**Runswick Bay**	1	480	Raw	At LWM	Sand and shingle.
	f ★★	**Staithes**	1	2,300	Raw	At LWM	Sand and rocks.

CLEVELAND

Beach No on Map	Rating	Resort	Sewage outlets	Population	Type of treatment	Discharge point	Remarks
		Skinningrove	1	7,700	Raw	At LWM	Sandy.
	★★	**Saltburn-by-Sea**	2	13,850 6,800	Raw Raw	At LWM At LWM	Sand and pebbles.
		Marske-by-the-Sea	1	12,800	Raw	At LWM	Sandy.
	★★★ ★★	**Redcar**	1	35,000	Screened/ macerated	1599 below	Sand and rocks. Improvement scheme
		Coatham Sands	1	1,200	Raw	25 below	Sandy.

Beach No on Map	Rating. The more stars the better. f=failed	Resort	Sewage outlets	Population Discharging from outlet	Type of treatment	Discharge point relative to low water mark, unless otherwise stated. Distance given in metres	Remarks
f	★	**Seaton Carew**	2	31,300	Macerated	At LWM	Sandy. £11.4 million improvement scheme.
				28,500	Macerated	25 below	
		Hartlepool	5	22,800	4×Raw 1×screened/ macerated	2x25 below 3xLWM	Sandy.

DURHAM

		Crimdon Park	1	4,000	Tidal tank	At LWM	Sandy.
		Blackhall	1	10,500	Raw	At LWM	Sand and pebbles.
		Denemouth	1	31,500	Tidal tank	At LWM	Sand with stones and coal waste.
		Horden	2	6,900 8,100	Raw Raw	Above LWM Above LWM	Sand with coal waste
		Easington	1	8,500	Raw	LMW	Sand with coal waste.
		Seaham (South of Harbour)	4	36,600	Raw	25 below	Improvement scheme.
f	★★/ ★★	**Seaham (North of Harbour)**					Sand.

TYNE AND WEAR

		Ryhope	2		Raw	At LWM	Sandy. Storm sewage overflows only.
		Sunderland	2	500	Tidal tank	At LWM	Rocky outfalls situated south of Wear Estuary.
				175,000	Screened	300 below LWM	
f	★★	**Roker**	1		Raw	25 below	Sand. Storm sewage overflow.
		Seaburn	1		Raw	At LWM	Sand. Storm sewage overflow.

Beach No on Map	Rating. The more stars the better. f=failed	Resort	Sewage outlets	Population Discharging from outlet	Type of treatment	Discharge point relative to low water mark, unless otherwise stated. Distance given in metres	Remarks
	★★★	**Whitburn**	1		Raw	At LWM	Sand. Storm sewage overflow.
	★★★	**Marsden Bay**					Sand.
	★★★	**South Shields**	2		Raw	At LWM	Sand. Storm sewage overflows only.
	★★/ ★★★	**Long Sands**	2		Raw	At LWM	
	f ★★	**Cullercoats**	1		Raw	At LWM	
	f ★★	**Whitley Bay**	5		Raw	At LWM	
	f ★★	**Seaton Sluice**	1	43,000	Tidal tank	60 below	Sandy.

NORTHUMBERLAND

Beach No on Map	Rating	Resort	Sewage outlets	Population Discharging from outlet	Type of treatment	Discharge point	Remarks
	★★	**Blyth:** **South Beach**					Sandy.
		North Beach	1	28,500	Maceration	30 below	Sandy.
	f ★★	**Newbiggin**	2	29,000 5,000	Maceration Raw	At LWM At LWM	Sand.
		Cresswell	1	1,800 summer (200 winter)	Other	At LWM	Sandy.
6	★★★	**Druridge Bay**	1	5,500	Maceration	At LWM	Sandy.
		Amble	1	8,000	Screens/ maceration	250 below	Rocky.
7	★★★	**Warkworth**					Sand.
8	★★★	**Alnmouth**					Sandy.
		Longhoughton Steel	1	3,000	Raw	At LWM	Sandy cove.
		Craster	2	400	Maceration	30 below	
10	★★★	**Newton Haven**					Sandy.
11	★★★	**Beadnell Bay**	1	2,000 summer (1,200 winter)	Maceration	At LWM	Sandy.

Beach No on Map	Rating. The more stars the better. f=failed	Resort	Sewage outlets	Population Discharging from outlet	Type of treatment	Discharge point relative to low water mark, unless otherwise stated. Distance given in metres	Remarks
	★★★	**Seahouses**	1	6,000	Screens/ maceration/ tidal tank	100 below	
12	★★★	**Bamburgh**	2	1,000 summer (700 winter)	Maceration/ tidal tank	At LWM	Sandy.
				100	Raw	At LWM	
		Holy Island	1	500 summer (200 winter)	Tidal tank	At LWM	Pebbles.
13		Cocklawburn Beach	1	300	Raw	20 above	Sand and rocks.
	★★	**Spittal**					Improvement scheme.
		Berwick-upon-Tweed	1		Raw	At LWM	Sandy.

1 Hornsea, North Humberside   OS Ref: TA2047

From Barmston just south of Bridlington to the shingle of Spurn Point is the fastest eroding section of coastline in Britain. Tens of feet of the clay cliffs are lost annually. This makes access to the coastline difficult with the erosion of roads, paths and steps. Hornsea is one of the few places where there is a break in the cliffs and sea defences attempt to stop the advancing sea. A sea wall and promenade face the mile-long beach of sand and pebbles which virtually disappears when the tide rises. A park and various seaside amusements line the promenade. Received a Tidy Britain Group Clean Beach Award in 1989. The quiet town of Hornsea is set back from the sea.

Water quality Beach monitored by the NRA and found to meet the EC standard for clean bathing water in 1989. One outfall serving 10,500 people discharges screened and macerated sewage ⅔ mile (1km) below low water mark. One storm sewage overflow.

Bathing safety Due to strong currents offshore, bathing is only safe close inshore. The central section of the beach is patrolled by lifeguards at weekends.

Access Steps and ramp from promenade to sands.

Parking Several car parks adjacent to the promenade.

Toilets On promenade.

Food 3 cafés at central section of beach.

Seaside activities Swimming, windsurfing, sailing and fishing. Golf course.

Wet weather alternatives Hornsea Pottery with zoo and butterfly world just south of town. Museum of village life. Amusements.

Wildlife and walks Hornsea Mere lies just south of the town. This 2 mile (3km) long lake is an RSPB reserve and its 5 acres (2 hectares) are an important wintering ground for wildfowl. There is a large population of reed warblers to be found in the reed swamps. A public footpath along the south shore, through woods and open fields, provides good views of the area. There are boat launching facilities on the Mere.

2 Bridlington, North Humberside   OS Ref: TA1866

'Good Old Brid' – a bustling holiday resort which has won a whole variety of awards in the past, including the Blue Flag. With its two beaches, it combines the traditional seaside holiday entertainments with new up-to-date facilities, and there is easy access to the natural beauty of the adjacent Flamborough Head Heritage Coast. Two safe, sandy beaches are separated by Bridlington harbour; stone quays enclose a tidal harbour which is a continually changing scene of fishing and pleasure craft. The south beach extends for 5 miles (8km) with the busy promenade giving way to steep cliffs south of the town. North beach is the most popular for water sports as it is sheltered by the sheer white cliffs that sweep north to Flamborough Head.

Water quality Beach monitored by the NRA and found to meet the EC standard for clean bathing water in 1989. One outfall at Bridlington South serving 50,000 people discharges screened sewage 1 mile (1.6km) below low water mark. Two storm water outfalls discharge storm overflow to the north beach at low water. There have been reports of solid sewage waste occasionally on the shore, probably resulting from these overflows.

Litter The beach is cleaned by the local council, but there are complaints about dog fouling. A by-law should be in place for the 1990 season, banning dogs from the beach during the summer.

Bathing safety Safe bathing.

Access Steps and ramps from promenade.

Parking Sea front and adequate spaces within town.

Toilets On promenade.

Food Selection of cafés and restaurants along promenade.

Seaside activities Swimming, windsurfing, diving, fishing, sailing, water skiing and paragliding. Windsurfing and sailing facilities are available for hire. Fishing tackle for hire and daily fishing trips from the harbour. Bridlington is the venue for the UK Windsurfing Championships.

Wet weather alternatives Old Town, Bayle Gate Museum, Harbour History Exhibition, Priory Church (organ recitals on Wednesdays during the season). Sewerby Hall (north of town, access by miniature train along cliffs). Leisure World – new water sports and entertainment complex. Amusement arcades.

Wildlife and walks To the north lies Flamborough Head, 300 feet (90m) of towering chalk cliff. The area is rich in magnificent scenery, with natural arches, stacks and caves to be admired or explored. Several guided walks are on offer and details can be obtained from the Heritage Coast Information Centre at the South Landing, Flamborough.

3 Cayton Bay, North Yorkshire   OS Ref: TA0685

Steep wooded cliffs surround the small arc of this bay, which is fringed by boulders, many of which have the imprints of fossil ammonites and belemites. The National Trust owns the northern half of the bay. At low tide, sandbanks are revealed which may trap the unwary if the incoming tide is not watched. It is also dangerous to cross the rocks at the southern end of the bay. The rockpools abound with marine life and will keep the amateur naturalist engrossed for hours.

Water quality Beach monitored by the NRA and found to meet the EC standard for clean bathing water in 1989. No sewage is discharged in the vicinity of the beach.

Bathing safety Safest at high water; at other times beware of incoming tide.

Access Signposted off the A165, with a path down from the holiday camp at the top of the cliffs.

Parking Car park with 50 spaces approximately 1 mile (1.6km) from beach.

Toilets None.

Food None.

Seaside activities Swimming, surfing, fishing.

Wet weather alternatives The woods at the top of the cliff will at least provide some shelter: for the less hardy, the resort of Scarborough is less than 3 miles (5km) away.

Wildlife and walks The Cleveland Way runs close by the beach; it can be followed north through Scarborough and into the North York Moors National Park.

4 Robin Hood's Bay, North Yorkshire   OS Ref: NZ9505

A wide sweeping bay framed by crumbling red cliffs stretches from Ness Point and the village of Robin Hood's Bay south to the 600 foot (180m) headland of Old Peak with its scattered housing of Ravenscar. Magnificent views of the bay can be obtained from the undulating farmland on the cliff top. There is a remnant cliff line inland. A 40 foot (12m) high sea wall protects the cluster of fishing cottages that make up Robin Hood's Bay village. Vehicle access to the older parts of the village is restricted and to get to the beach you have to park at the top of the hill and walk down through the village. Elsewhere there is limited access to the shore of this huge bay. Boggle Hole, where Mill Beck cuts through the cliffs, is a sheltered shingle and rock cove. Stoupe Beck Sands is an 880 yards (800m) stretch of sand in the middle of the bay. This area of the bay is very isolated with no facilities; the beach is reached by a paved track through a wooded valley. The headland at Ravenscar and the rock shore below are owned by the National Trust and offer excellent views north along the coast. All have a wild feel to them and mats of washed-up seaweed are commonplace, which some may find unpleasant. There is a National Trust information centre and shop.

Water quality Beach monitored by the NRA and found to meet the EC standard for clean bathing water in 1989. No sewage is discharged from the beach but there have been complaints about the stream across the beach, and reports of solid waste on the shore.

Bathing safety Safe bathing but beware of sharp rocks.

Access The main access to the beach is from Robin Hood's Bay village, signposted off the A171 south of Whitby. There is a regular bus service to the village and parking above.

Parking Pay-and-display car park at the top of the hill (267 spaces).

Toilets By the beach.

Food Various cafés, kiosks and pubs.

Seaside activities Swimming, diving and fishing.

Wildlife and walks The area is famed for its geology and fossils – there is a geological trail from Ravenscar. The Cleveland Way follows the bay and there is a network of paths on the cliffs. There is much to interest the beachcomber with rock pools full of life.

5 Runswick Bay, Runswick, North Yorkshire   OS Ref: NZ8016

From the picturesque hillside village of Runswick, the broad sandy beach backed by steeply sloping clay cliffs curves south-east to the rocky headland that bounds the bay. The crescent of sand gives way to rocky shore at either end. The old village of Runswick nestles at the base of the cliffs with the new one perched above. There is easy access to the beach and the area is not over commercialised. There are some beach huts and chalets on the scrub-covered cliffs. There are good views across the bay from the village of Kettleness on the southern headland.

Water quality Beach monitored by the NRA and found to meet the EC standard for clean bathing water in 1989. One outfall serving 480 people discharges raw sewage at low water mark.

Bathing safety Safe bathing.

Access A road off the A174 north of Whitby leads down to Runswick village. There is a ramp to the beach.

Parking Pay-and-display at the bottom of the hill with 104 spaces.

Toilets By car park.

Food Cafés and shops in village.

Seaside activities Swimming, sailing and fishing.

Wildlife and walks. The area is excellent for walking with the Cleveland Way skirting the bay. Following the route north for 2 miles (3km) you reach the tiny harbour of Mulgrave now falling into disrepair below the cliffs. Further north at the mouth of a tiny rocky inlet is Staithes Harbour. The village with its closely packed houses and network of alleyways nestles in the steep valley.

6 Druridge Bay, Cresswell, Northumberland   OS Ref: NZ2993

A 5 mile (8km) curving sweep of golden sand is fringed by dunes with rocky outcrops at either end, at Cresswell and Hadston Carrs. Cresswell is the easiest point of access and may be busy on a sunny afternoon, but a short walk along the shore will bring you to miles of quiet sand. There are views north along the bay to Coquet Island and its lighthouse.

Water quality Beach monitored by the NRA and found to meet the EC standard for clean bathing water in 1989. One outfall serving 5,500 people discharges untreated sewage at low water mark.

Bathing safety Swimming with extreme caution as the tides and currents are strong and unpredictable.

Access A road from Ellington on the A1068 leads to Cresswell. It is a short walk from the car parks across the dunes.

Parking Near Cresswell there is a car park with 100 spaces; at Cresswell Ponds there is space for 10 cars, and on Druridge Links a National Trust car park has 150 spaces.

Toilets In Cresswell Village and at Druridge Country Park at the northern end of the bay.

Food Café and tea room in village, mobile ice cream vans.

Seaside activities Swimming, sailing and fishing.

Wildlife and walks At the northern end of the beach is Druridge Country Park. There are also nature reserves at Druridge and Hauxley. Cresswell Ponds have been designated as a Site of Special Scientific Interest. A superb area for bird-watching, the Northumberland Wildlife Trust has recently opened its Druridge Pools Reserve to the public; hide facilities are available. The Trust also runs the Blakemoor Visitor Centre where details of bird numbers and species can be found. South of the bay, beyond the smaller Broadsands beach and the rocky outcrops of Snab Point, is the sharply contrasting Lynemouth beach, blackened by coal dust washed from waste tips that line the beach.

7 Warkworth, Northumberland   OS Ref: NU2606

Between Warkworth Harbour at the mouth of the Coquet Estuary and the Aln Estuary there lies 3 miles (5km) of fabulous sandy beach. The beach, margined by sand dunes, extends northwards for 2 miles (3km) to merge with Alnmouth Links. The town of Amble lies on the southern banks of the estuary and here fishing cobles may be seen in the harbour and yachts moored in the river or at the Braid Marina – winner for the past three years of a European Blue Flag for ports, awarded for environmental quality, and good facilities. Coquet Island lies one mile (1.6 km) offshore, sheltering the harbour entrance. The island is an RSPB reserve and boat trips are available from the harbour. The views back across the estuary, with the backdrop of Warkworth Castle, are most impressive. The near perfect medieval village of Warkworth, an idyllic spot with dramatic castle, Hermitage and unique fortified bridge, is set a mile inland and is almost enclosed by a meander of the river Coquet. Warkworth beach is signposted from here. The picnic site by the beach has panoramic views of the Coquet Estuary. There is access to Alnmouth Links south of Bilton on the A1068 but there is very limited parking behind the dunes.

Water quality Beach monitored by the NRA and found to meet the EC standard for clean bathing water in 1989. One outfall serving 8,000 people discharges screened and macerated sewage at Amble.

Litter Some marine litter and fishing debris is washed on to the beach.

Bathing safety Bathing is dangerous at high tide. There is an inshore and offshore rescue boat and coastguard station at Amble.

Access North of Warkworth, a turning off the A1068 is signposted to the beach.

Parking Car park at picnic site with space for 50 cars.

Toilets In car park.

Food None. Tea rooms in village a mile (1.6km) away.

Seaside activities Swimming, golf course (Warkworth), river and sea fishing from Amble.

Wildlife and walks. The picnic site and surrounding area at Warkworth beach is managed by the Northumberland National Park and the National Trust own the land to the north. A coastal path stretches the 3½ miles (6km) from Warkworth to Alnmouth and is described in a leaflet available locally. A walk to the south takes you through dunes to the long breakwater serving Warkworth harbour and some interesting salt marshes which were designated as a Site of Special Scientific Interest in 1988. Coquet Island, with its prominent lighthouse, is frequented by colonies of breeding sea birds – puffins, terns, eider. These may be viewed from boat trips around the island organised by the RSPB and bookable at the Amble Tourist Information Office.

8 Alnmouth, Northumberland   OS Ref: NU2410

A one mile (1.6km) expanse of sand stretches from the picturesque village of Alnmouth north to the Marsden Rocks. At low tide over a quarter of a mile (400m) of excellent sand is exposed. The beach is bordered by a large car park and golf course, behind which lies the village. Alnmouth was a port of some importance during the 18th century, but due to a change in the course of the river little can be seen of the old harbour. However, the old granaries have been carefully converted into pubs, shops, eating places and accommodation, retaining its unspoilt character.

Water quality Beach monitored by the NRA and found to meet the EC standard for clean water in 1989. No sewage is discharged in the vicinity of the beach.

Bathing safety There are dangerous currents at some states of the tide.

Access Alnmouth is signposted off the A1068 south of Alnwick. A road through the golf course north of the village leads to the beach car park.

Parking Parking for 150 cars adjacent to the beach.

Toilets In the village.

Food Numerous cafés and restaurants in the village.

Seaside activities Swimming, surfing, windsurfing, fishing and sailing in estuary. Two links golf courses north of village.

Wildlife and walks There is an excellent coastal walk north from Alnmouth along the rocky shore with a series of small sandy bays to explore. Fulmars glide effortlessly along these cliffs where a wide range of sea birds can be seen. At Howick Haven you can either continue north along the low cliffs to the fishing village of Craster or turn inland following the wooded valley for a mile (1.6km) to the grounds of Howick Hall, where the gardens are open in summer.

9 Embleton Bay, Northumberland   OS Ref: NU2329

This scenically outstanding bay is bounded to the south by the craggy headland on which stand the dramatic ruins of Dunstanburgh Castle. The steep basalt cliffs are known as Gull Crag because of the numerous nesting sea birds, especially kittiwakes and fulmars. The excellent sandy Embleton beach, bordered by sand dunes and a golf course, stretches north from the boulder strewn shore below the Crag to merge with the Newton Haven beach at the northern end of the bay.

Water quality No sewage is discharged on to the beach.

Litter A clean beach but with some marine debris washed up, particularly in winter.

Bathing safety Bathing is safe on the incoming tide; there are under-currents on the ebbing tide.

Access From Embleton village on the B1339 follow the road leading to the Golf Course or Dunstan Steads Farm. A path leads directly on to the beach and connects with the coastal footpath.

Parking Roadside parking for approximately 100 cars.

Toilets In the village.

Food In the village.

Seaside activities Swimming.

Wildlife and walks This stretch of coastline is owned by the National Trust. There are excellent views across the bay from the Heritage Coast path to the south. The path continues along the rocky foreshore to Craster, a classic fishing village with miniature harbour, rows of neat cottages and the stone sheds where the world-famous Craster kippers are smoked.

10 Newton Haven, Northumberland   OS Ref: NU2525

Newton Haven's ⅔ mile (1km) crescent of dune-fringed sand lies at the northern end of Embleton Bay. Low tide exposes a wide beach which is fringed by dunes. Sheltered by a grass headland to the north and an offshore reef, the beach is popular for water sports. The beach is overlooked by the village of Low Newton, an attractive square of fishermen's cottages and a pub, now owned by the National Trust. Behind the dunes lies Newton Pool, a freshwater lagoon which is a nature reserve.

Water quality Beach monitored by the NRA and found to meet the EC standard for clean bathing water in 1989. There is no sewage discharged in the vicinity of this beach.

Litter Some oil drums and fishing debris are washed up, particularly in winter.

Bathing safety Bathing is safe on the incoming tide; there are under-currents on the ebbing tide.

Access From the car park on the approach road to Low Newton, signposted off the B1339 from High Newton. It is a short walk down to the village with direct access to the beach. A path leads along Low Newton beach to Embleton Bay.

Parking There is a car park 330 yards (300m) from Low Newton and on the road sides with space for about 100 cars. Parking in the village is for residents and disabled badge holders only.

Toilets Adjacent to beach.

Food Pub with snacks and tea room in High Newton ⅔ mile (1km) away.

Seaside activities Swimming, windsurfing, sailing, diving, canoeing and fishing. Newton Sailing School provides tuition hourly or weekly and has dinghies, canoes and windsurfboards for hire.

Wildlife and walks There are bird hides at Newton Pool (one with disabled access) and a wide variety of species can be seen, particularly in winter. The Heritage Coast Path stretches south round Embleton Bay to Dunstanburgh Castle and north around Newton Point to the wide sweep of Newton Links and Beadnell Bay.

11 Beadnell Bay, Beadnell, Northumberland   OS Ref: NU2229

The golden sands of this superb dune-edged beach sweep south on a 2 mile (3km) long curve to the rocky outcrop of Snook Point. A stream meanders across the flat sands in the centre of the bay and to the south is a good area for collecting shells. At the northern end of the beach is the tiny harbour of Beadnell, still used by the traditional east coast fishing cobles. It has the distinction of being the only East Coast harbour to actually face west! Standing on the quay are some huge 18th century limestone kilns. These impressive structures have been restored and are owned by the National Trust.

Water quality Beach monitored by the NRA and found to meet the EC standard for clean bathing water in 1989. One outfall serving approximately 2,000 people discharges macerated and screened sewage at low water mark.

Litter A very clean beach: two wardens are employed to oversee the maintenance of the beach.

Bathing safety Bathing is safe on the incoming tide; there are dangerous undercurrents on the ebb.

Access A road from the B1340 in Beadnell village leads to the harbour. Short walk from car park to sand.

Parking Large car park at north end of bay near harbour with 200 spaces. Small car park at Newton Links at south end of bay with space for 30 cars.

Toilets In Beadnell car park.

Food Ice cream van at car park.

Seaside activities Swimming, windsurfing, sailing, diving, water skiing and canoeing. Outdoor sports hire centre at car park.

Wildlife and walks This stretch of coastline provides some splendid walking. To the south, a path around the edge of the bay leads to Newton Haven, the lovely Embleton Bay and the romantic ruins of Dunstanburgh Castle. To the north, the rocky shore gives way to sand that stretches to Seahouses.

12 Bamburgh and Seahouses, Northumberland   OS Ref: NU1834

A 150 foot (45m) rock outcrop towers above beautiful long sandy beaches and provides the magnificent setting for Bamburgh Castle. From the castle rock there are spectacular views of the sandy beach stretching north to Holy Island and south to Seahouses. Seaward lies the panorama of the Farne Islands. Their rocky cliffs fall steeply to the water below. It was from the Longstone lighthouse on Outer Farne in 1838 that Grace Darling set off to rescue the crew of the 'Forfarshire'. The row that made her a national heroine is remembered in the Grace Darling Museum in Bamburgh. Today the trip to the Islands is made from the little harbour at Seahouses. Inland, Bamburgh village nestles below the castle among undulating fields. Between Bamburgh and Seahouses are 4 miles (6.5km) of superb beach with sand which squeaks when walked over. Backed by the St Aidan's and Shoreston Dunes, the sands give way to rocky shore at Seahouses where the rock pools are full of marine life.

Water quality Both Bamburgh and Seahouses were monitored by the NRA and found to meet the EC standard for clean bathing water in 1989. There are two outfalls at Bamburgh: one, serving approximately 1,000 people, discharges macerated sewage through the tidal tank at low water mark; the other serves 100 people and discharges untreated sewage at low water mark. One outfall at Seahouses serving 6,000 people discharges screened and macerated sewage through a tidal tank 110 yards (100m) below low water mark.

Litter A little wood, plastic and fishing debris is washed on to the beach. Litter left by visitors is cleared by the National Trust.

Bathing safety Bathing is safe only on the incoming tide due to undercurrents as the tide ebbs; beware of offshore winds. Lifebelts are available at Seahouses. Inshore rescue boat and lifeboat.

Access There is access from both Bamburgh and Seahouses which lie on the B1340, with easy access to beach across dunes.

Parking Bamburgh: Large car park in Bamburgh has over 200 spaces. 3 dune car parks with approximately 25 spaces in each, plus space for about 50 cars along the road above dunes.
Seahouses: Car park in village has 500+ spaces. Space for 30 cars parking on verge of B1340 north of Seahouses.

Bamburgh

Toilets In village.

Food Café and hotel in village, and ice cream vans on or near beach.

Seaside activities Swimming, surfing, windsurfing, diving, sailing and fishing.

Wet weather alternatives Castle, Grace Darling Museum and grave in village.

Seahouses

Toilets In village.

Food In village.

Seaside activities Swimming. Golf course. Amusements.

Wet weather alternative Marine Life Centre.

Wildlife and walks This fantastic section of coastline falls within the Northumberland Heritage Coast and is also designated an Area of Outstanding Natural Beauty. Below the lofty position of Bamburgh Castle, a walk north along the shore leads to Budle Bay. The saltmarsh, mud and sand flats are part of the Lindisfarne Nature Reserve which covers the whole of the Fenham Flats, Holy Island Sands and most of the Island itself. The area provides feeding for thousands of waders and wildfowl. It is dangerous to cross the sands; access to the island is by the causeway which is covered for at least 11 hours each day. With its Castle and Priory, the island is steeped in history and its distinctive conical shape leaves a lasting impression on the memory. The beaches around the island are wide and sandy but unsafe for swimming because of strong currents. The Farne Islands to the south of Holy Island are of international importance for their large colonies of sea birds and grey seals. The 30 islands that make up the Farnes are a National Trust Nature Reserve and landing is permitted on Inner Farne and Staple Island. Boats make the hour-long trip from the harbour at Seahouses in good weather. Further information about the service is available from the National Trust shop in Seahouses. Access is restricted during the bird breeding season from mid-May until mid-July.

13 Cocklawburn, Scremerston, Northumberland   OS Ref: NU0349

The retreating tide exposes rock pools in the rocks which bound this ⅔ mile (1km) long section of sandy beach. This is the accessible end of an extensive sandy beach which stretches south as Cheswick Sands towards Holy Island. The further south-east you venture along the beach, the quieter it becomes. Wide flat sands revealed at low tide join Holy Island with the mainland. They should not be crossed by foot at low tide – use the causeway road from Beal. The influence of man is much in evidence at the Cocklawburn beach with the remains of lime kilns and waste heaps on the edge of the beach. The modern activity of man imposes on the beach at times too, with the sound of trains from the railway line to Edinburgh which runs parallel with the shore.

Water quality One outfall serving 300 people discharges raw sewage 22 yards (20m) above the low water mark.

Bathing safety Safe bathing on the incoming tide; undercurrents on the ebb tide make swimming dangerous; beware also of offshore winds.

Access Turning east from the village of Scremerston, a lane leads down to and then runs parallel with the shore. The beach is reached by a short walk through the dunes.

Parking Cars can be parked at several places along the lane on grassland behind the dunes. There is space for approximately 200 cars.

Toilets None.

Food None.

Seaside activities Swimming, surfing, windsurfing and fishing.

Wildlife and walks The dunes that margin the beach support a very good flora and an area at the southern end of the beach is a Northumberland Wildlife Trust Nature Reserve. The limestone outcrops are favoured by cowslips, cranesbills and vetches which add to the variety of plants to be found. A path north along the rocky shore leads to the mouth of the river Tweed where fishermen netting salmon can often be seen.

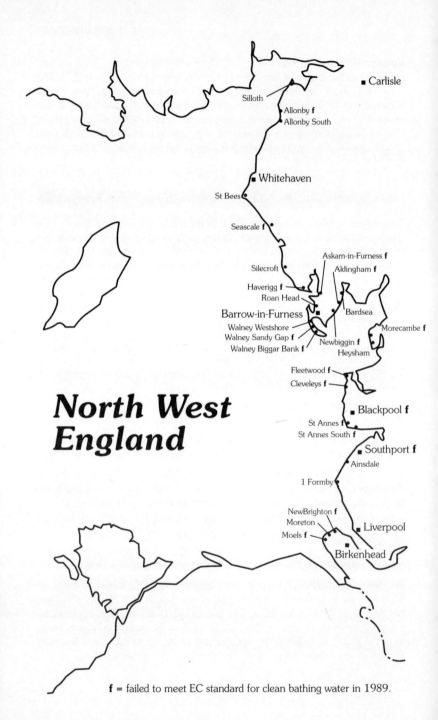

North West England

- Carlisle
- Silloth
- Allonby **f**
- Allonby South
- Whitehaven
- St Bees
- Seascale **f**
- Silecroft
- Askam-in-Furness **f**
- Aldingham **f**
- Haverigg **f**
- Roan Head
- Bardsea
- Barrow-in-Furness
- Walney Westshore
- Walney Sandy Gap **f**
- Newbiggin **f**
- Walney Biggar Bank **f**
- Heysham
- Morecambe **f**
- Fleetwood **f**
- Cleveleys **f**
- Blackpool **f**
- St Annes **f**
- St Annes South **f**
- Southport **f**
- Ainsdale
- 1 Formby
- NewBrighton **f**
- Moreton
- Moels **f**
- Liverpool
- Birkenhead

f = failed to meet EC standard for clean bathing water in 1989.

North-West England

For the region which pioneered the concept of the seaside resort, it's rather sad that the role the North-West can play in a guide such as this is so small. The North-West does have some lovely stretches of coastline; bird watching on Morecambe Bay, with the Lake District as a back drop, or the Victorian elegance of Southport are but two regional attractions.

However, the whole region suffers from major pollution problems which affect nearly all its shores. The Irish Sea is heavily polluted; it is the most radioactive sea in the world and it is more chemically contaminated than the North Sea. The Mersey Estuary and Liverpool Bay have suffered particularly. For example, 8.8lb (4kg) of mercury and cadmium, and 990lb (450kg) of lead are released into the bay each day, mostly from industrial and contaminated sewage discharged to the Mersey and its tributaries. In addition, at least 1.5 million tonnes of sewage sludge and 3.5 million tonnes of dredged spoil (sediments dredged from the estuary usually contaminated with heavy metals and other persistent toxic chemicals) are dumped into Liverpool Bay each year. Blackpool, the most famous (and still one of the most popular) seaside resorts of them all, looks out on to this toxic mess. As a result, its beaches remain some of the most grossly polluted in the whole of the UK.

Thus, any visitor to the beaches in this region must, unhappily, expect to see strands of foam resulting from excessive algal growth triggered by the very high nutrient inputs from sewage. They will also come across the refuse dumped from the boats and ships which continually use the waterway. Despite a considerable improvement in the water quality results (in 1988 only five of the designated beaches in the region complied with the EC standard for bathing water quality; in 1989 this rose to ten), most people would think twice about swimming. Although work is being undertaken to improve the situation (nearly £60 million for Blackpool alone), without more action it will be many years before there are major improvements.

Beaches receiving Clean Beach Awards from the Tidy Britain Group in 1989: Blackpool between the north and south piers, Southport (Ainsdale), Grannys Bay Beach (Lytham St Annes), Cleveleys, Silloth on Solway.

The Golden List *See page 26 for further details*

Beach No on Map	Rating. The more stars the better. f=failed	Resort	Sewage outlets	Population Discharging from outlet	Type of treatment	Discharge point relative to low water mark, unless otherwise stated. Distance given in metres	Remarks
	★★★	**Silloth**	1	2,600	Screened	60 below	Sand and shingle. Sewage treatment works planned.
	f ★★ ★★★	**Allonby**	1	600	Raw	50 below	Sand and rock slightly muddy. Popular beach. Safe bathing. Improvements planned.
		Maryport	1	11,500	Raw	At LWM	Sand, shingle. Fishing port.
		Flimby	3	500	Raw	150 above	
				1,500	Raw	150 above	Shingle/sand. Popular beach.
				100	Raw	150 above	
		Siddick (Low Seaton)	2	4,300	Raw	200 below	Shingle/slag. Mainly used by fishermen.
				50	Raw	200 below	
		Workington	4	6,000	Raw	At LWM	Sand, shingle and slag. Well used beach.
				8,000	Raw	10 above	Shingle/mud bank. Derwent Estuary.
				9,000	Raw	20 above	Shingle/slag. Low amenity.
				7,500	Raw	below HWM	Shingle/slag. Low amenity.
		Harrington	1	1,500 industry	Raw	At LWM	Shingle/slag. Popular beach.
		Parton	1	200+	Screened/macerated	800 below	Shingle/sand. Low amenity. Industrial.
		Whitehaven	3	500	Raw	Above HWM	Shingle/black sand and high cliffs. Little used.
				2,350	Raw	At LWM	
				23,500	Raw	At LWM	
	★★	**St Bees**	1	1,750	Primary	100 above	Sand/shingle. Strong tank currents. Proposed improvement scheme.
		Nethertown	1	400	Raw	50 below	Sand/shingle.
		Braystones	1	7,000	Raw	50 below	Sand/shingle.

Beach No on Map	Rating. The more stars the better. **f**=failed	Resort	Sewage outlets	Population Discharging from outlet	Type of treatment	Discharge point relative to low water mark. unless otherwise stated. Distance given in metres	Remarks
	f ✶✶	**Seascale**	1	2,200	Raw	Below LWM	Sand/shingle & rocks. £1.6 million improvement scheme.
		Ravenglass	1	250 +heavy tourist trade	Primary	To Esk Estuary at LWM	Shingle and mud.
	✶✶✶	**Silecroft**					Sand and shingle.
	f ✶	**Haverigg**					Sand dunes. High amenity. Improvement scheme.
		Millom	1	7,500	Primary	At LWM	Sand and shingle.
	f ✶✶	**Askam-in-Furness**	1	2,350	Primary	To Duddon Channel	Sand. Bathing safe inshore. Pollution in Duddon Estuary. Improvement scheme planned.
		Barrow-in-Furness	32	73,000	Raw/other	All discharge to Walney Channel	Beaches to the west of the island have sand dunes and normal bathing facilities. Walney Channel and east of the island is polluted and is used for boating only.
	✶✶	**Roanhead**					
		Rampside					
	✶✶	**Walney Island: West Shore**					
	f ✶✶	**Walney Island: Bigger Bank**					
	f ✶✶	**Walney Island: Sandy Gap**					
	✶✶	**Bardsea**					Sandy. Country park. Improvement scheme.
		Grange-Over-Sands & Kents Bank	3	11,500	Secondary	Discharges to Wyke Beck	Mud, shingle and sand. New sewage treatment works. Further work underway to remove overflows from promenade sewers.

Beach No on Map	Rating. The more stars the better. f=failed	Resort	Sewage outlets	Population Discharging from outlet	Type of treatment	Discharge point relative to low water mark, unless otherwise stated. Distance given in metres	Remarks
		Arnside	1	2,000	Tidal tank		Mud, shingle and sand. New pumping station has reduced the number of occasions when overflow operates.
		Hest Bank	2	2,850	Secondary	One above HWM and one below	Mud flats, sea retreats 5km. No bathing.
f ★★/ f ★		Morecambe	1	31,000	Raw	At LWM	North beach mud and shingle. South beach sandy with safe bathing. £20 million improvement scheme.
★★		Heysham	1	3,500	Raw	At LWM	Sand. Popular beach. Improvement scheme as above.
		Pilling Sands	1	1,000	Tidal tank	To Broad-fleet	Mud flats/salt marsh. Outfall has been moved.
		Knott End-on-Sea	1	1,100	Raw	To Wyre Estuary	Sand/mud flats.
f ★★		Fleetwood	1	31,000	Tidal tank	At LWM	Sand. Stormwater overflow at high water mark which often overflows on to the beach. Linked to Blackpool scheme.
f ★★		Cleveleys					Linked into Blackpool scheme. Sewage at present to Blackpool.
f ★★ f ★ f ★		Blackpool North Blackpool South Blackpool Lost Childrens Post	2	75,000 216,000	Screened Screened	950 below 500 below	Sand. Discharges of storm water directly on to the beach occur once or twice a year. £58.8 million improvement scheme, due for completion in 1993.
f ★/ f ★		Lytham St Anne's	1	37,000	Screened	At LWM	Sand. Outfall discharges into channel of the Ribble Estuary. Linked to new Blackpool scheme.

Beach No on Map	Rating. The more stars the better. f=failed	Resort	Sewage outlets	Population Discharging from outlet	Type of treatment	Discharge point relative to low water mark, unless otherwise stated. Distance given in metres	Remarks
		Marshside	5	91,500	Secondary	All above LWM	Sandy beaches. 3 storm sewage overflows used in emergency only, 2 stormwater overflows. Sewage is treated at Southport and Ainsdale sewage treatment works which is being extended in a £21 million scheme.
	f ★★	**Southport**					
	★★	**Ainsdale**					
1	★★	**Formby**					
		Hightown	2	2,100	Secondary		Sand and some muddy areas around Alt estuary. Emergency overflow into Alt Estuary. Sewage is treated at Formby sewage treatment works.
		Blundell Sands	5	48,100			New interceptor sewers carrying the sewage to a treatment works; part of a major scheme to clean up the Mersey.
		Brighton-Le-Sands					
		Crosby					
		Waterloo					
	f ★★	**New Brighton Egremont**	4	16,000			New Brighton to Egremont interceptor sewer completed. All crude outfalls along this length will be removed and flows diverted to Scottsfield for screening. Only one storm sewage overflow will remain and that will be screened.
		New Brighton Harrison Drive	5	30,000			1 crude and 1 storm sewage overflow (SSO) will be abandoned when new sewer complete leaving 3 SSOs.
	★★★	**Moreton**	1	65,000	Macerated	3000 below	A long sea outfall discharges macerated sewage through diffusers. The coast is normally free from sewage but see remarks above re the Mersey Estuary.
		Holylake					
	f ★★	**Moels**					
		West Kirby					

1 Freshfield, Formby, Merseyside   OS Ref: SD2907

Freshfield is the oasis in the desert of polluted, neglected, or industrialised beaches of the north-west. A massive expanse of sand is revealed as the tide retreats across the flat beach. Not an ideal beach for swimming from but good for walking, soaking up the sun or escaping from the surrounding urban sprawl and enjoying the 450 acres of unspoilt dunes and woodland. These are owned by the National Trust and stretch a mile inland from the beach. The 2½ mile (4km) long stretch of beach extends north to the Ainsdale National Nature Reserve, with views to Southport and Blackpool Tower beyond. To the south is the Raven Moels Nature Reserve, and there are views across the Mersey to the hills of North Wales.

Water quality Monitored by the NRA and found to meet the EC standard for clean bathing water in 1989. Formby sewage treatment works serving 34,000 people discharges secondary treated sewage to the channel at Formby Bank off the Signal Station.

Litter Litter causes quite a problem on the beach with a lot of plastics and other debris from boats being washed up. Some sewage solids have been observed.

Bathing safety Bathing is only safe close inshore: the incoming tide is very swift and can be dangerous.

Access A short walk through the dunes from the car park. Freshfields station is 1¼ miles (2km) from the beach along Victoria Road.

Parking National Trust car park for 770 cars at the end of Victoria Road within reserve. Sefton MBC car park at Lifeboat Road.

Toilets None.

Food Two ice cream vans during summer.

Seaside activities Swimming, fishing and windsurfing. Horse riding on marked way through dunes, woods and along the beach, by permit only. Golf course at northern end of beach beyond Pinetree Caravan Site.

Wildlife and walks The dunes and woodland behind the beach are owned by the National Trust. Throughout the area there are footpaths and board walks which you should use to protect this fragile environment. If followed inland from the beach, the footpaths will reveal the whole sequence of habitats associated with the developing dune system. These range from the sand and mud flats exposed at low tide, which provide for large numbers and varieties of migrating and breeding birds, to mature Scots pine woods planted to stabilize the sand. Between, there are mobile dune ridges and slacks (wet troughs) where Britain's largest population of breeding Natterjack toads can be seen and heard in the freshwater pools. Inland, the dunes become fixed by a continuous cover of heath-type vegetation, which is replaced landwards by scrub, characterised by creeping willow, and then deciduous woodland. At the Wicks Lane end of the reserve there is a lake that provides a further range of wetland habitats. Adjacent to Victoria Road there is a red squirrel reserve. They can be seen throughout the year in the pine woods. This whole area is covered by the Sefton Coastal Management Scheme and there is a programme of work to protect and improve the area and its wealth of wildlife. There is a full programme of guided walks organised by the Rangers – details from the Rangers' Office at Formby Council Offices.

Scotland

15 Sandside Bay
Thurso
Dunnet Bay
17 Balnakeil Bay
Farr Bay
14 Duncansby Head
18 Sandwood
16 Coldbackie
Sinclair's Bay
Wick
19 Scourie
21 Clachtoll
20 Clashnessie Bay
22 Achmelvich
23 Achnahaird
24 Achiltibuie
Ullapool
13 Dornoch
25 Gruinard Bay
38 The Coral Beaches
Invergordon
Lossiemouth Silversands
Inverboyndie Bay
26 Gairloch
Lossiemouth East
Fraserburgh
Banff f
9 Strathbe
27 Applecross
12 Burghead
10 Sandend
Peterheac
Nairn
11 Cullen
8 Cruden B
Inverness
Balmedie
Aberdeen Ball
Aberdeen
Aberdeen Footc
29 Morar
7 Muchalls
30 Camusdarrach
6 Stonehaven
31 Sanna Bay
5 St Cyrus
4 Montrose
32 Calgary Bay
Arbroath f
Camoustie f
33 Erraid
Oban
3 Tentsmuir Point
St Andrews West
St Andrews East f
Thorntonloch
Dunglass
1 Pease Sa
Edinburgh
White Sands
Coldinghar
Eyemouth
Glasgow
Saltcoats f
35 Brodick
Bay
Irvine f
34 Machrihanish
Troon
36 Blackwaterfoot
Prestwick f
Ayr f
Turnberry
Girvan
37 Southerness
Stranraer
Sandyhills

f = failed to meet EC standard for clean bathing water in 1989.
Numbered beaches appear in the following chapter.

Coastal walk
Forth Road Bridge to Newburgh (152km).

Shell Bay f
Largo
Crail
Lower Largo f
Anstruther
Lundin Links
Pittenweem
Kinghorn f
Elie/Earlsferry f
2 Gullane
North Berwick f
Burnt Island
Kirkaldy
Milsey Bay
Aberdour Silversands
Pettycur
Seacliff
Cramond
Dunbar f
Silverknowes
Belhaven
Edinburgh
Portobello f
Peffer Sands
Gosford f
Broad Sands
Longniddry

Scotland

If you are looking for a clean beach in the UK you are most likely to find one in Scotland. That is not to say that Scotland does not have problems around the coast. There are Scottish beaches that have failed to meet the EC bathing water quality standard. Sea borne rubbish is washed up on to shore. Sewage sludge and dredged spoil are dumped off the Clyde, Forth and Tay Estuaries. Industrial waste is discharged into coastal water, particularly the Clyde and Forth. Nuclear installations at Chapelcross, Hunterston, Torness and Dounreay contribute to pollution of the sea. There is development of the coastline detrimental to scenic value. The west coast lochs are studded with the floating cages of the rapidly expanding fish farming industry. The offshore structures of the North Sea oil and gas industry that dot the horizon have resulted in the growth of onshore terminals. The view along the Cromarty Firth is dominated by a string of massive platforms. By contrast there is probably some of the most spectacular coastal scenery in the country, including the long sand dunes of the east coast, and the rocky shore of Fife with its series of picturesque fishing villages. There are also the cliffs and stacks of Caithness, and of course the west coast, Highlands and Islands, sea lochs, towering mountains and fantastic sunsets. There are hundreds (if not thousands) of beaches, tiny sandy bays, mostly remote, deserted and beautiful. Many can only be reached by the keen walker but without a doubt the effort is well worth while. The beaches that follow are relatively easily accessible for a day at the sea or as a starting point to explore the delights of this coastline further. The sands of the Western Isles have not been included in the section; if you take the boat to the outer islands, beaches abound and every one is a good beach. If you are looking for peace and solitude combined with traditional hospitality then try Scotland.

Beaches receiving Clean Beach Awards from the Tidy Britain Group in 1989:

Croy and Troon.

The Golden List   See page 26 for further details

Beach No on Map	Rating. The more stars the better. f=failed	Resort	Sewage outlets	Population Discharging from outlet	Type of treatment	Discharge point relative to low water mark, unless otherwise stated. Distance given in metres	Remarks
BORDERS							
1 ★★★		**Pease Sands**	1	1,000	Secondary		Red cliffs and sand.
	f ★★	**Coldingham Bay**	1	200	Raw		Sandy. Safe bathing.
	f ★★	**Eyemouth**	2	4,500	Other		Rocks and sand. Bathing can be dangerous.
				1,000	Raw		
LOTHIAN							
	★★★	Thorntonloch					Mostly sandy.
	★★★	Whitesands Bay					Sandy.
	★★★	**Belhaven Beach**	1	4,200	Screens/ maceration	At LWM	Sandy.
	★★★	Peffersands					Sandy.
	★★★	**Milsey Bay**	2	2,100	Raw	At LWM	Sandy and rock outcrops.
	f ★★	North Berwick Bay	2	2,800	Raw	At LWM	Sandy and rock outcrops. Improvement scheme.
	★★★	**Yellowcraig (Broad Sands Bay)**	1	300	Raw	At LWM	Sandy.
2 ★★★		**Gullane Bay**					Sand and dunes.
	f ★★	Gosford Sands					Sand with rocky upper shore.
		Seton Sands	1	3,700	Primary	At LWM	Sand and rocks.
	f ★★	Portobello	1	4,500	Screened	At LWM	Mostly sand.
FIFE							
	★★★	**Aberdour Silversands**	1	2,500	Primary	At LWM	Sandy.

Beach No on Map	Rating. The more stars the better. f=failed	Resort	Sewage outlets	Population Discharging from outlet	Type of treatment	Discharge point relative to low water mark, unless otherwise stated. Distance given in metres	Remarks
	f ★★	**Kinghorn**	1	2,400	Primary	50 below	Sandy.
		Leven Links	1	110,000	Screens/maceration	100 below	Sandy.
	★★★	Lundin Links	1	1,100	Primary	200 below	Sandy to west.
	f ★★	Lower Largo	1	1,100	Primary	At LWM	Rocky with some sand.
	f ★★	Shell Bay	1	100	Primary	At LWM	Sandy.
	f ★★	**Elie**	2	1,000	Raw	At LWM	Muddy sand.
	★★★	Anstruther	7	4,200	Raw	Mostly LWM	Muddy sand.
	★★★	Roome Bay Crail	1	500	Primary	Above LWM	Sandy.
	f ★★	**St Andrews East**	1	16,000	Primary	At LWM	Sandy.
	★★★	**St Andrews West**					
	f ★★	**Carnoustie**					Sandy.
	f ★★	**Arbroath**	3	9,000 12,000 9,000	Raw Screened Primary	At LWM 900 below At LWM	Red sand.
		Lunan Bay					Sandy. Safe bathing except at river mouth.
4	★★★	**Montrose**					Sandy. Bathing safe except near river mouth.

GRAMPIAN

Beach No on Map	Rating	Resort	Sewage outlets	Population Discharging from outlet	Type of treatment	Discharge point relative to low water mark	Remarks
5	★★★	St Cyrus	1	820	Raw	At LWM	Sand/Saltmarsh.
6	★★★ ★★★	**Stonehaven**		9,780	Raw		
	★★★ ★★★	**Aberdeen Beach**		269,450	Raw		Sandy. New long sea outfall under construction.
	★★★	**Balmedie**					10 miles of sand and dunes.
8	★★★	**Cruden Bay**		2,220	Maceration		Sand and dunes.
	★★★	**Lido Peterhead**	1	20,450	Screened		Sandy.
	★★	**Fraserburgh**		15,690	Raw	Above HWM	Sand and dunes. Improvement scheme.

Beach No on Map	Rating. The more stars the better. f=failed	Resort	Sewage outlets	Population Discharging from outlet	Type of treatment	Discharge point relative to low water mark, unless otherwise stated. Distance given in metres	Remarks
f ★★		**Banff Links**		4,420	Raw		Sandy.
★★★		**Cullen**		1,500		Below LWM	Sandy.
		Findochty		1,050		Below LWM	Sandy.
		Strathlene, Buckie		15,000	Raw	LWM	Sandy.
★★		**Lossiemouth East**	3	42,700	Raw	1 long/ 2 short	Sandy.
★★		**Lossiemouth Silversands**					
		Hopeman	1	1,663	Raw	LWM	Water sports.
12		Burghead	1		Raw	Long east of harbour	Sandy. Bathing not recommended.

HIGHLAND

★★★		**Nairn**	3		2×Raw 1×Primary		Sandy. Improvement scheme.
		Cromarty			Raw		Untreated sewage discharges to beach.
		Sinclairs Bay	3	700	2×Raw	2×Above LWM	Sandy.
		Wick			1×Primary	1×tank	
		Dunnet Bay/ Murkle Bay	2	200 1,000	Maceration Primary	Above LWM Below LWM	Sand and dunes.
		Thurso	1	9,000	Maceration	450 below	Sandy.
		Sango Bay/ Balnakeil Bay	1	200	Primary	LWM	Sand/dunes.
19		Scourie	2	300	Primary	LWM	Sandy.
26		Gairloch	3		Primary		Sandy. Safe bathing.

STRATHCLYDE

		Kilchattan Bay	1	170	Raw	To LWM	
		Kames Bay	several	550	Raw		Sand and pebbles.

Beach No on Map	Rating. The more stars the better. **f**=failed	Resort	Sewage oulets	Population Discharging from outlet	Type of treatment	Discharge point relative to low water mark, unless otherwise stated. Distance given in metres	Remarks
		Dunoon (West Bay)	1	not known	Raw	Below LWM	Sand and pebbles.
		Ganavan	1	100		Above LWM	Sand and rocky outcrops.
34		Machrahanish	1	200	Raw	To LWM	Sandy.
		Carradale	2	480	Raw	To LWM	
		Helensburgh	1	13,200	Maceration		Sand and pebbles.
		Portkil/ Meiklecross	2	<100	Raw	Above LWM	Sand and rocks.
				<100	Raw	Below LWM	
		Gourock (West Bay)	4	2,600	Raw	Below LWM	Shingle and rocks.
		Lunderston Bay	3	not known	Other	Above LWM	Shingle and sand.
		Wemyss Bay	3	100	Other	Above LWM	
				100	Other	Above LWM	Shingle and sand.
				11,000	Maceration	Below LWM	
		Largs (Monument)	1	12,000	Other	Below LWM	Sand and rocks.
		Fairlie	2	700	Raw	Beyond LWM	Sand and rocks.
				800	Raw	At LWM	
		Millport	12	700	Varies	All at LWM	Sand and rocks.
		Seamill	3	4,500	Raw	All at LWM	Sand and rocks.
		Boydston	1	4,000	Maceration	At LWM	Sand and rocks.
	f ★★	**Saltcoats**	2	13,500	Raw	Both beyond LWM	Sandy.
		Stevenston	1	41,000	Screens	Beyond LWM	Sandy.
	f ★★	**Irvine (Beach Park)**	3	25,000	Raw	2 below LWM 1 at LWM	Sandy.
		Gailes	1	75,000	Screens	1.5km beyond LWM	Sandy.
		Brodick Bay	2	700	Raw	1 beyond LWM	Rocks and sand.
					Raw	1 above LMW	

Beach No on Map	Rating. The more stars the better. **f**=failed	Resort	Sewage outlets	Population Discharging from outlet	Type of treatment	Discharge point relative to low water mark, unless otherwise stated. Distance given in metres	Remarks
		Lamlash Bay	4	950	Raw	All at LWM	Rocks and sand.
		Whiting Bay	2	800	Raw	Beyond LWM	Sand and shingle.
		Troon (North)	1	6,300	Raw	At LWM	Sandy.
	★★★	**Troon (South)**					Sandy.
	f ★★	**Prestwick**					Sandy.
	f ★★	**Ayr**	1	16,200	Screens	140 beyond LWM	Sandy.
		Doonfoot	1	8,000	Maceration	220 beyond LWM	Sand/rocks.
		Butlins (Heads of Ayr)	1	8,000	Secondary	Beyond LWM	Sandy.
		Maidens	1	600	Primary	At LWM	Sandy and rocks.
		Turnberry	1		Primary	Beyond LWM	Sand and rocks.
	★★	**Girvan**	3	4,000	Screens/ maceration	10 below	Improvement scheme.
				500	Tidal tank	At LWM	Sandy.
				2,500	Tidal tank	At LWM	

DUMFRIES AND GALLOWAY

Beach No on Map	Rating	Resort	Sewage outlets	Population	Type of treatment	Discharge point	Remarks
		Southerness	1	3,500	Primary	500 above	Sand/rocks.
37	★★★	**Sandyhills**	1	200	Secondary	Tidal watercourse	Sandy.
		Brighouse Bay	1	400	Secondary	30 below	Sandy.
		Ardwell Bay	1	75	Primary	75 below HWM	Sand/shingle.
		Portlogan Bay	1	75	Primary	200 below HWM	Sandy.

1 Pease Sands, Cockburns Path, Berwickshire   OS Ref: NT7971

The deep wooded valley of Pease Burn opens out onto the sandy cove of Pease Bay. Framed by red cliffs, a shrub and grass-covered bank fringes the landward side of the sands beyond which is a large caravan and mobile home park. ¾ mile (1.2km) of good sandy beach is very much dominated by the caravan site that rings the bay.

Water quality Beach monitored by the River Purification Board and found to meet the EC standard for clean bathing water in 1989. One outfall serving 1,000 people discharges secondary treated sewage.

Bathing safety Safe bathing.

Access A steep road from the A1107, just south of its junction with the A1, leads down to the bay.

Parking Car park with 100+ spaces directly off beach.

Toilets At car park.

Food Small shop adjacent to beach.

Seaside activities Swimming and fishing.

Wildlife and walks Good walks are available in Pease Dean. A cliff path can be followed north of the beach passing the tiny village and harbour of Cove and leading to the Dunglass Gorge.

2 Gullane, East Lothian   OS Ref: NT4882

This is an absolutely beautiful and completely unspoilt 1½ mile (2.5km) sweep of sandy beach. The extensive flat sands exposed at low tide are backed by Gullane Bents, a series of 15 foot (5m) high dune ridges behind which scrubland slopes up 68 feet (20m) to flat grassland. Here there is parking and a picnic area, overlooked by the houses of Gullane village. The curve of sand is bounded at either end by outcrops of black pillow lava. To the east there is a series of tiny sandy bays only accessible by foot along the coast path. Muirfield golf course overlooks this lovely bay and the view across the beach is frequently seen as a backdrop to televised tournaments. All litter is cleared daily in summer.

Water quality Beach monitored by River Purification Board and found to meet the EC standard for clean bathing water in 1989. No sewage is discharged in the vicinity of the beach.

Bathing safety Bathing is safe from this beach.

Access The beach is signposted from Gullane village on the A198, there is a 110 yard (100m) walk down through the dunes to the beach.

Parking Car park with 500 places on grassland behind Gullane Bents.

Toilets Block at centre of beach sign-posted 110 yards (100m) from the beach.

Food Refreshment stand. Also in Gullane village.

Seaside activities Swimming and windsurfing. Riding track around the bay and three golf courses. Children's play area off path through the dunes.

Wet weather alternatives Golf museum adjacent to the golf professional J. Hume's shop. Luffness Castle and Myreton motor museum near Aberlady.

Wildlife and walks The beach has a large lug worm population as evidenced by the casts left on the sand. Rock outcrops at either end of the beach contain pools rich in marine life including mussels, crabs, anemones and numerous snails. The rocks at the west end of the beach are covered in barnacles but very little seaweed. Inland the dunes are stabilised by marram grass and the dune slacks (areas between the sand ridges) have a rich and diverse vegetation.

3 Tentsmuir Point, Tayport, Fife   OS Ref: NO5024

A large area of the extensive sand dunes north of the Eden Estuary dunes has been stabilised by the conifers planted in the 1920s by the Forestry Commission. The coastline can still be reached along roads cut through the forest giving access to parking and picnic areas beyond the forest. A wild and remote spot with a wide flat sandy beach backed by high sand dunes which are continually moving seawards.

Water quality No sewage is discharged in the vicinity of this beach. The beaches at the mouth of the Tay failed to comply with the EC bathing water quality standard in 1989 and poor water quality from the estuary may at times affect this beach.

Bathing safety Beware of offshore currents.

Access A turning off the road north-west of Leuchars leads to the forest. There are paths to the beach from the car park.

Parking Forestry Commission car park behind dunes.

Toilets At the car park.

Food None.

Seaside activities Swimming.

Wildlife and walks A large area of the shore, including dunes and developing scrub woodland, is a National Nature Reserve. There is a ranger service based at the car park where a nature trail commences. Wildlife is abundant. The area is a feeding ground for numerous waders and wildfowl and there is a rich vegetation. This is an excellent spot for walking with views across the offshore sand banks and away north across to the Tayside coast.

4 Montrose Links, Montrose, Tayside   OS Ref: NO7358

From the mouth of the South Esk 4 miles (6.5km) of magnificent beach stretches north to the mouth of the North Esk. At low tide there is 220 yards (200m) of firm clean sands backed by a 30 foot (9m) high dune ridge. Access is from the southern end of the beach where the delightful little town of Montrose is separated from the beach by two links golf courses. At the entrance a stretch of sea wall edges the beach, protecting the car park and facilities above. On a beach with so much space there should never be an overcrowding problem, and the further north you walk along it the quieter it should be. The beach is cleaned regularly by the local authority.

Water quality Beach monitored by the River Purification Board and found to meet the EC standard for clean bathing water in 1989. An outfall serving 8,000 people discharges macerated sewage at low water mark, another serving 6,000 people discharges untreated sewage at low water mark.

Bathing safety Safe bathing except near the river mouths at each end of the beach. Beach wardens patrol a clearly designated area of the beach.

Access The beach is signposted from the A92. A road through the golf course leads to car parks at the south end of the beach. Steps lead down on to the sands.

Parking 2 car parks adjacent to beach with approximately 350 spaces.

Toilets At the car park.

Food Café at the car park.

Seaside activities Swimming, windsurfing and fishing. Children's amusement play area. Small amusement arcade.

Wet weather alternatives Museum, amusement arcade and indoor swimming pool.

Wildlife and walks The tidal basin to the west is a nature reserve. Low tide reveals extensive mud flats which are an important feeding ground for wintering birds.

5 St Cyrus, Grampian   OS Ref: NO7565

From the cliff-top path at St Cyrus there is a superb view along this lovely beach that forms the northern half of Montrose Bay. Below the steeply sloping lava cliffs of Milton Ness, 2 miles (4km) of golden sand sweep south to the mouth of the River Esk. The cliffs retreat slightly inland and there is a ridge of dunes at their base which gives way to salt marsh close to the river. The cliffs, dunes and beach fall within the St Cyrus Nature Reserve and this has ensured that the beach remains natural and undeveloped.

Water quality Montrose at the southern end of the bay was monitored by the River Purification Board and found to meet the EC standard for clean bathing water in 1989. One outfall serving 820 people discharges raw sewage at low water mark.

Bathing safety Bathing is safe away from the river mouth at the southern end of the beach. Beware of rocks at the northern end of the beach.

Access The main entry to the beach is at St Cyrus on the A92 where there is a car park with a paved pathway leading along the cliff top. There is also access to the southern end via a side road from the A92 which leads to parking at Nether Warburton where board walks across the salt marsh to the dunes.

Parking Car parks at St Cyrus and Nether Warburton.

Toilets None.

Food None.

Seaside activities Swimming.

Wildlife and walks The whole beach forms part of the St Cyrus National Nature Reserve. The reserve with its cliffs, dunes, salt marsh and beach contains a wide range of wildlife. Over 300 wild flower species have been recorded and 47 bird species are said to breed here. There are many more visiting species. You may also see grey seals off shore, as well as traditional salmon netting at the river mouth. Walks along the cliff tops provide wonderful views over Montrose Bay.

6 Stonehaven, Grampian   OS Ref: NO8786

At a break in the rugged sandstone cliffs the waters of Cowie and Carron flow to the sea at Stonehaven. Nestling between the Downie and Garron headlands is Stonehaven itself, which retains the atmosphere of a traditional fishing village, its quaysides busy with boats. The fishing has declined but the twin-basin habour is used by pleasure craft in summer. A ⅔ mile (1km) sand and pebble beach curves away north of the harbour below the rolling farmland which rises beyond the town. The beach is not popular for swimming but often busy with people taking advantage of the promenade facilities. Steep 200 foot (60m) cliffs rise on either side of the bay and offer excellent walking with splendid views over the cliffs and Stonehaven Bay.

Water quality Beach monitored by the River Purification Board and found to meet the EC standard for clean bathing water in 1989.

Bathing safety Some currents can make swimming dangerous. Inshore rescue boat and lifeboat station.

Access From promenade.

Parking Ample on seafront and adjacent to the leisure centre.

Toilets On seafront.

Food Café.

Seaside activities Swimming and windsurfing. Sailing, diving and fishing trips from the adjacent harbour. Cliff-top golf course. Open air heated swimming pool and leisure centre.

Wet weather alternatives Dunnottar Castle, Tolbooth museum of local history, indoor pool and leisure centre, amusement arcades.

Wildlife and walks The promenade leads north to the fishing village of Cowie. North from Cowie, a grass cliff path beside the golf course provides glorious sea views across Stonehaven Bay. 2 miles (3km) along the cliff-top is a steep valley which leads down to two secluded pebbly coves at Skatie Shore. South from Stonehaven, a mile (1.6km) walk along the cliffs leads to the War Memorial giving panoramic views of the coast and inland. Continuing south for 2 miles (3km), the path leads to Dunnottar Castle. This impressive castle stands on an isolated sandstone cliff 170 feet (50m) above the sea. The connection between the castle rock and mainland was cut through to allow easier defence. A further 4 miles (6.5km) south lies the Fowlsheugh Bird Reserve, one of the largest bird colonies with 2 miles (3km) of cliff providing a home to thousands of birds. Parking at Crawton village provides easy access to the reserve.

7 Muchalls, Nr Stonehaven, Grampian   OS Ref: NO9292

This is a spectacular stretch of coastline whose rock formations include stacks, arches and caves with an underground waterfall. There are several rock and pebble coves below the steep cliffs but take care as some are cut off at high tide with no escape routes. Swimming is out of the question due to dangerous rocks offshore but the cliff-top scenery and the interesting coves with their numerous rock pools make the area worth a visit.

Water quality No outfalls discharge in the vicinity of the beach.

Bathing safety There are unsafe rocks off shore.

Access From Muchalls village, just off the A92, are two access routes – a very steep path and a road under the railway lead to the shore.

Parking In village.

Toilets None.

Food Pub and hotel in village.

Seaside activities Fishing.

Wet weather alternatives Muchalls Castle (check opening times as only open on occasional days in summer).

Wildlife and walks A cliff-top path gives fine views of the cliff formations to the north and the numerous nesting sea birds that frequent the rocky ledges. Rock pools on the shore contain a wealth of interest for the beach walker but remember to keep an eye on the tide.

8 Cruden Bay, Grampian   OS Ref: NK0936

The red granite cliffs of Buchan are very impressive. Predominantly steep and rocky, they form a series of holes, stacks and rocky inlets. The largest indent is Cruden Bay where the cliffs give way to a 2 mile (3km) sandy beach fringed by dunes and golf links. On the low headland at the northern end of the beach is the village of Cruden Bay and Port Erroll harbour. The waters of Cruden flow across the northern end of the bay separating the harbour from the beach. Access is from Cruden village on the north shore of the river; a bridge gives access to the sands. This is an excellent spot to combine a coastal walk with relaxation on the sands. Along this stretch of coast, debris from fishing boats and oil and gas supply boats causes litter problems. The beach is cleaned by the local authority.

Water quality Beach monitored by the River Purification Board and found to meet the EC standard for clean bathing water in 1989. One outfall serving 2,200 people discharges macerated sewage some way from the beach.

Bathing safety There are some currents, therefore bathing with care is advised.

Access There is parking in Cruden village, signposted off the A975 and a bridge leads on to the beach.

Parking There is a car park with 50–60 places.

Toilets In village at north end of the beach.

Food Café and shops in the village.

Seaside activities Swimming, windsurfing, sailing, diving and fishing. Championship golf course.

Wildlife and walks The route north of the bay passes the ruins of Slains Castle above the original harbour of Cruden and follows the cliffs to the village of Bullers of Buchan. The path follows the edge of a narrow inlet with a sheer 100 foot (30m) drop to the water below. The precipitous drops along the route mean that great care is needed when using the path; don't take small children on this route. North of Bullers of Buchan, the cliffs are a Scottish Wildlife Trust nature reserve, where a whole host of bird species and a rich variety of plant life can be seen.

9 Strathbeg Bay, Grampian   OS Ref: NK0663

This little-frequented beach has 3¾ miles (6km) of sand and substantial dunes stretching from the rocky Cairnbulg Point south, past the fishing villages of Inverallochy and St Combs to Rattray Head. This beach is not particularly scenic, but if you seek solitude on a remote and peaceful beach the wind-swept sands of Rattray should meet your requirements. The lighthouse off the headland indicates the presence of a reef which causes swift currents and makes swimming dangerous. South of Rattray Head, a further 7 miles (11km) of deserted sandy beach stretches to Peterhead, but the shore is dominated by the St Fergus gas terminal. Marine litter is a frequent problem along these shores.

Water quality No sewage is discharged in the vicinity of this beach.

Bathing safety Care is required as the currents off Rattray Head are dangerous.

Access There is a path through the dunes at St Combs, off the B9033 south east of Fraserburgh and another at Rattray Head, reached via a road off the A952 south of Crimmond.

Parking There is a car park at St Combs and very limited parking at Rattray Head.

Toilets None.

Food None.

Seaside activities Swimming, sailing, diving and fishing.

Wildlife and walks The Loch of Strathbeg RSPB reserve, with its Visitor Centre and observation hides, lies just behind the dunes. It is the largest dune slack pool in Britain and an important site for wintering wildfowl. Admission is by permit only, available from the warden, Jim Dunbar (Lonmay 2522).

10 Sandend, Grampian   OS Ref: NJ5566

From Fraserburgh to Inverness is a stretch of coast known as the Banffshire Riviera. It is characterised by towering cliffs, small sheltered sandy bays and fishing villages. Clear waters wash this most attractive sandy beach. ⅔ mile (1km) of dunes fringe the beach landwards and the bay is framed by high cliffs.

Water quality No sewage is discharged in the vicinity of the beach.

Bathing safety Heavy surf on occasions.

Access Sandend is signposted off the A98, it is a short walk from the car park to the beach.

Parking Car park with 100 spaces.

Toilets Public conveniences in village.

Food Small shop and restaurant.

Seaside activities Swimming, surfing, windsurfing, sailing, diving and fishing.

Wildlife and fishing East of the bay the coast path climbs over the cliffs on to the headland which offers excellent sea and coastal views. The path continues to Portsoy, a charming fishing village with a small harbour which has won awards for its architectural restoration. West of Sandend the cliff path can be followed to the ruins of Findlater Castle with its impressive

147

position 165 feet (50km) above the waves. Below the ruins is the lovely secluded Sunnyside Beach, its sweep of golden sand nestling below the steep cliffs.

11 Cullen Sands, Cullen, Grampian   OS Ref: NJ5167

The dipping Cullen quartzites form a spectacular rocky coastline and create the extremely scenic Cullen Bay. From the curving quays of the harbour, sheltering below the cliffs at the eastern end of the bay, an arc of rock-studded sand sweeps west to the isolated stacks known as the Three Kings. Beyond, the Boar's Craig rises and the sands give way to rocks below the cliffs of Portknockie headland. Here there are caves, known as the Preacher's and the Whale's Mouth, to explore and numerous rock pools to investigate. Relax on the sands (but watch the tide), or stretch your legs to enjoy the wonderful scenery around the bay. The railway once passed through Cullen but all that remains is a series of graceful viaducts. They separate the narrow streets of Seatown that cluster around the harbour from the upper town with its open square and wider streets.

Water quality Beach monitored by the River Purification Board and found to meet the EC standard for clean bathing water in 1989. One outfall serving 1,500 people discharges sewage below low water mark.

Bathing safety There are strong cross tides so care is required when bathing.

Access From Seatown and from the road to the golf course.

Parking Car park close to harbour. Large car park beside beach next to golf course.

Toilets Public toilets at the harbour are open all year.

Food Tea room at beach. Two hotels in Seatown. Cafés and hotels in upper town.

Seaside activities Swimming, putting, bowls, tennis and a golf course. Sea-angling and boat trips from the harbour.

Wildlife and walks From the harbour a path leads east along the shore to the excellent sandy cove of Sunnyside Bay. The path climbs to the cliff top and continues to Findlater Castle, a 15th century ruined castle sitting on a rocky promontory 165 feet (50m) above the sea. A return journey can be made along the cliff top, giving excellent views along the coast and across to Sutherland and Caithness. Alternatively you may head east to Sandend Bay, another of the lovely coves along this coastline complete with its own small harbour. West from Cullen there is a well marked path alongside the golf course. The path leads up from the rocky shore to the quiet fishing village of Portknockie on the cliff top. There are superb views of this magnificent rocky coast; just off-shore lies Bow Fiddle rock, where erosion of the dipping rock strata has produced an arch resembling the tip of a violinist's bow. Further west from Portknockie the cliff path leads to Findochty with its sheltered sandy cove and harbour; there are superb views of the Moray Firth and Black Isle.

12 Burghead Bay, Burghead, Grampian   OS Ref: NJ1169

The solid fishing cottages that make up Burghead stand on a low rocky promontory overlooking the 6 mile (10km) curve of Burghead Bay. At the western end of these long flat sands is Findhorn, situated at the mouth of the large, tidal Findhorn Bay. The quiet but somewhat windswept beach of fine sand and pebbles is rimmed by dunes, on which there is a Forestry Commission conifer plantation. A road has been made through the mature pines and there are parking and picnic facilities. Wartime concrete defences once stood on grassland well back from the beach, but the retreating beach means that they now stand on the tidal sands.

Water quality No significant sewage discharges in the vicinity of the beach.

Bathing safety There are strong currents at the western end where the River Findhorn flows out of Findhorn Bay. Bathing is not recommended in the bay but is safe from the beach of Burghead.

Access At either end of the bay at Findhorn or Burghead and also by paths from Roseisle Forest.

Parking At Findhorn dunes and picnic site, Roseisle Forest picnic site and at Burghead.

Toilets At Findhorn and Roseisle picnic sites (including disabled facilities). Public toilets at the harbour in Burghead.

Food Pubs, hotels and fish and chips available at Findhorn and Burghead. Wholefood café at Findhorn Bay Caravan Park.

Seaside activities Swimming, diving, fishing, windsurfing and waterskiing. The bay is a sailing centre with racing throughout the summer. Rowing, sailing and motor boats are available for hire at Findhorn. Sea-angling trips from Burghead harbour.

Wet weather alternatives Distillery, Falconer Museum and Burghead Well. Findhorn Foundation (a spiritual community based south-east of Findhorn village. They run a craft shop and take conducted tours during the summer).

Wildlife and walks There is a walk from Burghead to Findhorn along the shore, where rock and sand pools contain a variety of marine life. 2 miles (3km) south-west of Burghead is the Foresty Commission Rosesile Forest. Pathways from the beach lead to glades in the Corsican and Scots pines planted in the 1930s. Continuing along the shore the walk leads on to the Findhorn peninsula where the extensive tidal bay provides excellent birdwatching.

13 Dornoch, Highland   OS Ref: NH7989

The excellent Royal Dornoch Links golf course attracts many visiting players but the lovely sandy beach remains quiet and uncommercialised. The approach to the beach from Dornoch is unassuming; the low lying lands do not permit any view of the beach until you cross the dunes. To the south of the beach is the entrance to the Dornoch Firth which stretches almost 20 miles (32km) inland. The wide sands stretch 3 miles (5km) north narrowing towards Loch Fleet, a small sea-loch. There is access to the beach from the village of Dornoch, and at the northern end at Embo. Further north in Sutherland the main A9 hugs the shore which is only a ribbon of sand.

Water quality Sewage is treated by septic tank and discharged at Blackburn away from the beach.

Bathing safety There are currents at the north and southern ends of the beach; safe bathing in the main bay at Dornoch.

Access One road from the Square in Dornoch leads to the shore and golf courses, another takes you to Embo; there is a short walk across dunes to the sand.

Parking Dornoch: Two car parks, one overlooking the sea with spaces for 20 cars, the other close by has a further 20 spaces. Embo: car park with 25 spaces.

Toilets New toilet block at caravan site backing beach.

Food None (At Embo: Grannie's Heilan Hame Café and fish and chip shop – seasonal).

Seaside activities Swimming. Royal Dornoch Golf Course, local pipe band parade during the summer and Highland Games during August.

Wet weather alternatives Dornoch Cathedral. Local social club is open for supervised games during the season.

Wildlife and walks Loch Fleet, a sea-loch at the northern end of the beach, is the last of the Firth indents into this coastline going north. The loch and the alderwoods behind the mound embankment are nature reserves which contain a wide variety of wildlife. The Scottish Wildlife Trust Reserve Warden runs a series of guided walks during the summer. These include an exploration of the woodland and estuary or the sand dunes and sea shore. Otherwise, access to the reserve is restricted. In the nearby Skelbo Wood, the Forestry Commission has laid out several forest trails; the walks start from the Commission's car park off the B9168.

14 Duncansby Head, John o'Groats, Highland   OS Ref: ND4173

Travellers taking the A9 north beyond Inverness are normally heading for John o'Groats as the most northerly point. Not to be missed is Duncansby Head, without doubt one of the finest pieces of coastline in Britain. The road from John o'Groats takes you to the Duncansby lighthouse. From the small car park the view to the islands is hard to beat. On a clear day the panorama laid out before you can be breathtaking. Just offshore beyond the white foaming waters are the Pentland Skerries and Stroma, on which you can see many abandoned dwellings. Beyond, Swona, South Ronaldsay, Hoy and the mainland of Orkney complete the picture. Tucked below the headland, just off the lighthouse approach road, is a tiny beach. A mere 110 yards (100m) in length, the narrow strip of sand is shadowed by the red sandstone of the headland. A delightful spot, this may not be the beach to seek out for a day by the sea, but after enjoying a stroll in the headland, relax a while and watch the seals that bob around offshore. This is one of many little beaches along the north coast between the Duncansby and Dunnet headlands, although most are difficult to get to and are not as attractive, lacking the backdrop of sheer red cliffs.

Water quality No sewage is discharged in the vicinity of this beach.

Bathing safety The beach shelves steeply and swimming is dangerous.

Access Duncansby Head is signposted from the A9 south of John o'Groats. A short walk from the parking area down the hill across turf leads on to the sands.

Parking Car park at Duncansby Lighthouse with approximately 25 spaces.

Toilets None.

Food None.

Wildlife and walks A short walk over the headland passes a narrow inlet or geo whose cliff walls rise nearly 200 feet (60m) above the waves. A short distance further and you are rewarded with the marvellous view of Duncansby Stacks, their steeple-like outlines pointing skywards. These are also known as Muckle Stack. Boat trips around this stretch of coast are available from John o'Groats.

15 Sandside Bay, Reay, Highland   OS Ref: NC9774

This area has some of the best rocky exposed coastline in Britain. Low cliffs, rocky outcrops and dunes bound this long, flat sandy beach. At the western end of the bay is the tiny harbour of Fresgoe: a tranquil old world air prevails around the little-used harbour. A sharp contrast to the view along the coast east to the Dounreay Fast Reactor. A remote and quiet beach.

Water quality No sewage is discharged in the vicinity of the beach.

Bathing safety Safe bathing.

Access The road to Fresgoe runs alongside the bay, and it's a short walk from the road down a track between dunes to the beach.

Parking Parking in area along the side road.

Toilets Toilet block on road close to the car parking area.

Food None. The closest shop is in Reay village 2 miles (3.5km) away.

Seaside activities Swimming.

Wet weather alternatives Dounreay Exhibition Centre.

Wildlife and walks There is a short cliff walk from the beach.

16 Coldbackie, Tongue, Highland   OS Ref: NC6160

The half-moon of Coldbackie Sands faces Tongue Bay at the mouth of the Kyle of Tongue, one of the three deep indents into the north coast. The undulating turf-covered moorland which dominates this corner of Scotland, slopes down to the grass-covered dunes which flank the beach. Below Meall Mor, low grass-covered cliffs flank the beach. From the road above the beach a bank of dunes descends to the sands.

Water quality No sewage is discharged in the vicinity of this beach.

Bathing safety Safe bathing.

Access From the A836 north of Tongue, banks of dunes descend to the beach. There is no proper footpath but it is an easy walk down to the sand.

Parking There is limited car parking in a layby off the main road above the beach.

Toilets None.

Food None.

Seaside activities Swimming

Wildlife and walks The 1000 feet (300m) peaks of Cnoc an Fhreiceadan and Ben Tongue rise behind the beach. From the road a footpath inland skirts the sides of the hills, passing a tiny loch to reach Tongue and the shores of the Kyle.

17 Balnakeil Bay, Durness, Highland   OS Ref: NC3869

There are in fact three beaches at Durness all worthy of note. All have clean white sands, are unspoilt and are quiet, even at the height of summer. To the east of Faraid Head peninsula, below the steep limestone cliffs on which Durness stands, are the twin beaches of Sango Bay and Sangobeg. The best beach, however, is on the western side of the peninsula, Balnakeil Bay, a long curve of white sand and dunes. There is easy access at the southern end of the beach close to the ruined Balnakeil church. The extensive wind-sculptured dunes stretch north along the low rugged headland. The bare and treeless landscape is dominated by wild windswept moorland. It is in sharp contrast to the coastline made up of warm red sandstone cliffs, folded and faulted limestone, collapsed caverns, geos, rocky shores and sandy bays.

Water quality No sewage is discharged in the vicinity of the beach.

Bathing safety Safe bathing although in this part of the country some might find it rather cold.

Access The road off the A838 from Durness village leads to a car park behind the beach, and from here an easy path leads to the sand.

Parking Car park with 30 spaces.

Toilets Portaloo at car park.

Food Sango Sands Oasis Restaurant in Sango.

Seaside activities Swimming.

Wet weather alternatives ½ mile (800 m) inland is a craft village in the building of a disused early warning station. The workshops are open to the public during the summer months.

Wildlife and walks There are walks on the cliffs surrounding the bay, with much evidence of 1000 years of human activity, including slight remains of an ancient fortress on the Faraid Headland. Steps lead down from Durness village to the beach at Sango Bay where the high arched entrance to the Smoo Cave can be found. The Allt (river) Smoo flows from the cave and the first of the three chambers can be entered. The Highland Regional Ranger Service organises guided walks in the area, and further information can be obtained from the information centre in Durness. The remote north-western tip of Scotland, Cape Wrath, can be reached by a small ferry across the Kyle of Durness followed by a minibus service to the Cape. The bus takes you across the wild moorland to the Cape Wrath Lighthouse and there is fantastic cliff scenery along this most isolated stretch of coastline. The most spectacular cliffs are along the northern coast, where in places the sheer cliffs fall 800ft (250m) to the waters below.

18 Sandwood Bay, Highland   OS Ref: NC2364

Sandwood Bay must be one of the most remote beaches in Britain, but equally one of the most magnificent. Lying on the west coast of Scotland between Kinlochbervie and Cape Wrath, a 4 mile (7km) walk from Blairmore brings you to this outstanding beach with its huge sand dunes and gently sloping pink sands, studded with rock outcrops. Towering sandstone cliffs extend away on either side of the bay, and to the west is a most impressive rock stack. For those who do not want to venture to such an isolated and exposed beach, there are a series of pocket-handkerchief-sized sandy beaches that surround Blairmore, the starting point for the walk to Sandwood.

Water quality No sewage is discharged in the vicinity of this beach.

Bathing safety Very dangerous.

Access The B801 leads along Loch Inchard to Kinlochbervie, and beyond this a steep and twisting road continues to Sheigra. Sandwood can only be reached on foot, 4 miles (7km) along the track which turns off the road between Blairmore and Sheigra.

Parking Limited parking at Blairmore.

Toilets None.

Food None.

Wildlife and walk The walk to Sandwood crosses the peat moorland of Sutherland before making a steep descent to the bay. This area is both wild and beautiful, but anyone thinking of walking here should be fully aware of the dangers of this remote and difficult terrain. Only those completely prepared should undertake the trip.

19 Scourie, Highland   OS Ref: NC1544

Unlike most of the crofting villages along the west coast, Scourie has some facilities to cater for the visitor. It boasts two hotels, a shop, a post office and a camp site, thus enabling the tourist to stop a while and enjoy this most picturesque district. Scourie is set at the head of a 1 mile (1.5km) rocky inlet on the banks of a small river draining from a loch a short distance inland. There is a lovely sheltered beach on the southern flank of the bay. The wide, gently sloping sands are backed by a narrow storm beach, where small boulders and pebbles edge the sand. The irregular hummocks of this grey-green rocky landscape come down to the water's edge in the outer bay. This exposed rocky coast is coloured by bands of lichens and encrusted with barnacles and seaweed below high water mark, where there are many rock pools to explore. This is a deservedly popular spot.

Water quality Two outfalls, each serving 100-200 people, discharge primary treated sewage at low water mark.

Bathing safety Safe bathing.

Access There are gently sloping grass slopes down to the sand.

Parking Parking space available adjacent to the beach.

Toilets In village.

Food Hotel and shop in village.

Seaside acativities Swimming.

Wildlife and walks A stroll around the loch, village and its quayside can be a most pleasant way to spend an afternoon. Alternatively follow the path north of the bay to Tarbet Handa Island, lying just across the South of Handa, is an RSPB reserve. The numerous ledges on its vertical cliffs provide nesting sites for thousands of sea-birds including guillemots, kittiwakes and fulmars. The island can be visited by boat from Tarbet daily, except Sunday, from April to August.

20 Clashnessie Bay, Lochinver, Highland   OS Ref: NC0631

Steep rocky cliffs, wide bays dotted with tiny islands, clean clear waters, beautiful sunsets, sea birds and seals: the perfect ingredients to make a good beach. Clashnessie is an attractive and safe beach. The 660 yards (600m) of gently sloping pink sands are framed by red sandstone cliffs. There are superb views north towards Oldany Island and east along the rugged cliffs of the Stoer Peninsula.

Water quality No sewage is discharged in the vicinity of the beach.

Bathing safety Safe bathing.

Access A side road from the B869 at Clashnessie leads down to the shore, and then there is a short walk down to the beach.

Parking Car park at beach with 10-15 spaces.

Toilets None.

Food None.

Seaside activities Swimming.

Wildlife and walks To the east there is a cliff-top walk onto the Stoer Point with views of the fine cliff scenery including the Old Man of Stoer, an isolated sea stack rising 200ft (60m) above the waves. Further along the coast stands the Stoer lighthouse. A good variety of birds can be seen on the beach and cliffs. There are also a number of walks on the wide flat moors inland.

21 Clachtoll, Lochinver, Highland   OS Ref: NC0427

This is one of a series of sandy coves along this stretch of coastline, north of Loch Inver, which is scenically stunning. Clachtoll is a small cove, 275 yards (250m) of beautiful white shell sand backed by machair banks and grey and red cliffs. The quiet beach is washed by clear waters and seals can often be seen close to the shore. There is a camp site behind the beach.

Water quality No sewage is discharged in the vicinity of this beach.

Bathing safety Safe bathing within the bay.

Access There is parking off the B869 which runs along this stretch of coast. It is a short walk across the dunes to the beach.

Parking Car park with 20 spaces.

Toilets Toilets and showers at beach car park.

Food Take-away meals and snacks at the camp site.

Seaside activities Swimming, windsurfing, diving, sailing, canoeing and fishing. Boats can be hired for fishing. Details are available from the local Ranger.

Wet weather alternatives Teas and games at Stoer village hall.

Wildlife and walks There is a diverse range of plant and animal life around the bay, and an interesting variety of birds and mammals, including seals and whales, can be seen. Many rare plants can also be found. There is a wealth of material for those interested in conservation and the history of the area. Full details are available from the interpretative centre at the beach, and coastal walks can be arranged by the Ranger.

22 Achmelvich, Lochinver, Highland   OS Ref: NC0625

This is a small sandy cove at the southern end of Achmelvich Bay which can be reached fairly easily. The white sands of the bay are backed by an area of machair grassland. This sand dune-type vegetation is very fragile and easily eroded, so great care must be taken not to cause damage in this area. Steep grey, rocky cliffs rise on either side of the sands, creating a marvellous setting for the bay. Litter on the beach is collected by local volunteers. Dogs are permitted on the beach under strict control; but they are not allowed on the surrounding land.

Water quality No sewage is discharged in the vicinity of this beach.

Bathing safety Safe bathing.

Access A side road off the B869 north of Lochinver leads to Achmelvich. The car park gives direct access to the turf sloping to the sand.

Parking Car park with 60 spaces.

Toiletsd Public toilets in car park.

Food None.

Seaside activities Swimming, surfing, windsurfing, diving, sailing and fishing.

Wildlife and walks There is a 1 mile (1.6km) nature trail along the coast to the small sandy bay of Alltan na Bradhan. The walk leads from the machair grassland over the sand hills and then passes through heath and bog vegetation. A leaflet describing the whole trail is available from the Countryside Ranger Centre at the rear of the car park at Achmelvich. This area also has interesting geology. There is a combination of red sandstone and grey Lewisian Gneiss (pronounced 'nice') with igneous dyke intrusions – dark rock squeezed in bands up through the surrounding rock.

23 Achnahaird, Enard Bay, Highland   OS Ref: NC0214

Flat windswept moorland with outcrops of grey Gneiss leads down to the shore of Enard Bay, a magnificent island dotted prospect. On the western side of the Rudha Mor headland is the narrow inlet of Achnahaird Bay. The bay, in the southern corner of Enard Bay, stretches nearly a mile (1,300m) inland and low tide reveals an expanse of flat white sand. On the western side of the inlet there are extensive dunes which give way to salt marsh at the head of the bay. Irregularly layered sandstone cliffs flank the eastern side of the inlet and a stream meanders across the centre of the sands.

Water quality No sewage is discharged in the vicinity of this beach.

Bathing safety Bathe with caution as there may be some currents that could cause problems for the swimmer.

Access A side road from Achnahaird village leads to parking behind the beach. There is access to the sands on a path down the rocks (can be difficult) or through the camp site behind the dunes.

Parking There is limited parking behind the dunes.

Toilets None.

Food None.

Seaside activities Swimming.

Wildlife and walks The shores of Enard Bay are part of the Inverpolly National Nature Reserve, a huge area of moorland, including the huge bulk of Suilven. There is a visitors' centre at Knockan some way inland, where there is an interpretative centre, a nature trail and a geology trail. This helps to introduce the visitor to an area that abounds in wildlife including red deer and otters. 100 bird species and 300 types of plant have been recorded within the reserve. Achnahaird Bay combines a wide variety of vegetation types: dunes, salt marsh, rocky and sandy shore. The salt marsh attracts waders and wildfowl. There is a comprehensive range of wildlife supported by the diverse habitats. The rocky shore is banded with lichen and there are rock pools among the barnacle encrusted rocks.

24 Achiltibuie, Badentarbat Bay, Highland OS Ref: NC0309

Smooth heather-clad slopes descend to the crofting village of Achiltibuie which straggles 3 miles (5km) along the shore of Badentarbat Bay. The beach, which curves round the bay, lacks the sand so common on the west coast but to compensate is a marvellous view across the bay to the Summer Isles. A patchwork of islands and rocky skerries lies just offshore and provides the most wonderful seascape. From the pier at the northern end of the bay, the shingle and cobble beach stretches south to the rocky headland of Rubha Dunan.

Water quality No sewage is discharged in the vicinity of this beach.

Bathing safety Bathe with caution as there may be some currents that could cause problems for the swimmer.

Access The road through the village continues along the edge of the bay and the sand can be reached across the grass which slopes below the road.

Parking Car park on the grass between the road and the beach.

Toilets None.

Food Shops in village.

Seaside activities Swimming and fishing.

Wildlife and walks The Summer Isles fall within the Ben More Coigach Nature Reserve (Scottish Wildlife Trust – Royal Society for Nature Conservation). 6,075 hectares include the peak which gives the reserve it name, and whose purple and red slopes dominate the views inland from Achiltibuie. There is good walking along the Coigach Peninsula west of the bay. The Summer Isles can be viewed at closer range by taking a boat trip from the pier at Achiltibuie.

25 Gruinard Bay, Laide, Highland   OS Ref: NG9092

There are several excellent beaches dotted around Gruinard Bay, all of which overlook the lovely Gruinard Island, centrepiece of the bay. The island was used for anthrax experiments during the last war and has been out of bounds ever since. It is now being cleaned up, so hopefully the warning signs that have prohibited landing for so long will soon disappear. The A832 skirts the southern and eastern shores of the bay giving easy access to the three lovely cove beaches on the eastern shore. Their pink sands are set among sandstone rock outcrops. In contrast, the south eastern shore at Little Gruinard has the bulging hummocks of Lewisian Gneiss as a most attractive backdrop. Gruinard Hill provides the best views of the bay, the island, and of the Summer Isles on the horizon. Wooded slopes above the beach provide a sharp contrast to the grey rocky outcrops. At Laide, the road runs parallel with the beach behind the machair turf, which slopes to the sand of this 1 mile (1.6km) beach. This most picturesque of bays, like most of the west coast beaches, is relatively quiet and unspoilt. A holiday spent walking the coast or exploring the lochans that speckle the surrounding countryside is an ideal way to escape and relax. Facilities for the tourist are limited and there is restricted parking. In many parts of the bay parking along the back-shore causes severe erosional problems for the machair grass. It is important that the grass cover is maintained and parking should be limited accordingly.

Water quality No sewage is discharged in the vicinity of this beach.

Bathing safety Safe bathing.

Access The A832 follows the shore round most of the bay with easy access to the beach.

Parking There are two car parks in the south eastern corner of the bay near Little Gruinard and another at Laide.

Toilets In Laide.

Food Hotel and shop in Laide.

Seaside activities Swimming and fishing.

Wildlife and walks There are trips around the bay available during the summer months which allow the visitor to take a closer look at Gruinard Island and enjoy the spectacular panoramas across the bay towards the mountains inland.

26 Gairloch, Highland   OS Ref: NG7679

Set among the stunning mountains of Wester Ross, Gairloch, although it is no more than a sizeable fishing village, is one of the few 'holiday resorts' on the west coast. It overlooks a fine sandy beach which curves north from the rocky promontory at Charlestown, round Strath Bay at the head of the loch, extending west of Gairloch to Big Sand. The bay enjoys the mild climate resulting from the North Atlantic Drift, and gardens nearby are filled with plants more commonly found in more southern locations. The A832 follows the shore at the head of the beautiful Loch Gairloch, where there are rocky outcrops of Gneiss. The outer section of the bay is red sandstone with safe, sandy beaches at Shieldaig and Badachro on the southern shores, and Big Sand on the northern shore. There is a large caravan site behind the extensive beach which is sheltered by Longs Island just offshore.

Water quality Three outfalls discharge primary treated sewage into the River Sand. Complaint of sewage contamination at Redpoint beach.

Bathing safety Safe bathing.

Access The A832 runs parallel with the shore between Charlestown and Gairloch. There are paths to the beach.

Parking Parking at Big Sand, in Gairloch and off the A832 to the south.

Toilets In Gairloch.

Food In Gairloch.

Seaside activities Swimming, windsurfing, sailing and fishing.

Wet weather alternatives Gairloch Heritage Museum.

Wildlife and walks From Badachro there is a footpath which leads south-west inland. It passes a small loch and leads to the cliffs of Redpoint, where there are superb views across the Minch to the Hebrides. For those less able, there is road access and a car park at Redpoint. A further mile to the south, there is a beautiful and remote sandy beach backed by dunes. The path continues to the south-east along the shores of Loch Torridon to Diabaig. This walk follows a spectacular length of coast which can only be reached on foot.

27 Applecross, Highland   OS Ref: NG7144

The dramatic and tortuous 'Pass of the Cattle' climbs over 2,000ft (620m) as it twists its way from the A896, at the head of Loch Kishorn, across the wild mountains and moorlands to Applecross. There is a wooded approach to the cluster of white cottages which make up this remote village, on the southern shore of a wide bay. The sweeping sandy beach lies below limestone cliffs from which there are superb views across the Inner Sound to Raasay and Scalpay, with the Cuillin Hills of Skye on the distant horizon. Having crossed desolate moorland, negotiated precipitous roads and revelled in vast panoramic views, one could be at the edge of the world. This lovely beach with its magnificent setting provides an ideal spot to rest and unwind.

Water quality No sewage is discharged in the vicinity of this beach.

Bathing safety Safe bathing.

Access The Pass from Loch Kishorn should not be attempted by the caravanner or the faint-hearted; the alternative route which approaches the village along the coast from Loch Torridon is an easier drive. The village stands on the shore with easy access to the sands.

Parking Limited at Applecross.

Toilets None.

Food Shop in village.

Seaside activities Swimming and fishing. Picnic site behind the beach.

Wildlife and walks There are good walks along this beautiful stretch of coast with eider duck, mergansers and other sea birds to be seen in the bays.

28 The Coral Beaches, Dunvegan, Skye   OS Ref: NG2354

A pleasant, easy, half-mile (1km) walk across grassland takes you to two small beaches which are beautiful and totally unspoilt. Known locally as the Coral Beaches, they are in fact white sand made up of broken shells. Grass banks slope gently down to the sand. The bays, each about 220 yards (200m) in length, are separated by a low grassy promontory around which there are rocky outcrops. There are lovely views across Loch Dunvegan whose clean clear waters wash the beach.

Water quality No sewage is discharged in the vicinity of this beach.

Bathing safety Safe bathing.

Access The road north from Dunvegan becomes a narrow lane beyond Claigan. From the lane ending there is a well defined path across the grassland to the sand.

Parking Limited parking along the lane.

Toilets None.

Food None.

Seaside activities Swimming and snorkelling.

Wildlife and walks There is excellent walking to the Coral Beaches and along the beautiful peninsula beyond. Numerous seals can be seen in the waters of the loch. They are often visible close inshore, and a short boat trip from Dunvegan takes you to the rocky islands where they can be seen basking on the shore. They are unconcerned by the little boat which passes within feet of them.

29 Morar, Highland   OS Ref: NM6793

This stretch of coastline between Mallaig and Arisaig has to be one of the most memorable in Scotland. When you try to imagine the silver sands of the west coast you probably create a picture closely resembling this stretch of shore. The green crofting land, dotted with white cottages, slopes down to the white sands of the bays. South of Mallaig, with its busy harbour that links to the Islands, is the wide sheltered Morar Bay. ⅔ mile (1km) of white sands fringe the wide 'Y'-shaped bay which is set below undulating hills. The bay was originally the mouth of a sea loch similar to many others that penetrate this coastline. The long finger of Loch Morar was cut off from the sea by an uplift of the land and glacial deposits. A fast flowing river drains the fresh water lake over a weir, which is all that remains of once impressive falls which were sacrificed to a hydro-electric power scheme. The river meanders across the southern edge of the bay to the narrow sea opening.

Water quality There have been reports that some sewage from Morar village and other villages along this coast end up on the sands.

Bathing safety Bathing is only safe close inshore due to strong undercurrents 110 yards (100m) from the shore.

Access The main road runs parallel with the beach and it is a short walk across the turf banks down to the sand. The railway runs alongside the road and some trains will stop at Morar.

Parking Along the road above the beach.

Toilets None.

Food None.

Seaside activities Swimming and sailing.

Wildlife and walks At the southern end of the bay a turning off the main coast road leads along the shore of Loch Morar. Beyond the tiny hamlet of Bracora the road gives way to a path which can be followed through some spectacular scenery to Tarbet on Loch Nevis. Walking the shoreline around Morar there are stunning views east to the Inner Hebrides.

30 Camusdarrach Beach, Highland   OS Ref: NM6592

This beach was made famous in Bill Forsyth's film, *Local Hero* (although the actual village scenes were shot on the east coast). The mile (1.6km) of gleaming white sands backed by dunes and undulating grassland is popular, but remains beautiful and unspoilt. There is easy access to the beach by paths from the road above the beach. A series of delightful secluded bays can be reached by walking over the hills edging the shore, forming rocky outcrops. The area is popular with tourists and in summer many caravans appear. The approach to the beach is vulnerable to erosion and visitors should use the paths to avoid damaging the dunes. Those staying late at this beach will enjoy the most breathtaking sunsets, as the sun sinks behind the rugged mountains of Skye.

Water quality No outfall in the vicinity of this beach.

Bathing safety Safe bathing but beware of some offshore currents.

Access Camusdarrach is situated just south of Morar Bay. The road runs parallel with the shore between Morar and Arisaig. There are paths giving access at various points across the low turf-banks that descend to the beach.

Parking At various points along the road, cars can park on the turf behind the beach.

Toilets None.

Food None.

Seaside activities Swimming and windsurfing. Golf course.

Wildlife and walks All along the western coast there is much to interest the naturalist; underwater there is a rich and varied marine life which can only be glimpsed from the shore. The bobbing heads of seals are common; the outline of the basking shark a rarer occurrence. On the rocks that edge these beautiful beaches cormorants, shags, gannets and terns may be seen.

31 Sanna Bay, Sanna, Highland   OS Ref: NM4368

On the northern side of Ardnamurchan Point, the most westerly point of mainland Britain, are the lovely white sands of Sanna bay. This is a beautiful and unspoilt beach backed by impressive marram-covered dunes and ringed by craggy hills. There are a series of island skerries off Sanna Point at the northern end of the bay, as well as rocky outcrops along the beach, dividing the bay into three sections. The sands are washed by clean clear seas. The south side of the bay is covered by extensive rocks encrusted with barnacles and many types of seaweed. To the south is a second sandy cove which is shadowed by cliffs and the Ardnamurchan Lighthouse; from here, excellent views are obtained seawards to Rhum and Eigg.

Water quality No sewage is discharged in the vicinity of the beach.

Bathing safety Offshore currents necessitate bathing with caution.

Access The B8007 from Kilchoan leads to the southern end of the bay, Portuairk, and from here it is a short walk across the dunes to the beach.

Parking Limited parking behind the dunes.

Toilets None.

Food None.

Seaside activities Swimming, sailing and fishing.

Wildlife and walks There is a string of small sandy bays along the north coast of Ardnamurchan, only accessible on foot. These deserted beaches offer much to interest the naturalist. Ardnamurchan Point is itself notorious in sailing circles for unpredictable weather, so don't be surprised if you see boats motoring past as quickly as possible!

32 Calgary Bay, Mull OS Ref: NM3652

Calgary Bay has been described as Mull's most beautiful bay. It might best be considered as a small sea loch with a sandy beach at its head. The gently sloping white sands are backed by small dunes and flat machair grassland. Rocky shores extend at right angles from both sides of the beach. There are areas of both flat rock and boulders amongst which are numerous rock pools rich in animal and plant life. Steep cliffs and grassy slopes rising behind the rocky shore enclose the bay. This lovely beach is understandably popular with visitors in the summer. Emigrants from this area may well have founded the Canadian city which bears the same name.

Water quality No sewage is discharged in the vicinity of this beach.

Bathing safety Safe bathing.

Access The B8073 from Tobermory leads south to Calgary. The road skirts the grassland behind the beach and continues along the southern shore.

Parking There is a car park at the northern end of the beach and a small parking area at the southern end.

Toilets At the southern end of the beach, on the road behind the dunes.

Food None.

Seaside activities Swimming and fishing.

Wildlife and walks From the car park at the northern end of the beach, a track leads to an old pier. This track continues for a short distance as a footpath above the rocky shore where a series of lava dykes can be seen as grey bands where the molten lava has pushed up between the surrounding rocks.

33 Erraid, Fionnphort, Mull OS Ref: NM3120

Mull has 300 miles (500km) of breathtaking coastline including sheer cliffs, stacks and arches. There are also tiny bays nestling below the cliffs with a backdrop of brooding mountains. The Ross of Mull, a long low peninsula to the south of the island, has some of the best coastal features. There are cliffs of basalt columns, the Carsaig Arches at Malcolm's Point, numerous caves and secluded sandy bays which can only be approached on foot. The extensive sands at the western tip of the Ross are much more accessible. A road from Fionnphort, the departure point for the ferries to Iona, proceeds south along the Sound of Iona to extensive sandy beaches sheltered by Erraid Island. Between the island and the mainland, the Sound of Erraid is a sandy beach at low tide backed by sand dunes and machair grassland. At either end of the Sound are rocky outcrops, and a host of islets and skerries lie just offshore. The grassland behind the beach is used for camping and as a result the beach can be quite crowded in summer. Those wanting to get away from the busier beaches should seek out the bays along the southern coast. There is easy access to Ardchiavaig, with limited parking.

Water quality No sewage is discharged in the vicinity of this beach.

Bathing safety Bathing can be dangerous due to the numerous skerries and associated currents.

Access A side road from the A849 at Fionnphort leads south to Fidden skirting the dunes south to Knockvologan.

Parking Parking space is available behind the dunes.

Toilets None.

Food None.

Seaside activities Swimming.

Wildlife and walks The lovely island of Iona is well worth a visit; boat trips leave from Fionnphort. There are sites of great historical interest including the St Oran Chapel and the Iona Cathedral. The island also has much to offer scenically with its beautiful shoreline, clear blue seas, and white sands set amongst fringing green grassland.

34 Machrihanish, Campbeltown, Strathclyde   OS Ref: NR6521

A ribbon of pale sand edges the underdeveloped west coast of the Mull of Kintyre, from West Loch Tarbert to Machrihanish. All along this western shore there are sea views north to the mountains of Jura and the low lying Islay. Ireland, only 20 miles (32km) away, is clearly visible on a good day. 4 miles (6km) of sandy beach studded with rocky outcrops sweep north from the headland at Machrihanish. Pounding surf washes the gently sloping sands which are backed by mountainous dunes. There is a championship golf course at the southern end of the beach and an airfield on the flat grassland stretches inland from the dunes. This delightful beach is popular in summer.

Water quality One outfall serving 200 people discharges untreated sewage at low water mark.

Bathing safety Dangerous undertows just offshore can cause problems for bathers.

Access There is access from either end of the beach with a short walk to the sands. The B843 from Campbeltown leads to Machrihanish at the southern end of the beach. The A83 hugs the western shore from Tarbert to Machrihanish Bay where it swings inland crossing the Mull towards Campbeltown.

Parking There is off-the-road parking at Machrihanish and at Westport off the A83 at the north end of the beach.

Toilets None.

Food None.

Seaside activities Swimming, surfing and fishing.

Wildlife and walks The plain that spans the peninsula from Campbeltown on the east coast to Machrihanish is in contrast to the tree-clad slopes to the north and the windswept Mull to the south. The Mull coast has cliffs dotted with caves, and most of its length can only be reached on foot – it is well worth the effort. There are often seals, basking sharks or porpoises to be seen offshore.

35 Brodick Bay, Brodick, Isle of Arran   OS Ref: NS0237

Below the bare granite summit of the magestic Goat Fell, wooded slopes descend to the water's edge of Brodick Bay north shore. The busy pier on the rocky southern shore at Brodick is the main landing point for the island. The rocky shore gives way to a mile-long (1.6km) arc of sand and pebble beach extending around the head of the bay. The beach is bisected by a river which meanders across flat grassland behind the beach before crossing the sands. The beach has a most beautiful setting, overlooked by the impressive Brodick Castle. The bay enjoys a particularly mild climate which is reflected in the Castle Gardens where thriving semi-tropical plants can be found.

Water quality 2 outfalls serving 700 people discharge untreated sewage, one below and one above low water mark. There have been reports of sewage solids and litter washing onto the beach.

Bathing safety Safe bathing.

Access The car park at Brodick is adjacent to the beach. A few steps from the car park take you to the sands.

Parking Parking for 100 cars at Brodick and Claddach.

Toilets At Brodick and Brodick Country park.

Food Several small cafés.

Seaside activities Swimming, windsurfing, canoeing and fishing. Canoes, rowing boats, windsurfboards and fishing tackle are all available for hire. Golf course.

Wet weather alternatives Brodick Castle, Heritage Museum and Transport Museum.

Wildlife and walks On the northern side of the bay is the Brodick Country Park. Its 173 acres include the formal gardens and woodland of Brodick Castle which have a notable rhododendron collection. There is a self-guided nature trail and access to a path climbing Goat Fell. There is a permanent Ranger Naturalist Service and a series of guided walks are organised during the summer months, including a seashore life walk. A walled Victorian garden has been restored and in addition there is an ice house, Bavarian summer house and a children's adventure play area.

36 Blackwaterfoot, Arran   OS Ref: NR8928

The northern half of Arran is scenically outstanding, with lush glens cutting deep in to the massive granite mountains. This area has been classed as a National Scenic Area. Beaches attractive to the tourist predominate around the south of the island and include Lamlash Bay sheltered by Holy Island, Whiting Bay and Blackwaterfoot. The latter, on the western shore of the island, has 1 miles (1.6km) of sand and shingle with rocky outcrops containing rock pools that are worth exploring. Sand dunes and a links golf course stretch south around the bay.

Water quality No sewage is discharged in the vicinity of this beach.

Bathing safety Safe bathing.

Access There is a short walk from car park to the beach.

Parking There is a car park next to the golf club and Kinloch Hotel has 200 spaces.

Toilets At Blackwater harbour.

Food Kinloch Hotel.

Seaside activities Swimming.

Wet weather alternatives Kinloch Hotel has a swimming pool, squash court, sauna and solarium.

Wildlife and walks The lane past the golf course leads towards Druma-doon Head where there is a most impressive sill, produced when molten rock is forced upwards through other rocks. The path continues north along the line of a raised beach to the King's Cave. The path can be followed along the wooded slopes to Tormore and Machrie Bay. There is much evidence of man's past activities in the area with standing stones and hut circles on the hillside.

37 Mersehead Sands, Southerness, Dumfries   OS Ref: NX9855

An endless sky seems to dominate these wide flat sands that face the Solway Firth. From Southerness Point 6 miles (10km) of flat sands backed by low dunes stretch west to the cliffs of Port O'Warren and Sandyhills. On the low rocky headland of Southerness stands a lighthouse which once directed boats into Dumfries. East of the headland the sands narrow to the Arbigland estate. Behind the dunes is the holiday village of Southerness.

Water quality Sandyhills was monitored by the River Purification Board and found to meet the EC standard for clean bathing water in 1989. One outfall serving 200 people discharges secondary treated sewage to the tidal water course.

Bathing safety Due to the very flat nature of the beach the tide flows in very quickly and swimming is therefore only safe close inshore.

Access This very large beach can be accessed from both ends, from Sandyhills on the A710 or at Southerness signposted to the east from the A710.

Parking Car park with 50 places at Southerness.

Toilets Near beach.

Food Café (seasonal opening).

Seaside activities Swimming and fishing.

Wet weather alternatives Paul Jones Cottage. (Paul Jones was a local boy who became a famous admiral in the American Navy. The cottage is where he was born and brought up.)

Wildlife and walks The wide sand flats are a rich feeding ground for numerous waders and sea ducks.

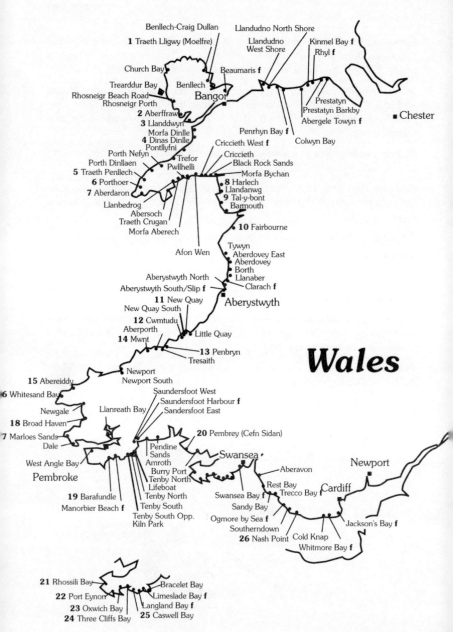

Benllech-Craig Dullan
Llandudno North Shore
1 Traeth Lligwy (Moelfre)
Llandudno West Shore
Kinmel Bay **f**
Rhyl **f**
Church Bay
Beaumaris **f**
Trearddur Bay
Benllech
Rhosneigr Beach Road
Bangor
Rhosneigr Porth
Prestatyn
Prestatyn Barkby
Abergele Towyn **f**
2 Aberffraw
3 Llanddwyn
Penrhyn Bay **f**
Colwyn Bay
Morfa Dinlle
4 Dinas Dinlle
Pontllyfni
Criccieth West **f**
Porth Nefyn
Trefor
Criccieth
Porth Dinllaen
Pwllheli
Black Rock Sands
5 Traeth Penllech
Morfa Bychan
6 Porthoer
8 Harlech
7 Aberdaron
Llandanwg
9 Tal-y-bont
Llanbedrog
Barmouth
Abersoch
Traeth Crugan
10 Fairbourne
Morfa Aberech
Tywyn
Afon Wen
Aberdovey East
Aberdovey
Borth
Aberystwyth North
Llanaber
Aberystwyth South/Slip **f**
Clarach **f**
11 New Quay
Aberystwyth
New Quay South
12 Cwmtudu
Aberporth
Little Quay
14 Mwnt

Wales

13 Penbryn
Tresaith
Newport
15 Abereiddy
Newport South
16 Whitsand Bay
Saundersfoot West
Newgale
Saundersfoot Harbour **f**
Llanreath Bay
Sandersfoot East
18 Broad Haven
17 Marloes Sands
20 Pembrey (Cefn Sidan)
Dale
Pendine
West Angle Bay
Sands
Swansea
Newport
Amroth
Pembroke
Burry Port
Aberavon
Tenby North
Rest Bay
Cardiff
Lifeboat
Trecco Bay **f**
19 Barafundle
Tenby North
Swansea Bay **f**
Manorbier Beach **f**
Tenby South
Sandy Bay
Tenby South Opp.
Ogmore by Sea **f**
Jackson's Bay **f**
Kiln Park
Southerndown
Cold Knap
26 Nash Point
Whitmore Bay **f**

21 Rhossili Bay
Bracelet Bay
22 Port Eynon
Limeslade Bay **f**
23 Oxwich Bay
Langland Bay **f**
24 Three Cliffs Bay
25 Caswell Bay

Chester

f = failed to meet EC standard for clean bathing water in 1989.
Numbered beaches appear in the following chapter.

Coastal walk
Pembrokeshire Coast Path
Cardigan to Tenby 180 miles (290km) mostly in the
Pembrokeshire National Park.

Wales

Sand dunes of Anglesey, pounding surf on the Lleyn, miles of sand, cliffs and secluded coves of West Wales and the beautiful Gower – this is the coast of Wales. There are numerous lovely beaches which are comparable with the best anywhere in the country and they have the added advantage of not being too crowded. Unfortunately there are individual beaches throughout the region that have failed to meet the minimum EC standard for clean bathing water due to the inadequate disposal of sewage from their shores. The north and south coasts suffer from the close proximity of large industrial centres. The large conurbations of South Wales – Swansea, Cardiff, Port Talbot and Newport – all contribute to the pollution of the south coast with discharges of domestic and industrial waste. The north coast is affected by pollution from Merseyside and the Wirral. Milford Haven has suffered from oil pollution problems from the terminals and refineries that line its shore. Further west, away from the centres of population, beaches remain on the whole clean and unspoilt; definitely worth exploring.

Beaches awarded a European Blue Flag (for Ports) in 1989:

Milford Haven and Swansea Marina.

Beaches receiving Clean Beach Awards from the Tidy Britain Group in 1989:

Plas Beach Aberporth, Borth, Aberystwyth North and South, Tenby North and South and Castle, Barry Island, Langland Bay, Caswell Bay, Cefn Sidan and North Shore Llandudno.

The Golden List See page 26 for further details

Beach No on Map	Rating. The more stars the better. **f**=failed	Resort	Sewage outlets	Population	Discharging from outlet	Type of treatment	Discharge point relative to low water mark, unless otherwise stated. Distance given in metres	Remarks
CLWYD								
	★★★	**Prestatyn**	1	16,246		Screens/ maceration	1000 below	Sandy. Safety patrols.
	f ★★ ★★	**Rhyl**	1	22,600		Maceration/ tidal tank	400 below	Sandy. Safety patrols. Bathing safe inshore except near river mouth. £8 million LSO scheme.
	f ★★	**Kinmel Bay**						Sandy. Bath safe except near river mouth.
	f ★★	Abergele (Towyn)	1	4,237		Screens/ maceration/ tidal tank	100 above	Sand/shingle. Safe bathing.
		Abergele (Pensarn)	1	7,487		Screens/ maceration/ tidal tank	100 above	Sand at low tide. Safe bathing.
	★★★	**Colwyn Bay**	1	3,000		Screens/ maceration/ tidal tank	75 below	Sand/shingle. Storm overflow on beach LSO improvement scheme.
GWYNEDD								
		Penrhyn Bay	1	25,800		Screens/ maceration/ tidal tank	1000 below	Some complaints. Improvements planned.
				3,500		Screens/ maceration/ tidal tank	100 above	Sand/shingle.
	★★	**Llandudno (North)**						Sandy. Good bathing.
	★★	**Llandudno (West Shore)**	1	34,000		Screens/ maceration/ tidal tank	LWM	Sand/shingle. Bathing safe at high tide only. Some complaints due to unsatisfactory discharges in Conwy Estuary. £7.8 million improvement scheme.
	f ★★/★	Penmaenmawr (Conwy Bay)	1 2	8,000 160		Raw Raw	200 above 200 above	Sand/shingle. Improvements planned.

ANGLESEY

Beach No on Map	Rating. The more stars the better. f=failed	Resort	Sewage outlets	Population Discharging from oulet	Type of treatment	Discharge point relative to low water mark, unless otherwise stated. Distance given in metres	Remarks
	f **/ f **	Beaumaris					Shingle/sand. Bathing safe on incoming tide, dangerous on the ebb.
	f **	Red Wharf Bay					Bathing safe except at ebb tide.
	***	**Benllech**	1	2,284	Raw	200 below	Sandy.
1	***	Moelfre	1	894	Raw	100 below	Shingle. Safe bathing.
		Amlwch (Bull Bay)	1	11,000	Raw	50 below	Outfall half mile east of bay. Storm overflow below LWM.
		Caemes Bay	1	1,000	Maceration/ tidal tank	70 below	Sandy.
		Holyhead	5	11,000	Raw	All above LWM	Docks area.
	***	**Trearddur Bay**					Sand and rocks. Good swimming.
	***	Rhosneigr	1	1,532	Raw	150 below	Outfall discharges from rocks.
2	***	Aberffraw Bay	1	534	Screens/ maceration	At HWM	Sandy.

GWYNEDD cont

Beach No on Map	Rating. The more stars the better. f=failed	Resort	Sewage outlets	Population Discharging from oulet	Type of treatment	Discharge point relative to low water mark, unless otherwise stated. Distance given in metres	Remarks
	***	**Morfa Dinlle**					Sandy.
		Trefor	1	582	Secondary	At LWM	Sand/shingle.
		Nefyn	1	2,800	Raw	At HWM	Sand. Surfing.
	***	Morfa Nefyn	1	2,100	Raw	At LWM	Sand/rocks.
	***	Porth Dinllaen					Sand/rocks.
		Rhos-y-Llan	1	420	Primary	Off rocks	Sandy.
7	***	Aberdaron					Sandy. Surfing.
	***	**Abersoch**	1	1,356	Secondary	100 below	Sandy.
	***	Llanbedrog	1	672	Maceration/ tidal tank	50 below	Sandy.
	***	**Pwllheli**	1	4,107	Maceration/ tidal tank	At harbour mouth	Sandy. LSO planned.
		Morfa Aberech					Sandy.

Beach No on Map	Rating. The more stars the better. f=failed	Resort	Sewage outlets	Population Discharging from outlet	Type of treatment	Discharge point relative to low water mark, unless otherwise stated. Distance given in metres	Remarks
		Afon Wen	1	46	Maceration/ tidal tank	At LWM	Sand/shingle.
	f ★★ ★★★	**Criccieth**	1	800	Tidal tank	50 below	Sand/shingle. New LSO proposed.
	★★★	**Morfa Bychan**	1	800	Tidal tank	50 below	Sandy beach. Contaminated by local streams. Safe bathing except SE end.
8	★★★	**Harlech**	1	1,291	Primary	At LWM	Sandy beach. Bathing unsafe.
	★★★	**Llandanwg**	1	258	Primary	At LWM	Sand/rock. Bathing safe at high tide.
	★★★	**Barmouth**	2	800 1,400	Raw Macerated	At LWM At HWM	Sandy. Estuary unsafe for swimming. New outfall near to completion.
10	★★★	**Fairbourne**	1	474	Primary/ tidal tank	400 below	Sandy.
	f ★★	Llwyngwril	1	370	Raw	At LWM	Sand/shingle.
	★★★	**Tywyn**	1	2,811	Macerated/ tidal tank	At LWM	Sandy. Surfing. Scheme under investigation.
	★★★	Aberdovey	1	6,000	Primary/ tidal tank	At LWM	Bathing safe from beach north of village. Sewage outfall in estuary.

DYFED

	★★★	**Borth**					Bathing dangerous near mouth of the estuary. Good elsewhere.
	f ★★	Clarach Bay					Bathing safe close inshore.
	f ★★ f ★★/ ★★★ ★★★	Aberystwyth Harbour **Aberystwyth South Aberystwyth North**	1	9,100	Screened		Bathing safe centre of prom and south of harbour in calm seas. New LSO planned.
		Llanrhystud	1	500	Primary		Shingle. Sand at low tide.
		Llansantffraid	1	1,160	Primary	At LWM	Sand and shingle.

Beach No on Map	Rating. The more stars the better. **f**=failed	Resort	Sewage outlets	Population Discharging from outlet	Type of treatment	Discharge point relative to low water mark, unless otherwise stated. Distance given in metres	Remarks
		Aberarth	1	470	Primary	At LWM	Shingle beach.
		Aberaeron	1	5,000	Raw	At LWM	Sand and shingle. Under investigation.
	★★★	Little Quay Bay					Sand. Safe bathing.
11	★★★ ★★★	**New Quay**	1	6,000	Macerated	1300 below	Long sea outfall off Llanina Point.
	f ★★	Llangranog	1	400	Primary	75 below	Sand/shingle.
13	★★★★/ ★★★	**Penbryn**					Sandy.
	★★	Tresaith	1	180	Macerated	75 below	Sand and shingle. Safe bathing. Lifeguards.
		Aberporth	1	1,842	Macerated	75 below	Sandy. Bathing safe except when strong north winds blow.
	★★★	**Poppit Sands**			Secondary		Sand and shingle. Estuary polluted by outfalls at Cardigan. Bathing safe only at slack water.
	★★★	**Newport**	1	1,400	Macerated	At LWM	Bathing safe in centre of beach except on ebb tide or when rough. Sand/shingle.
		Pwllgwaelod	1	880	Secondary	At LWM	Grey sand.
		Fishguard	1	2,480	Screens/ maceration	At LWM	
	★★★	Goodwick	1	2,710	Raw	At LWM	Ferry terminal.
16	★★★	**Whitesands Bay**					Surf bathing. Strong currents.
	★★★	**Newgale**					Shingle and sand. Surfing.
18	★★★	**Broadhaven**	1	2,200	Secondary	At HWM	Sandy. Surfing.
		Dale	1	600	Maceration/ tidal tank	Above LWM	Shingle and sand.
		Sandy Haven	1	1,360	Secondary	At LWM	Red sand.
		Angle Bay	1	500	Secondary	At LWM	Shingle and muddy sand.
	★★★	Freshwater East	1	600	Raw	At LWM	Sandy.

Beach No on Map	Rating. The more stars the better. f=failed	Resort	Sewage outlets	Population Discharging from outlet	Type of treatment	Discharge point relative to low water mark, unless otherwise stated. Distance given in metres	Remarks
	f ★★ ★★★	Manorbier Beach Manorbier West	1	520	Secondary	At LWM	Sand and shingle.
	★★★	**Tenby**	1	25,000	Screened/ macerated	2.7km below	Sandy.
	  ★★★ ★★★ ★★ f ★	**Saundersfoot:** West East **Beach** Harbour	1	11,000	Primary	50 below	Sand and shingle.
	★★★	**Amroth**					Sand and shingle.
	★★★	**Pendine Sands**					Sand and dunes. Part of beach often closed for MOD firing range.
20	★★★	**Pembrey Sands**	1	3,832	Other	Above HWM	Sand and dunes. Bathing safe except on spring high water.
		Burry Port	1	6,020	Secondary	Below LWM	Industrial and muddy. Bathing unsafe.

WEST GLAMORGAN

Beach No on Map	Rating	Resort	Sewage outlets	Population Discharging from outlet	Type of treatment	Discharge point	Remarks
	★★★	Broughton Bay					Sandy, bathing unsafe.
21	★★★	**Rhossili Bay**					Sandy.
		Mewslade Bay	1	270	Primary	Below LWM	Sandy.
22	★★★	**Port Eynon Bay**	1	1,208	Secondary	At LWM	Sand and dunes.
23	★★★	**Oxwich Bay**					Sand and dunes.
		Southgate	1	1,400	Other	Below LWM	Rocky.
		Brandy Cove	1	2,000	Secondary	Below LWM	Rocky.
25	★★★	**Caswell Bay**					Sandy. Surfing safe except on ebb tide.
	f ★★	**Langland Bay**					Sandy.
	f ★★	**Limeslade Bay**					Sandy.
	★★	**Bracelet Bay**					Sandy.

Beach No on Map	Rating. The more stars the better. **f**=failed	Resort	Sewage outlets	Population Discharging from outlet	Type of treatment	Discharge point relative to low water mark, unless otherwise stated. Distance given in metres	Remarks
	f ★★ **f** ★	**Swansea Bay:** The Mumbles	1	170,000	Screened/ tidal tank	Below LWM	Subject of many complaints. New projects totalling over £2 million for whole bay area.
	★★★	Aberavon	1	60,000	Macerated	2.4km below	Improvements planned as above.
		Port Talbot	1	60,000	Macerated	3.1km below	Improvements as above.

MID GLAMORGAN

Beach No on Map	Rating	Resort	Sewage outlets	Population Discharging	Type of treatment	Discharge point	Remarks
	★★★	**Rest Bay**					Sand and rocks. STW planned.
		Porthcawl	1	19,000	Raw	Below LWM	Sand and rocks.
	★★★	**Sandy Bay**					Sand and rocks.
	f ★★	**Trecco Bay**	1	31,000	Raw	Below LWM	Sand and rocks. STW planned (as for Rest Bay).
	f ★★	Ogmore by Sea	1	78,240	Secondary/ other	At LWM	Sand and rocks. Lifeguards.
	★★	**Southerndown**					Sand and rocks. Strong currents off Trwyn y Witch headland. Lifeguards. Surfing except at high tide.

SOUTH GLAMORGAN

Beach No on Map	Rating	Resort	Sewage outlets	Population Discharging	Type of treatment	Discharge point	Remarks
		Tresilian Bay	1	8,000	Macerated	At LWM	Rocky. Bathing unsafe.
		Limpert Bay	1	4,500	Macerated	At LWM	Rocky. Overlooked by power station.
		Font-y-Gary Bay	2	3,045 936	Raw Raw	At LWM At LWM	Rocky. Lifeguards.
	★★★	**Cold Knap Beach**					New scheme proposed for completion in 1995, with Whitmore and Jacksons Bay.
	f ★★	**Whitmore Bay**	2	21,000 23,000	Maceration Raw	At LWM At LWM	Sand, shingle and mud.
	f ★★	**Jacksons Bay**					
	f ★	St Mary's Well					Shingle and rocks.
	f ★	Penarth	4				Shingle and rocks. Bathing dangerous.

175

1 Traeth Lligwy, Moelfre, Anglesey   OS Ref: SH4987

A hard flat sandy beach ⅔ mile (1km) wide is revealed at low tide, ideal for sand castles and ball games. There are some areas of mud on the sand surface but signs indicate the areas to avoid. Gently sloping, grass-covered cliffs ring the bay to the south of the dunes that back the centre of the beach. A cliff path along the low rugged cliffs that rise to the north of the beach leads to the adjacent Dulas Bay. This more secluded bay has a fine sandy beach which can only be reached on foot.

Water quality Beach monitored by the NRA and found to meet the EC standard for clean bathing water in 1989. One outfall serving 894 people discharges raw sewage 110 yards (100m) below low water mark at Moelfre south of the bay. The stream which crosses the beach may well be polluted; presence of solids and an unpleasant smell at times.

Bathing safety Safe bathing but beware of offshore winds.

Access Three lanes off the A5025, one at the Moelfre roundabout and two slightly further north, lead to the bay. The car park is adjacent to the sand.

Parking Two privately run car parks with 500 spaces, rough surfaced.

Toilets One block at car park.

Food Refreshment caravan.

Seaside activities Swimming.

Wildlife and walks Cliff-top paths can be followed in both directions from the beach. Walking south, the path over the headland provides excellent views of the rocky coastline. It leads to the picturesque little fishing village of Moelfre. Above the beach, in the rolling green field which slopes down to the shore, there are the remains of a 4th-century fortified village, Din Lligwy, and also a megalithic burial chamber.

2 Aberffraw, Anglesey   OS Ref: SH3568

A wide flat sandy beach, bounded landwards by a series of sand dune ridges behind which flat grassland extends inland. This makes the dunes a prominent feature in a landscape that seems to be dominated by the sky. Aberffraw village is set back from the beach on the higher ground that rises to the west. The beach extends about ⅔ mile (1km) from low cliffs at the western end, below which the river flows. The beach is cleaned during the summer.

Water quality Beach monitored by the NRA and found to meet the EC standard for clean bathing water in 1989. One outfall serving 534 people discharges screened and macerated sewage at high water mark west of the beach.

Bathing safety Safe bathing, although the estuary area should be avoided on the ebb tide.

Access A lane off the A4080 just south of Aberffraw leads to car parking behind the dunes. Easy walk through the dunes to the beach.

Parking Parking for several hundred cars ½–1 mile (800–1,600m) from beach, on grassed common land.

Toilets In village and at Llywelyn.

Food In village and at Llywelyn.

Seaside activities Swimming.

Wildlife and walks The marram grass covered dunes are well developed; depressions between the ridges (wet slacks) abound with wild flowers and low scrub, for example creeping willow. There is a 2 mile (3km) walk along the cliffs from Aberffraw leading to the church of Llangwyfan. This area was the site of Llewelyn the Great, Prince of Gwynedd's summer palace, although no trace remains.

3 Llanddwyn, Newborough, Anglesey   OS Ref: SH4163

From the rocky Llanddwyn Island, a lovely sand beach curves 3 miles (5km) east to Abermenai Point, the end of a sand spit at the mouth of the Menai Strait. The beach is backed by the extensive sand dunes of Newborough Warren. At the western end there is a conifer wood planted by the Forestry Commission. This remote gently shelving beach is usually quiet and has superb views of Snowdonia and the Lleyn Peninsula.

Water quality No sewage is discharged in the vicinity of this beach.

Bathing safety Safe bathing except at the eastern end; currents at the entrance to the Menai Strait can cause problems.

Access Road from Newborough village leads to a Forestry Commission car park within their plantation, and a path leads to the beach.

Parking Car park with space for several hundred cars in cleared forest areas behind beach.

Toilets At car park.

Food None.

Seaside activities Swimming and sailing.

Wildlife and walks There is a forest trail starting from the car park. The dunes of Newborough Warren behind the beach and Llanddwyn Island are both nature reserves. There is restricted access to the dunes to prevent damage. The island can be reached by a causeway, and you get good views back along the beach and to the mountains in the distance. There is a ruined church and navigation beacon on the island. There are extensive cockle beds on the Strait side of Abermenai Point. Across the sand flats, a footpath leads through the Warren to Newborough Village.

4 Dinas Dinlle, Gwynedd   OS Ref: SH4456

3 miles (5km) of wide open beach stretches from Dinas Dinlle (a 100 foot (30m) hill which dominates the surrounding flat coastal plain) north to the mouth of the Menai Straits. The hill shadows the small village of the same name, with its string of bungalows, cafés and shops facing the beach. A moderately steep bank of large pebbles gives way to sand at low tide. The adjacent grassland, on which stands the Caernarfon airport, is protected by a low sea wall. Good surfing conditions frequently prevail. There is easy access to this unspoilt beach which is cleaned regularly throughout the summer.

Water quality No sewage discharged in the vicinity of this beach.

Bathing safety Safe bathing except at the northern end.

Access Dinas Dinlle is signposted from the A499 south of Caenarfon. The road runs along adjacent to the beach, with easy level access from or through gaps in the low sea wall.

Parking Parking along the whole length of the road, with about a mile (1.6km) of pebbled parking areas.

Toilets Blocks at either end of the beach and one at the centre.

Food Several shops and cafés at the southern end of the beach.

Seaside activities Swimming, surfing, and fishing.

Wet weather alternatives Airport viewing pavilion.

Wildlife and walks Good for a bracing winter walk.

5 Traeth Penllech, Tudweiliog, Gwynedd   OS Ref: SH2034

A super beach, a wide sandy arc stretching over ⅔ mile (1km) below the rocky, grass-topped cliffs that fall steeply to the shore. A long strip of soft sand remains at high water, and wide flat sands studded with rocks towards the southern end are exposed at low tide. Traeth Penllech forms part of a larger indented bay on the northern coast of the Lleyn Peninsula. There are good views from the cliff-top to the headlands in either direction. By following the cliff-top path, small sand and shingle coves can be reached. The relentless waves that wash this coast make for excellent surfing conditions.

Water quality No sewage is discharged in the vicinity of this beach.

Bathing safety Safe bathing.

Access From the B4417 take the road through Penllech, turning left at the T-junction. There is parking off this road, above the beach. A steep path down a narrow valley leads to the shore ⅔ mile (1km) away.

Parking During the summer there is parking in a private field off the road north-east of Pen-y-graig.

Toilets None.

Food None.

Seaside activities Swimming, surfing, windsurfing, diving and fishing.

Wildlife and walks The area is popular with divers because of its rich marine life; the rock pools below the cliffs give a hint of what can be seen below the waves. A path along the cliff top, above which choughs may be seen, leads to other delightful little sandy coves.

6 Porthoer, Gwynedd   OS Ref: SH1630

This is the last and most accessible in a series of long secluded bays along the north coast of the Lleyn Peninsula. This small cove is ringed by steep grass-covered cliffs, typical of this whole coastline. It is also called 'Whistling Sands' because the white sands seem to whistle or squeak as they are walked on. To really get away from it all, try Porth Iago and Porth Colman further north.

Water quality No sewage is discharged in the vicinity of this beach.

Bathing safety Safe bathing.

Access From the B4413 south of Pey-y-groeslon lanes lead down to car park just before Carreg. Steep path down from cliff-top.

Parking Car park on cliff-top 220 yards (200m) from beach.

Toilets At car park.

Food Café on beach.

Seaside activities Swimming and fishing.

Wildlife and walks Low tide reveals rockpools at the western end containing a wide variety of marine life.

7 Aberdaron, Gwynedd   OS Ref: SH1726

A sheltered sandy bay, except when a south or south-west wind blows and the waves come crashing in. The mile long (1.6km) sandy beach, below the cluster of houses that make up the fishing village of Aberdaron, completely disappears at high tide. Take care not to get caught below the rocky cliffs that fringe the bay and extend south to the toe of the Lleyn.

Water quality Beach monitored by the NRA and found to meet the EC standard for clean bathing water in 1989. No sewage is discharged in the vicinity of the beach.

Bathing safety Safe bathing.

Access Ramp to beach.

Parking Adjacent to ramp.

Toilets Adjacent to ramp.

Food Cafés and two pubs in village.

Seaside activities Swimming, windsurfing, diving, fishing and sailing.

Wildlife and walks Cliff-top walks lead south to the 500 ft (150m) hill Mynydd Mawr that rises above the end of the peninsula. There are spectacular views of the rocky coast and of Bardsey Island, 2 miles (3km) offshore. Westwards, the cliff paths lead to the cove of Porth Ysgo, which is inaccessible by road. Boat trips to Bardsey Island leave from Aberdaron.

8 Harlech, Gwynedd   OS Ref: SH5831

From Harlech, with its castle perched on a rocky cliff 60 yards (55m) above the coastal plain, there are superb views over the dunes and golf links below and across Tremadoc Bay to the Lleyn Peninsula. 4 miles (6km) of soft sands, edged by a wide belt of dunes, extend from Harlech Point south to Llandanwg. There is masses of room on the extensive flat rather windswept sands. The fragile dunes have suffered from erosion, and restoration work is being undertaken to help them recover; please assist this work by avoiding any further damage. There is also access to the beach at Llandanwg, where board walks lead across the dunes to the beach. The church of old Llandanwg village can be seen half buried by sand.

Water quality Harlech and Llandanwg are monitored by the NRA and were found to meet the EC standard for clean bathing water in 1989. One outfall at Harlech serving 1,291 people discharges primary treated sewage at low water mark. One outfall at Llandanwg serving 258 people discharges macerated and primary treated sewage at low water mark. A new sewage treatment works is planned for operation in 1995.

Litter Some marine debris is washed onto the shore.

Bathing safety The estuary and the area around Harlech point are unsafe for bathing due to strong currents. Further south, the beach is safe for bathing. HM Coast Guard search unit post at the car park. Emergency phone on path to beach and lifebuoys.

Access The beach is signposted from the A496 at Harlech. The road leads to car parking behind the dunes. A path leads through dunes.

Parking Car park with 300 spaces behind the dunes.

Toilets At the car park.

Food None.

Seaside activities Swimming, surfing, windsurfing, diving, sailing, canoeing, and fishing. St David's Golf Course.

Wet weather alternatives Harlech Castle, Sports Hall with indoor swimming pool, galleries and craft shop in Harlech.

Wildlife and walks The northern end of this beach and the shore of the estuary fall within the Morfa Harlech nature reserve; access is by permit only. The Snowdonia National Park Information Centre is situated in the town.

9 Tal-y-Bont, Gwynedd   OS Ref: SH5921

A first-class beach; miles and miles of golden sand backed by dunes – 15 miles (24km) in all, unspoilt and set against the magnificent scenery of North Wales. The beach stretches from Shell Island Peninsula in the north, so called because of the variety of shells to be found there, towards Barmouth in the south. A road just north of Tal-y-bont leads to car parking behind the dunes. There are a lot of caravan parks along this section of coastline. At Tal-y-bont they remain hidden behind the dunes but it does mean that the sands can be popular in summer. However, the wide flat sands revealed at low tide provide plenty of space. Beach cleaned by local authority.

Water quality No sewage is discharged in the vicinity of this beach.

Bathing safety Safe bathing. Emergency phone at the car park.

Access Beach signposted off the A496 north of Tal-y-bont, road leads to a car park behind the dunes. Good paths through the dunes to the beach.

Parking National Park car park behind the dunes has 120 spaces.

Toilets At the car park.

Food None, cafés in village.

Seaside activities Swimming, surfing, windsurfing, canoeing and fishing.

Wildlife and walks The dunes at the north end of the beach form the Morfa Dyffryn Nature Reserve; access is by permit only.

10 Fairbourne, Gwynedd   OS Ref: SH6116

Fairbourne has a magnificent setting at the mouth of the beautiful Mawddach estuary with the back drop of the Welsh mountains. 2 miles (3km) of sandy beach stretches north from the small resort of Fairbourne to the mouth of the estuary. The promenade gives way to the dunes of Morfa Mawddach, a sand spit. A narrow gauge railway runs from Fairbourne along the beach to the point, where a ferry will take the visitor across the estuary to the old quay of Barmouth on the opposite shore. There are lots of shells to be found on this beach.

Water quality Beach monitored by the NRA and found to meet the EC standard for clean bathing water in 1989. One outfall discharges macerated and primary treated sewage through a tidal tank 440 yards (400m) below low water mark. A £1.7 million scheme will extend this outfall further out to sea.

Bathing safety Safe bathing except near the estuary mouth.

Access Beach signposted from the A493 through the town. Direct access from the promenade. Disabled access.

Parking Extensive car parking near the beach.

Toilets Near main access to beach.

Food Refreshment kiosks and cafés on the seafront. Restaurant at the point.

Seaside activities Swimming, windsurfing, sailing, canoeing and fishing. Amusements. Narrow gauge railway. Windsurfing boards available for hire.

Wet weather alternatives Fairbourne railway and Butterfly Safari.

Wildlife and walks There is excellent walking country within easy reach of Fairbourne; footpaths lead along the estuary. The panorama walk above Barmouth provides superb views of mountains, river and sea.

11 New Quay, Dyfed   OS Ref: SN3959

This traditional fishing town perched on the steep slopes above the harbour has three beaches. Traeth y Dolau to the north of the harbour is backed by contorted shale cliffs. The harbour beach, bounded by the stone pier, and Traethgroyn, stretching around the curve of New Quay Bay, are both gently sloping sandy beaches. At low tide Llanina Point to the north can be rounded to reach Cei Bach beach, a quiet half mile (1km) of sandy beach, backed by a shingle ridge and shrub-covered slopes.

Water quality Beach monitored by the NRA and found to meet the EC standard for clean bathing water in 1989. One outfall serving 6,000 people discharges macerated sewage from a tidal tank at low water mark off New Quay Head.

Bathing safety Safe from all beaches.

Access Short walk along the road which slopes from the town to the beach.

Parking Car parks with 60 spaces in town.

Toilets Close to the beach.

Food Hotels, motels and cafés.

Seaside activities Swimming, surfing, windsurfing, sailing and fishing. Boats and surf boards for hire.

Wet weather alternatives Bird hospital and lifeboat station.

Wildlife and walks Ceredigion Heritage Coast Path provides walks with views of dramatic cliff scenery. Ceredigion District Council produce leaflets describing the many beaches from Borth in the north to Gwbert-on-Sea in the south.

12 Cwmtudu, New Quay, Dyfed OS Ref: SN3558

A small secluded cove among the rugged cliffs south west of New Quay, it lies at the mouth of the wooded Afon Fynnon Ddewi valley. A group of houses nestles in the valley. The shingle beach has small amount of sand at low tide and is edged by cliffs with striking rock formations. Caves among the folds and faults were once used by smugglers.

Water quality No sewage is discharged in the vicinty of this beach.

Bathing safety Safe.

Access Signposted from the A487 south of New Quay. Several miles' drive along lanes to the cliff top car park. Steep path down to the cove.

Parking Car park with 30 spaces.

Toilets None.

Food Café.

Seaside activities Swimming.

Wildlife and walks The Ceredigion Heritage Coast Path, 110 yards (100m) up the road from the beach, leads around the headland to the north and gives views over the bay. Earth banks above the craggy inlet are the remains of an Iron Age fort. From here the path continues along the coast for 3 miles (4.8km) to New Quay Headland and Birds Rock.

13 Penbryn, Dyfed OS Ref: SN2953

A wooded valley cuts through the steep cliffs to reach the beach: ½ mile (1km) of golden sand with small dunes on either side of the River Hoffnant. The headland to the east is blue-grey shale and mudstone smoothed at its base by the waves. Access to the sandy bay beyond the headland is possible at low tide, but beware of the rising tide as there is no escape at high tide. Dogs are banned from the beach from May to September.

Water quality No sewage is discharged in the vicinity of the beach.

Bathing safety Safe bathing.

Access Penbryn is signposted from the A487. Short walk from the car park to the beach.

Parking National Trust car park with 150 spaces.

Toilets In the car park (disabled facilities).

Food Café, half a mile (1km) from the beach.

Seaside activities Swimming.

Wildlife and walks Footpath to the west of the sand dunes leads to St Michael's Church which commands good views of the Hoffnant valley. A track from Llanborth car park leads up between hedges and banks to give coastal views westwards.

14 Mwnt, Cardigan, Dyfed OS Ref: SN1952

A natural suntrap, this beautiful undeveloped sandy beach is quite easily accessible and can be very popular in summer. The 330 yards (300m) of gently sloping sands are fringed by folded and faulted shale and mudstone cliffs. The beach is shadowed by the imposing form of Foel y Mwnt, a conical hill on the headland. The tiny white-washed church of The Holy Cross nestles in a hollow at its foot. The only other obvious sign of man is the remnant of a limekiln adjacent to the path down to the beach; limestone was landed in the bay and fired ready for use by the local farmers. Dogs are banned from the beach from May to September.

Water quality No sewage is discharged in the vicinity of this beach.

Bathing safety Safe bathing inshore; care is required as surface currents, due to waves breaking on the headland, deflect across the bay. Emergency phone on cliff path.

Access Mwnt is signposted from the B4548 north of Cardigan. Lanes lead to the car park above the beach. Steps and a steep path down the cliff to the beach.

Parking National Trust car park with 50 spaces.

Toilets At the head of the steps to the beach (disabled facilities).

Food Refreshments available from Easter to October.

Seaside activities Swimming.

Wildlife and walks National Trust cliff-top walks. A pack detailing walks in the Cardigan area is available from local tourist information centres. Foel y Mwnt hill on the headland provides good views of the bay south to Cardigan Island and the narrow rocky inlet to the north. On the cliff tops above the beach there is a small remnant dune system where marram grass covers the wind-blown sand.

15 Abereiddy Bay, Abereiddy, Preseli, Dyfed OS Ref: SM8031

One of the many small bays that have known a very different and more active past. The slate that gives the small beach its dark grey sand was quarried, and the remains of the workings can still be seen at the northern end of the beach. A small harbour on the north side of the headland where the rock has been cut away forms a deep blue pool: ⅔ mile (1km) along the coast path north, there is the sandy bay of Traeth Llfyn. Here the sheltered beach (known locally as Ynys Barri) is enclosed by steep cliffs.

Water quality No sewage is discharged in the vicinity of this beach.

Bathing safety Dangerous undercurrents and undertows off parts of the beach; life saving equipment and an emergency telephone are available.

Access Lanes from the A487 north of St David's lead to the hamlet of Abereiddy and Porthgain. Access along coast footpath.

Parking Large car park at Yyns Barri Hotel.

Toilets At car park.

Food Available at the hotel.

Seaside activities Swimming, diving, canoeing, surfing and fishing.

Wildlife and walks The Pembrokeshire Coast Path leads in both directions along this most impressive and unspoilt stretch of rocky coastline, several stretches of which are owned by the National Trust.

16 Whitesand Bay, St David's, Preseli, Dyfed   OS Ref: SM7327

Gorgeous sunsets framed in the wide arc of Whitesand Bay, from the remote rocky headland of St David's to St John Point, are an added attraction of this lovely beach. There are splendid views away to Ramsey Island and the Bishops and Clerks; the South Bishop can be identified on the far horizon by its lighthouse. The wide white sands stretch for ⅔ mile (1km). Large pebbles are thrown to the top of the beach by waves that frequently crash on to this beach, much to the delight of many surfers. At the north end of the beach a rocky promontory separates the small cove of Pwlleuog from the main beach. The two merge at low tide, but take care, as the smaller cove is cut off by the tide and there is no escape. Open fields slope down to the shore from the imposing craggy hill Carn Llidi, which provides good walking with excellent sea views. St David's Head is owned by the National Trust.

Water quality Beach monitored by the NRA and found to meet the EC standard for clean bathing water in 1989. No sewage is discharged in the vicinity of this beach.

Bathing safety Dangerous and unpredictable currents off parts of the beach and at some states of the tide; warning signs indicate where to bathe. Flags indicate when it is safe to bathe. Lifeguards patrol the beach during the summer. Weaver fish.

Access Road off A487 north of St David's, signposted to Whitesand, leads directly to car park a few yards from the sand.

Parking Car park behind beach, with approximately 160 spaces.

Toilets At car park.

Food Café/shop at car park.

Seaside activities Swimming, surfing, canoeing, diving, windsurfing and fishing.

Wildlife and walks The coast path to the north provides an interesting circular walk, taking in St David's Head with the remains of a fort and a burial chamber, and returning around Carn Llidi Hill. A guide describing the route is published by the Pembrokeshire Coast National Park and can be obtained at information offices locally. Ramsey Island lies just south of the bay, and boat trips from Whitesand (12-person inflatables, May-September) take you round the island to view the sea-bird breeding colonies.

17 Marloes Sands, Marloes, Preseli, Dyfed   OS Ref: SM785075

'Magnificient Marloes' a mile (1.6km) of wide flat golden sands, stretch from the imposing bulk of Gateholm Island in the north west to Red Cliff and Hooper's Point to the south-east. Beds of rock laid flat on a sea bed long ago are tilted and seem to be pushing up through the sands. Their jagged outlines point skywards along the length of this glorious bay. The steep cliffs that bound the beach reflect these dipping strata; do not attempt to climb them as they are dangerous. The barnacle and seaweed-covered rocky outcrops allude to the fact that the whole beach disappears at high water. There is only one access point to the beach where a tiny stream flows through a narrow valley, so take care not to get cut off at the extremities of the beach by the incoming tide.

Water quality No sewage is discharged in the vicinity of this beach.

Bathing safety Beware of currents and rocks. Safe bathing. Life-saving equipment is available. Take care as some areas of the beach are quickly cut off by the rising tide. The cliffs are dangerous; do not climb.

Access From Marloes village a lane, signposted Marloes Sands, takes you to the National Trust car park. From here take the lane to the YHA, and just beyond the Youth Hostel a footpath to the beach is marked. Walk across the field and a path leads steeply down to the beach. There is an alternative footpath down to the beach just before the car park.

Parking National Trust car park with about 50 spaces.

Toilets None.

Food None.

Seaside activities Swimming and fishing.

Wildlife and walks The coast path that follows the cliff-top round the bay provides excellent views of the sands. There is a 2 mile (3km) nature trail starting from the National Trust car park. Walkers using the trail are guided by a leaflet produced by the Dyfed Wildlife Trust (DWT). To the south-west, the coast path leads to West Dale Bay and a series of secluded sandy beaches around the Dale Peninsula that can only be reached on foot. To the north-east, the path heads towards Martin's Haven. A National Park guide, available from the DWT Information Centre describes a walk around the headland. Boat trips run from Martin's Haven to Skomer Island, renowned for its sea birds, wild flowers and seal colonies.

18 Broadhaven South, Bosherston, Dyfed   OS Ref: SR9893

A classic golden beach with a clear stream meandering across a wide flat 'V' of golden sands, backed by dunes and with rocky cliffs rising at either side. A distinct rocky outcrop lies just offshore. This unspoilt beach is only accessible by foot across the dunes but still gets busy in summer. It is perfect for relaxation or for exploration. There are lily ponds in the nature reserve behind the dunes and surprises around every headland: tiny rocky inlets, deep crevices, stacks and blow holes, not to mention the wildlife. Beach cleaned regularly by the National Trust.

Water quality No sewage is discharged in the vicinity of this beach.

Bathing safety Safe bathing. Lifesaving equipment available.

Access A lane from Bosherston leads to the National Trust car park; a path leads to the beach, and there is also a steep path to the beach from Bosherston a mile (1.6km) inland.

Parking National Trust car park on headland above beach, National Park car park in Bosherston.

Toilets At car park in summer.

Food None.

Seaside activities Swimming.

Wildlife and walks Separated from the beach by the dune ridge are the Bosherston lily pools, three lakes created in the late 18th century by damming three narrow valleys behind the beach. Water lilies and freshwater wildlife abound. Paths and causeways form circular walks around the area, starting at the car park in Bosherston. To the south of the bay, the coast path proceeds along the cliff-top to the tiny rocky inlet where St Govan chapel stands at the foot of a long flight of steep steps up the cliffs. Further south there is a 130 foot (40m) deep cleft in the cliff known as the Huntsman's Leap: a local huntsman is said to have died of fright after realising what his horse had just leapt! The path continues along this most beautiful rocky coastline towards the Elugug Stacks, a series of impressive limestone stacks, about 3 miles (5km) away. A large arch carved by the waves from the limestone cliffs is known as 'the Green Bridge of Wales'.

19 Barafundle Bay, Stackpole, Dyfed   OS Ref: SR9995

The National Trust owns an 8 mile (13km) section of the coast around Stackpole, including the beautiful Barafundle Bay. The beach can only be reached by foot with a mile (1.6km) walk along the cliff top from Stackpole Quay. One of the many tiny harbours that once proliferated in West Wales, the stone quay in this tiny inlet has been restored by the National Trust. From the cliff top path you have your first glimpse of the bay, an impressive view of soft golden sands backed by high dunes, with steep limestone cliffs rising on either side. The cliffs, with distinctive dark bands at their base due to the encrusting sea weeds, barnacles and lichens, extend to Stackpole Head which shelters the bay. In summer the beach is cleaned daily by the National Trust.

Water quality No sewage is discharged in the vicinity of this beach.

Bathing safety Safe bathing. Lifesaving equipment at top of steps down cliff.

Access A lane east of Stackpole, signposted to Stackpole Quay and Barafundle, leads to the car park at Stackpole Quay. A 10 minute walk along the coast path, signposted from the car park, leads to the bay; follow the steps down the cliff to reach the sands.

Parking National Trust car park at Stackpole Quay with about 230 spaces.

Toilets At car park.

Food None.

Seaside activities Swimming.

Wildlife and walks The coast path from Stackpole Quay crosses the beach and, climbing through the trees, the path tracks around Stackpole headland, passes Rame Blow Hole, and on to Broad Haven Bay. There are excellent views of the rocky coastline, and north-east the ranks of red sandstone headlands extend to the horizon. Walking south-east there are views down onto tiny sandy coves which cannot be reached due to the steep limestone cliffs that tower above.

20 Pembrey Sands, Llanelli, Dyfed   OS Ref: SN3802

A marvellous beach with 7 miles (11km) of sand edged by a belt of sand dunes, known locally as Cefa Sedan. A past Blue Flag winner, the beach falls within the Pembrey Country Park which also covers the extensive grassland and forest behind the dunes. The middle of the beach near the visitors' centre can be very busy on a warm sunny afternoon, but the extremities remain relatively quiet although they are often used for marine sports. Land yachting by the local club is well worth watching. Whether you want to relax on the sand and enjoy the clear views to the Gower on the horizon or be more active, the country park has lots of facilities, both natural and man-made, to keep the whole family happy. A lot of litter gets washed up and left on this beach, but it is cleaned regularly. Dogs are not permitted in the central ¾ mile (1.2km) section of the beach.

Water quality Beach monitored by the NRA and found to meet the EC standard for clean bathing water in 1989. One outfall serving 3,832 people discharges treated sewage above high water mark.

Bathing safety Safe bathing. Lifeguards patrol the beach near the main access point from June to September.

Access Country Park signposted from the A484. Bus services 173 and 174 from Llanelli to the Country Park. Board walks from the car parks lead through the dunes to the beach.

Parking Several car parks behind dunes with about 1,000 spaces.

Toilets One toilet block with facilities for the disabled.

Food Permanent kiosk with outdoor seating provides snacks, drinks and ices.

Seaside activities Swimming, windsurfing, canoeing and fishing. Pitch and putt golf, miniature and narrow gauge railways, adventure play area, and dry ski slope. Events are regularly staged on the beach, for example sand sculpture competitions and treasure hunts.

Wet weather alternatives Kidwelly Castle and Industrial Museum, Pembrey Motor Sports Centre. The Country Park Information Centre presents displays and exhibitions about the surrounding beach and country park (open all year).

Wildlife and walks There are four self-guided nature trails around the country park; woodland walk, floral trail, the yellow post walk (which includes the beach, dunes, forest and grassland), and the leisure route, suitable for wheel chairs and push chairs. There is a permanent orienteering course, a programme of guided walks by the Ranger service and a nature quiz for children. Full information is available from the visitor's centre.

21 Rhossili Bay, Rhossili, West Glamorgan   OS Ref: SS4287

A spectacular 3 miles (5km) sweep of golden sands edges Rhossili Bay, stretching from Worms Head north to Burry Holms. The sands are shadowed by Rhossili Down, whose grass slopes rise 600 feet (200m) above the beach and are popular with hang gliders. The southern end of the beach is ringed by steep cliffs which fall away northwards where the Down is replaced by sand dunes. Contrary to its name, Worms Head is in fact an island and is only linked to the mainland at low tide. The remains of a wreck can sometimes be seen at low tide. This lovely beach and the adjacent Down are owned by the National Trust.

Water quality Beach monitored by the NRA and found to meet the EC standard for clean bathing water in 1989. No sewage is discharged from this beach. Complaints of visible sewage have been received.

Bathing safety Safe bathing.

Access The B4247 leads to Rhossili village. There is a good path down the cliffs to the beach.

Parking Car park in village.

Toilets At the car park.

Food In the village.

Seaside activities Swimming, surfing and fishing.

Wildlife and walks Worms Head island and the adjacent stretch of coast are a National Nature Reserve. The limestone cliffs are rich in flora, and nesting birds can be seen on the nature trail. The limestone rocky shore of the Gower is one of the best examples in Britain. There is a network of paths on the headland and the adjoining Down where superb views can be obtained.

22 Port Eynon, West Glamorgan   OS Ref: SS4685

The rocky headland of Port Eynon Point to the south shelters this sandy cove. The road from the post office leads down to the shore where a short section of newly built promenade gives access to the beach. On either side, high dunes back the wide flat sands. High cliffs rise on either side of the bay with rocky outcrops at their base. On the eastern side of the bay stands the newly excavated remains of a salt house and workings. The wide, gently sloping sands are safe for bathing, and an ideal spot for building sand castles or playing cricket. The beach is cleaned daily in summer and twice weekly in winter. A dog-restriction by-law is being considered.

Water quality Beach monitored by the NRA and found to meet the EC standard for clean bathing water in 1989. One outfall serving 1,200 people discharges primary and secondary treated sewage at low water mark off Overton Mere, east of Port Eynon Point.

Bathing safety Warning notices indicate where it is safe to bathe. The beach is patrolled by lifeguards from May until September.

Access From the village a road leads to main access point where there is direct access to the sands. There are also board walks and marked paths through dunes to the beach.

Parking Car park behind the dunes with 500+ spaces.

Toilets At beach entry point.

Food Shop and café at beach entrance.

Seaside activities Swimming, surfing, windsurfing, diving, canoeing and fishing. A boat ramp leads from the car park to the tidal sand, providing easy access to the beach for boats.

Wildlife and walks The South Gower Coast Nature Reserve stretches from Port Eynon to Worms Head at Rhossili, comprising 6 miles (10km) of rocky shore with faulted and folded grey limestone cliffs. There is most interesting limestone flora, and nesting birds can be seen on some ledges. The limestone rocky shore of Gower is one of the best examples in Britain. A footpath on to Port Eynon Point climbs the cliff from the eastern end of the beach; the path leads to the Culver Hole, a deep cleft in the cliff which has been sealed off with a wall. There is a nature trail from the Rhossili Bay car park at the opposite end of the Nature Reserve.

23 Oxwich Bay, Oxwich, West Glamorgan   OS Ref: SS4986

A superb beach, from the steep tree-clad slopes of Oxwich Point a sweep of very fine soft sand backed by high dunes curves 2 miles (3km) round the bay to Great Tor – a stretch of towering rocky limestone cliffs. At low tide wide flat sands are revealed. There is only one indentation into the crescent of sand, where the dunes are interrupted by the river Nicholaston Pill which meanders through marshland before crossing the beach. The main access is from Oxwich village where there are full facilities. The North Devon Coast can be seen on the horizon and in the evening it appears as a string of lights. At low tide Oxwich Bay links with Three Cliffs Bay to the east giving 3 miles (5km) of continuous south-facing sands.

Water quality Beach monitored by the NRA and found to meet the EC standard for clean bathing water in 1989. No sewage is discharged in the vicinity of this beach.

Bathing safety Safe bathing; lifeguards from May to September.

Access Narrow lanes lead to Oxwich village at the western end of the bay. A car park next to the dunes faces directly on to the beach. There is a ramp for launching boats which could be used for easier access to the hard tidal sand. There is also access to the other end of the beach; a 15-minute walk from Penmaen along the footpath marked Tor Bay leads to a steep path down the cliff.

Parking Large car park at Oxwich village, plus limited parking at Penmaen. In summer, additional space is provided in a National Trust seasonal car park (a farmer's field) at Penmaen.

Toilets Two blocks at Oxwich car park.

Food The Oxwich Bay Hotel which stands at the eastern end of the beach provides meals and bar snacks. There is a kiosk for refreshments at the car park, and cafés and a shop within the village.

Seaside activities Swimming, windsurfing, sailing, diving, canoeing and fishing. A slipway across the sand enables boats to be launched and makes the bay popular with water skiers. There is a windsurfing school on the beach.

Wildlife and walks The Oxwich National Nature Reserve covers most of the beach, backshore and the Oxwich Point headland. The reserve includes a wide variety of habitats: sandy beach, dunes, salt and freshwater marshes, cliffs, woods and grassland. There are marked footpaths throughout the reserve and board walks give access to the dunes. A path west of the hotel leads through the trees past St Illtyd's Church to steps which climb to the headland and along the coast to Horton. There is an interpretative centre at the car park at Oxwich. At the western end, barnacle and mussel encrusted rocks are found below the cliffs, and low tide reveals pools full of life.

24 Three Cliffs, Parkmill, Glamorgan   OS Ref: SS5488

The ruins of the Pennard Castle stand aloft the river valley which opens out to the eastern corner of this lovely sandy bay, ringed by steep cliffs. A three pointed outcrop of rock curving out from the cliffs on the eastern side gives the bay its name. Wind-blown sand has built a series of burrows at the back of the beach. At low tide the river 'Pennard Pill' completes a wide oxbow meander behind the burrows and then flows across the beach. Beyond the three cliffs there are wide flat sands that merge at low tide with the sands of Oxwich Bay to the east.

Water quality No sewage is discharged in the vicinity of this beach.

Bathing safety It is dangerous to swim at middle tide near the three cliffs due to severe tidal conditions; notices at the entrance to the beach indicate where it is safe to bathe.

Access From Penmaen a lane leads to a steep path down the cliff to the beach. Another path leads from Parkmill. The beach can also be reached from Oxwich Bay along the beach.

Parking Car park at Penmaen, limited spaces at the post office, and a National Trust seasonal car park (a field) close by for summer use.

Toilets None.

Food None.

Seaside activities Swimming, diving, surfing, fishing, windsurfing, and canoeing from the beach.

Wildlife and walks Footpaths criss-cross the bracken- and heather-covered headlands, offering good views of the bay and adjacent Oxwich Bay.

25 Caswell Bay, Mumbles, West Glamorgan   OS Ref: SS5987

Another of the lovely bays to be found on the Gower and the recipient of a 1989 Clean Beach Award from the Tidy Britain Group. High rocky cliffs shadow this ⅔ mile (1km) of golden sand. There are only 55 yards (50m) of soft sand remaining at high tide but low tide reveals wide flat sands with rocky, wave-cut platforms bounding either side of the beach. Beyond the rocks there is the small Brandy Cove which can only be reached down a very steep cliff path or over the rocky shore. There is easy access to the main beach: the road runs adjacent to the beach and a few steps lead down to the sand from a neat paved area with shop and refreshment facilities.

Water quality Beach monitored by the NRA and found to meet the EC standard for clean bathing water in 1989. One outfall serving 2,000 people discharges secondary treated sewage below low water mark in Brandy Cove. Both beaches will benefit from a proposed £12.4 million scheme for a long sea outfall in the vicinity.

Bathing safety Bathing with care due to severe tidal conditions; the beach is patrolled by lifeguards from May to September.

Access From the road there are steps down on to the sand.

Parking Car park on the landward side of the access road with 500 spaces.

Toilets In the car park. Disabled facilities.

Food Shop, and refreshments available at the beach entrance.

Seaside activities Swimming, surfing, windsurfing, diving, canoeing and fishing.

Wildlife and walks A network of paths covers the wooded headlands above the beach and follows the Bishopston Valley inland from Pwlldu Bay.

26 Nash Point, Marcross, South Glamorgan   OS Ref: SS9263

From the headland at Nash Point with its two lighthouses (one now disused) there are good views of the North Devon coast across the Bristol Channel and north-west to Swansea and the Gower. Paths lead down into a deep valley which opens out on to the beach. Impressive layered limestone cliffs, typical of this area of Heritage Coast, extend away in both directions. The sheer walls are very unstable so do not sit too close to them or attempt to climb on them. There is one small area of sand, otherwise the beach is composed of large flat rocks where the cliffs have been eroded backwards. There are numerous rockpools exposed as the tide falls. Although the main beach area has continuous access, the extremes of the beach can become tide traps as the beach becomes covered at high tide.

Water quality No sewage is discharged in the vicinity of this beach.

Bathing safety Bathing is very dangerous because of submerged rocks and tidal races. Do not climb on the cliffs.

Access There are steep paths from the headland car park to the valley which leads on to the beach.

Parking Parking in private field on headland adjacent to lighthouse.

Toilets None.

Food Car park kiosk sells ice cream.

Seaside activities Fishing.

Wildlife and walks There is a nature trail through the wooded valley behind the beach. A coast path follows the cliffs in both directions.

Northern Ireland

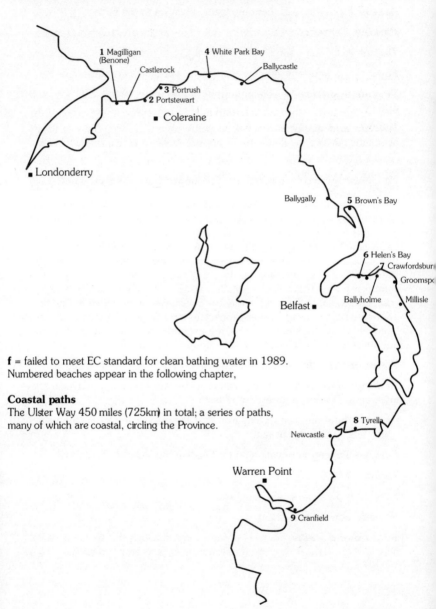

1 Magilligan (Benone)

Castlerock

3 Portrush

2 Portstewart

4 White Park Bay

Ballycastle

■ Coleraine

■ Londonderry

Ballygally

5 Brown's Bay

6 Helen's Bay

7 Crawfordsburn

Groomsport

Millisle

Belfast ■

Ballyholme

f = failed to meet EC standard for clean bathing water in 1989.
Numbered beaches appear in the following chapter,

Coastal paths
The Ulster Way 450 miles (725km) in total; a series of paths,
many of which are coastal, circling the Province.

8 Tyrella

Newcastle ●

Warren Point ■

9 Cranfield

Northern Ireland

The coast of Northern Ireland remains largely undiscovered to those outside the province although its most famous feature, the Giant's Causeway, is one of the natural wonders of the world. It consists of huge basalt columns that disappear below the waves like a stairway to the depths. Rich in geology, the coastline is made up of a succession of bays and rugged headlands. There are the strands of County Londonderry with their popular holiday resorts, and the nine glens of County Antrim, each with a little beach nestling at its mouth. There are also the magnificent sea loughs of County Down: Belfast, Strangford and Carlingford, all rich in wildlife. Unfortunately, undiscovered does not necessarily mean unthreatened, and Strangford Lough in particular has been suffering from the effects of the scallop dredge in recent years. While this may not necessarily affect the quality of its beaches, the rape of such a beautiful and unique habitat should concern anyone who cares for our coasts and coastal life.

The Golden List   *See page 26 for further details*

Beach No on Map	Rating. The more stars the better. **f**=failed	Resort	Sewage outlets	Population Discharging from outlet	Type of treatment	Discharge point relative to low water mark, unless otherwise stated. Distance given in metres	Remarks
1	★★★★	**Benone**					*Miles of sandy beach.*
	★★	**Castlerock**	1	2,000	*Primary*	*At LWM*	*Sandy.*
2	★★★	**Portstewart**	1	4,000+	*Raw*	*At LWM*	*Miles of sandy beach.*
3	★★★	**Portrush**	1	5,000	*Maceration*	*At LWM*	*Sandy.*
	★★★	**Ballycastle**	1	3,700+	*Primary*	*At LWM*	*Sandy. Safe swimming.*
5	★★★	**Browns Bay**					*Sandy. Safe swimming.*
6	★★★	**Helen's Bay**	1	1,600	*Tidal tank*	*At LWM*	*Sandy. Safe swimming.*
7	★★★	**Crawfordsburn**	1	200+	*Secondary*	*Discharges to stream*	*Sandy.*
	★★★	**Ballyholme**					*Sandy.*
	★★★	**Groomsport**	1	40,000+	*Screened*	*At LWM*	*Sandy.*
	★★★	**Millisle**	1	1,000+	*Primary*	*At LWM*	*Sandy.*
8	★★★★	**Tyrella**					*Sandy and very safe beach.*
	★★	**Newcastle**	2	5,000+	*Raw*	*At LWM*	*Sandy.*
9	★★★★/ ★★★	**Cranfield**					*Long sandy south facing beach.*

1 Benone, Limavady, Co. Londonderry   OS Ref: C7037

From Magilligan Point at the entrance to Lough Foyle, 7 miles (11km) of firm flat golden sand stretch east to the cliffs at Down Hill. Dunes fringe the wide curving beach, with sand hills covering the peninsula. The eastern end of the beach is backed by 750 foot (225m) cliffs, which are themselves shadowed by a heather-clad land plateau and the Binevenagh Mountains. The new leisure complex provides excellent facilities close to the beach. If you prefer to get away from the sand castles and games, the miles of sand offer solitude with only the sea and sky for company. The 110 yards (100m) of sand virtually disappear at high tide, covered by waters which were only one of a handful to achieve a ★★★★ Good Beach Guide grade. The beach is cleaned regularly.

Water quality Beach monitored by the DoE and found to meet the EC standard for clean bathing water in 1989. No sewage is discharged in the vicinity of the beach.

Bathing safety Bathing from some areas of the beach is unsafe due to currents; notices indicate where not to bathe. The beach is patrolled by lifeguards from June to September.

Access It is a short walk from the car park on to the beach at Benone.

Parking There is a car park behind dunes with 300 spaces. Car parking is also permitted on the sands but should be avoided on any beach.

Toilets Public toilets at beach and also facilities at the leisure complex.

Food Refreshments are available at the leisure complex.

Seaside activities Swimming, surfing, windsurfing, sailing and fishing from the beach. Golf course, tennis, and children's activity area are available at the leisure complex. A concrete ramp to the beach allows access to launch boats.

Wet weather alternatives Benone Tourist Complex.

Wildlife and walks It is claimed that up to 120 different species of shell have been found on Benone beach in one day, and an outdoor field studies recreation centre at Magilligan reflects the fact that the whole area is excellent for those interested in flora and fauna. 140 acres of the sand dune system around the Martello Tower on Magilligan Point form a Nature Reserve and there is restricted access to protect this fragile environment. The coastline is the limit of the North Derry Area of Outstanding Natural Beauty. Inland, the Binevenagh mountains are good for hill walking and afford good views of the coast.

THE GOOD BEACH GUIDE

2 The Strand, Portstewart, Co. Londonderry   OS Ref: C8338

This is a small quiet resort compared to its near neighbour, Portrush. The town, set around its harbour, is located on a promontory. To the west are 2 miles (3km) of beautiful sandy beach, backed by 185 acres of dunes owned by the National Trust. The flat sands are safe for swimming and good for fishing. There is good cliff scenery extending east towards Portrush, and the North Antrim Coast Path follows the cliff-top. The beach is cleaned regularly.

Water quality Beach monitored by the DoE and found to meet the EC standard for clean bathing water in 1989. One outfall serving over 4,000 people discharges untreated sewage at the low water mark.

Bathing safety Beware of currents that may affect bathing safety; the beach is patrolled by lifeguards during July and August.

Parking On the beach at low tide, but motor cycles are not permitted.

Toilets One male and one female.

Food One confectionery shop at the beach entrance.

Seaside activities Swimming, surfing, windsurfing, sailing, diving and fishing. Two golf courses. Pleasure boat trips from the harbour along Causeway Coast.

3 West Bay Strand, Portrush, Co. Antrim   OS Ref: C8740

Portrush is the largest seaside holiday centre in Northern Ireland. The Victorian and Edwardian resort is located on rocky Ramore Head and has all the facilities and amusements that might be expected of a traditional holiday town. From its elevated position there are excellent views along the coast to Donegal in the west and Rathlin Island in the east. A low sea wall bounds the soft sands of the west bay which curves gently south from the small harbour. The promenade which runs along the sea wall is on two levels separated by grassy banks. The larger East or Curran Strand is also backed by a sea wall but this gives way to dunes and a links golf course.

Water quality Beach monitored by the DoE and found to meet the EC standard for clean bathing water in 1989. One outfall serving 5,000 people discharges macerated sewage at low water mark.

Bathing safety Beware of currents that may affect bathing safety. The beach is patrolled by lifeguards during July and August.

Access Steps and a ramp from the promenade.

Parking 150–200 spaces at West Strand, 250-300 at East Strand.

Toilets Male and female at each end of West Strand, and on East Strand.

Food Promenade café.

Seaside activities Swimming, surfing, windsurfing, sailing, diving and fishing. Boat trips from the harbour.

Wet weather alternatives 'Water World' alongside the old harbour has a swimming pool complete with flumes and jacuzzis. Its facilities include an aquarium and entertainments. Amusements.

Wildlife and walks A section of the rocky shore on the eastern side of Ramore Head between the Portandoo Harbour and Bath Road is a Nature Reserve noted for its fossil ammonites. Adjacent to the reserve is the Portrush Countryside Centre, an interpretative centre which can provide further information about the reserve and surrounding area. East of Portrush there is superb cliff scenery, including towering limestone cliffs eroded by the ceaseless waves to form arches and caves. The white cliffs are replaced by the brown basalt which forms the famous Giant's Causeway further east. The coastal path follows the cliff-top to the picturesque ruin of Dunluce Castle. Surmounting its rocky headland, if offers superb views along the coastline; (the castle is closed on Sunday mornings and on Mondays during the winter).

4 White Park Bay, Portbradden, Co. Antrim   OS Ref: DO245

Stacks and rocky outcrops stud this magnificent bay owned and managed by the National Trust. The long curve of flat white sand is backed by dunes and circled by white chalk cliffs. On the western shore the whitewashed houses of Portbradden sit below the cliffs. The village's tiny church, St Gothan's, is the smallest in Ireland, a mere 11 feet by 6 feet (3.3m by 1.8m). Portbradden marks the junction between the chalk cliffs and the brown basalt of the Dunseverick and Causeway coast. The stretch of coast from Gid Point, the western boundary of White Park Bay, to Benbane Head is the Dunseverick Coast. The dipping rocks and basalt columns are less well defined than those of the Giant's Causeway beyond Benbane Head. However, the series of rugged headlands and small indented bays with the cliff-top ruins of Dunseverick Castle and the numerous offshore stacks makes this section of quieter coastline extremely attractive. The bay is popular with naturalists, for nearly every type of maritime vegetation can be found along this section of coastline, including strand line, salt marsh, cliff grassland, maritime scrub and heath. There is a wide variety of bird and marine life to be seen. The beach is cleaned regularly.

Water quality No sewage is discharged in the vicinity of this beach.

Bathing safety Strong currents make bathing dangerous.

Access There is car parking to the east of Templastragh on the A2 and on a minor road to Portbradden on the eastern shore of the bay. There is also a path from Ballintoy, 1½ miles (2.4km) east of the bay. During July and August an open topped bus makes the journey between Coleraine and Bushmills with stops at Portstewart, Portrush, Portballintrae and the Causeway.

Parking Car park near the youth hostel east of Templastragh and on the cliff-top near Dunseverick Harbour.

Toilets Near car park.

Food In village.

Seaside activities Swimming and fishing.

Wildlife and activities There is a 1 mile (1.6km) nature trail at White Park Bay, and a leaflet guide is available from the National Trust shop at the Giant's Causeway. The North Antrim Coast Path follows the cliffs west of the bay. It skirts Dunseverick harbour and castle and continues beyond Benbane Head to Giant's Causeway. 40,000 basalt columns, formed by cooling lava, create the unique features of the Causeway. It has been estimated that somewhere in the region of 500,000 people view the Causeway each year. The main access point for those not wanting to walk the 5 miles (8km) to Benbane Head from White Park Bay is at Causeway Head off the B146 north of Bushmills. There is parking and a National Trust Information Centre. The centre houses an exhibition of the history, geology, fauna and flora of the area. During the summer a bus will take visitors from the centre to the top of the Grand Causeway. To really appreciate this magnificent scenery to the full, a walk to Benbane Head is recommended. There is a path along the base of the cliffs passing the Grand Causeway, and other features including the Organ, the Amphitheatre, the Wishing Well, and Lovers' Leap. The return journey can be made along the cliff-top. 2½ miles (4km) along the coast path east of White Park Bay is the Carrick-a-rede rope bridge. The fragile swinging bridge spans a 60 foot (18m) wide and 80 foot (24m) deep ravine which separates Carrick-a-rede island from the mainland. The bridge is constructed each May by fishermen to provide access to their salmon fisheries. The walk across and back is not for the faint hearted! A National Trust car park at Larrybane gives closer access.

5 Brown's Bay, Whitehead, Co. Antrim   OS Ref: D4303

Brown's Bay is at the northern end of Island Magee, a long peninsula which bounds Lough Larne. At the northern end of the peninsula two headlands, Barr's Point and Skernaghan Point, frame a deeply indented bay. A ⅔ mile (1km) crescent of sandy beach with rocky outcrops, containing numerous rock pools, is revealed by the falling tide. The beach is easily accessible and is a good amenity beach, suitable for a family day by the sea. The beach is cleaned regularly by the local council.

Water quality Beach monitored by the DoE and found to meet the EC standard for clean bathing water in 1989. No sewage is discharged in the vicinity of the beach.

Bathing safety Safe bathing.

Access The B90 circles the northern half of Island Magee and runs parrallel with the bay. A sea wall and promenade edge the sand.

Parking Council car park with 124 spaces.

Toilets Public toilets at car park.

Food Nearby shop for confectionery and ice cream.

Seaside activities Swimming, windsurfing, diving, and fishing. Golf courses.

Wildlife and walks There are local walks on the headlands at either side of the bay.

6 Helen's Bay, Bangor, Co. Down   OS Ref: J4683

This small sandy beach is sheltered by headlands at either end. From the Horse Rock below Grey Point, the beach stretches to Quarry Point in the east and is backed by a stone promenade and a golf course on the grassland sloping up from the promenade. Grey Point with its disused fort commands an excellent view of Belfast Lough and the Antrim coast. A wooded avenue leads from Grey Point 2½ miles (4km) inland. It was once a private carriageway built by the first Marquess of Dufferin and Ava, after whose mother, Helen Sheridan, the bay is named. The beach is cleaned regularly.

Water quality Beach monitored by the DoE and found to meet the EC standard for clean bathing water in 1989. One outfall serving 1,600 people discharges sewage through a tidal tank at low water mark.

Bathing safety Safe bathing.

Access Helen's Bay Halt is ⅔ mile (1km) away and the car park only 50m from the beach.

Parking There is a car park at the west end of the bay.

Toilets Ladies, gents and disabled in the car park.

Food None.

Seaside activities Swimming and golf course.

Wildlife and walks. The beach lies on the North Down Coastal Path. To the east is Crawsfordsburn beach and country park. Seals and a variety of sea birds are just some of the wildlife of interest in this area.

7 Crawfordsburn, Bangor, Co. Down   OS Ref: J4783

Crawfordsburn and Helen's Bay are both within very easy reach of Belfast, by road along the A2 and also by train. As a result they can be very popular in summer. The 550 yard (500m) sandy beach at Crawfordsburn is divided in two by the stream that flows from the glen behind the sands. The beach and the glen fall within the Crawfordsburn Country Park. On the right bank of the stream stands the house of the Scottish family who settled here in the 17th century and gave the bay their name. The house is now a hospital and its extensive lawns are a caravan park. For those wishing to escape from the busy part of the beach. Swinerley Bay to the east is more secluded.

Water quality Beach monitored by the DoE and found to meet the EC standard for clean bathing water in 1989. One outfall serving 200+ people discharges macerated and secondary treated sewage to the stream flowing across the beach.

Bathing safety Safe bathing.

Access Crawfordsburn Halt is ¾ mile (1.2km) from the beach along the road through the Country Park. The Country Park car park is ¼ mile (400m) from the beach.

Parking Large car park in Country Park.

Toilets Ladies, gents (with disabled facilities in the car park).

Food Café.

Seaside activities Swimming, golf course. Orienteering courses held in the country park.

Wildlife and walks The stream from Crawfordsburn village flows through a steep sided valley, wooded with some exotic species. Below the village, it descends to a waterfall and flows under one of the railway viaduct's 80 foot (24m) high arches. Marked footpaths provide circular walks of varying lengths. Information about the park, including its walks and wildlife, is available from the interpretative centre. The beach is part of the North Down Coastal Path and also forms part of the Ulster Way. It follows the coast from Holywood, passes through the glen to the Clandeboyne Estate and on to Newtonards.

8 Tyrella Beach, Clough, Co. Down   OS Ref: J4535

Situated in Dundrum Bay, Tyrella is a 3 mile (5km) stretch of unspoilt sandy beach facing south and backed by dunes. The clean, shallow water and safe bathing make this a very popular beach on sunny Sundays in the holiday season: at other times it is blissfully quiet. There are six golf courses within a 12 mile (20km) radius of the beach, including the excellent Royal County Down.

Water quality Beach monitored by the DoE and found to meet the EC standard for clean bathing water in 1989. No sewage is discharged in the vicinity of this beach. The water quality is among the best in the UK.

Bathing safety Safe bathing.

Access The A2 between Clough and Killough passes directly behind the beach.

Parking At present, some cars do park on the beach: this is a practice that the Marine Conservation Society strongly disapproves of. Alternative parking should be found.

Toilets On the beach.

Food Snack vans visit the site.

Seaside activities Swimming.

Wet weather alternatives Leisure centres at Newcastle and Downpatrick, each about 6.5 miles (10km) away.

Wildlife and walks. The Murlough Nature Reserve is close by – a dune system with plenty of wildlife and vegetation. There are signs of man's early habitation of the area: castles, dolmens (ancient cairns) and some of the earliest Christian remains (a result of St. Patrick landing in the area). The Ulster Way goes past the beach.

9 Cranfield, Kilkeel, Co. Down OS Ref: J2611

An Area of Outstanding Natural Beauty adjoining an area of Special Scientific Interest, Cranfield Bay is situated at the entrance to Carlingford Lough. The south-facing sand and shingle beach is backed by dunes and has the magnificent Mourne mountains as a backdrop. The beach stretches from the rocky outcrops at Greencastle Point to the boulders at Cranfield Point. There are good views across the Lough to Ballagan Point and away down the coast beyond Dundalk Bay. The water is some of the cleanest you will find in the UK – in 1989 it achieved ★★★★ Good Beach Guide grading at one of the monitoring sites.

Water quality Beach monitored by the DoE and found to meet the EC standard for clean bathing water in 1989. No sewage is discharged in the vicinity of the beach.

Bathing safety Safe.

Access A road leads from Cranfield to the car park, from which there is a short walk across grass to the beach.

Parking Car park with 150 spaces.

Toilets Public conveniences.

Food Hotel, two cafés and three shops.

Seaside activities Swimming, windsurfing, diving, water skiing and fishing. Beach entertainment and band concerts. Golf course.

Wet weather alternatives Analong cornmill and marine park.

Wildlife and walks. Mourne mountains are excellent for walking, with the Silent Valley Reserve just north of Kilkeel. A 3,000 million gallon (14,000 million litres) reservoir is set among the peaks and there is some fine parkland on the approaches to the dam.

Index

Join the Fight to Save our Seas

Yes, I want to join the Marine Conservation Society.
Please enrol me as a (tick box)

Annual Member £12☐   Family Member £16 ☐   Life Member £200 ☐
(overseas members add £3 a year postage. Institutions may join for £30 a year)

NAME _____

ADDRESS _____

_____

I enclose a cheque for Membership fee   £
                      Donation (if you wish) £
                      Total   £

☐ Please send me details of how to make my subscription worth nearly £3 more with a Deed of Covenant and how to pay by banker's order. (please tick)

Send this form to: **Marine Conservation Society**
                       9 Gloucester Road
                       Ross-on-Wye HR9 5BU

Keep the Good Beach Guide Up to Date

A use of a guide such as this relies on the Marine Conservation Society being made aware of any changes at the beaches listed. If you come across a change or discrepancy at a site, or disagree with any of our comments, please let us know.

I have a potential alteration for the next edition of the Good Beach Guide:

Page number:

Name of beach:

Alteration/comment:

☐ Beach survey forms are also available for any interested volunteers who wish to help expand our beach database. Please tick the box if you would like to be sent copies of the survey forms.